Cultural Migrants
and Optimal Language
Acquisition

SECOND LANGUAGE ACQUISITION

Series Editors: **Professor David Singleton**, *University of Pannonia, Hungary* and Fellow Emeritus, *Trinity College, Dublin, Ireland* and **Dr Simone Pfenninger**, *University of Zurich, Switzerland*

This series brings together titles dealing with a variety of aspects of language acquisition and processing in situations where a language or languages other than the native language is involved. Second language is thus interpreted in its broadest possible sense. The volumes included in the series all offer in their different ways, on the one hand, exposition and discussion of empirical findings and, on the other, some degree of theoretical reflection. In this latter connection, no particular theoretical stance is privileged in the series; nor is any relevant perspective – sociolinguistic, psycholinguistic, neurolinguistic, etc. – deemed out of place. The intended readership of the series includes final-year undergraduates working on second language acquisition projects, postgraduate students involved in second language acquisition research, and researchers and teachers in general whose interests include a second language acquisition component.

Full details of all the books in this series and of all our other publications can be found on http://www.multilingual-matters.com, or by writing to Multilingual Matters, St Nicholas House, 31-34 High Street, Bristol BS1 2AW, UK.

SECOND LANGUAGE ACQUISITION: 91

Cultural Migrants and Optimal Language Acquisition

Edited by
Fanny Forsberg Lundell and Inge Bartning

MULTILINGUAL MATTERS
Bristol • Buffalo • Toronto

Library of Congress Cataloging in Publication Data
A catalog record for this book is available from the Library of Congress.
Cultural Migrants and Optimal Language Acquisition/Edited by Fanny Forsberg Lundell and Inge Bartning.
Second Language Acquisition: 91
Includes bibliographical references and index.
1. Linguistic minorities—Europe. 2. Second language acquisition—Europe. 3. Language and languages—Study and teaching—Europe. 4. Language and culture—Europe. I. Lundell, Fanny Forsberg, editor. II. Bartning, Inge, editor.
P119.315.C85 2015
306.44'94–dc23 2015009701

British Library Cataloguing in Publication Data
A catalogue entry for this book is available from the British Library.

ISBN-13: 978-1-78309-403-5 (hbk)
ISBN-13: 978-1-78309-402-8 (pbk)

Multilingual Matters
UK: St Nicholas House, 31-34 High Street, Bristol BS1 2AW, UK.
USA: UTP, 2250 Military Road, Tonawanda, NY 14150, USA.
Canada: UTP, 5201 Dufferin Street, North York, Ontario M3H 5T8, Canada.

Website: www.multilingual-matters.com
Twitter: Multi_Ling_Mat
Facebook: https://www.facebook.com/multilingualmatters
Blog: www.channelviewpublications.wordpress.com

Copyright © 2015 Fanny Forsberg Lundell, Inge Bartning and the authors of individual chapters.

All rights reserved. No part of this work may be reproduced in any form or by any means without permission in writing from the publisher.

The policy of Multilingual Matters/Channel View Publications is to use papers that are natural, renewable and recyclable products, made from wood grown in sustainable forests. In the manufacturing process of our books, and to further support our policy, preference is given to printers that have FSC and PEFC Chain of Custody certification. The FSC and/or PEFC logos will appear on those books where full certification has been granted to the printer concerned.

Typeset by Deanta Global Publishing Services Limited.

Contents

Contributors — vii

Cultural Migrants: Introducing a New Concept in SLA Research — 1
Fanny Forsberg Lundell and Inge Bartning

Part 1: Focus on Cultural Migrants

1 Beyond Native-like? The Lexical Profile of a Cultural Migrant in Italy — 17
 Anna Gudmundson and Camilla Bardel

2 Successful Profiles in High-level L2 French – 'c'est un choix de vie' — 59
 Fanny Forsberg Lundell and Inge Bartning

3 Reported Use and Perception of *tu* and *vous* Among Less Integrated and Highly Integrated Anglophone Cultural Migrants in France — 83
 Amanda Edmonds and Catherine Guesle-Coquelet

4 L2 English Vocabulary in a Long-residency Swedish Group Compared to a Group of English Native Speakers — 115
 Britt Erman and Margareta Lewis

Part 2: Culture as a Decisive Factor in L2 Attainment

5 Migratory Experience and Second Language Acquisition Among Polish and Chinese Migrants in Dublin, Ireland — 137
 Chloé Diskin and Vera Regan

6   Acculturation as the Key to the *Ultimate* Attainment?
    The Case of Polish-English Bilinguals in the UK   178
    Kate Hammer and Jean-Marc Dewaele

7   The Role of Sociopsychological Factors in Long-term L2
    Achievement of L1 Chinese Learners of L2 Spanish   203
    Gisela Granena

    Concluding Chapter: What Can SLA Learn From Cultural
    Migrants?   221
    Fanny Forsberg Lundell and Inge Bartning

    Index   228

Contributors

Camilla Bardel is professor of modern languages and language education at Stockholm University, Sweden. Her research interests lie in the field of second language acquisition with special focus on crosslinguistic influences in vocabulary and syntax. She also has an interest in lexicographical issues. She has coordinated research projects and published several articles, book chapters and co-edited works on the learning of French, Italian, Swedish and other languages, often with a focus on the learning of a third or additional language, and questions related to multilingualism. She has recently participated in the research program *High Level Proficiency in Second Language Use*.

Inge Bartning is professor emerita of French at Stockholm University. She has taught and published in the domain of French syntax, semantics and pragmatics. In the two last decades, her main interest has been in French L2 acquisition, in particular, the domain of developmental stages, advanced learners and ultimate attainment of morphosyntax, discourse and information structure. She is currently participating in a joint project, *High Level Proficiency in Second Language Use*. She has (co-)authored articles in *Studies in Second Language Acquisition*, *IRAL*, *Journal of French Language Studies*, *EUROSLA Yearbook*, *AILE*, *LIA*, *Langue française*, *Lexique*, *Revue Romane* etc.

Jean-Marc Dewaele is professor of applied linguistics and multilingualism at Birkbeck, University of London. He does research on individual differences in psycholinguistic, sociolinguistic, pragmatic, psychological and emotional aspects of second language acquisition and multilingualism. He has published over 150 papers and chapters, and a monograph *Emotions in Multiple Languages* in 2010 (2nd edn in 2013). He is vice-president of the *International Association of Multilingualism* and former president of the *European Second Language Association*. He became general editor of the *International Journal of Bilingual Education and Bilingualism* in 2013. He is the father of a trilingual daughter and holds a black belt in Go Kan Ryu karate.

Chloe Diskin is an Irish Research Council postgraduate scholar in sociolinguistics and second language acquisition (SLA) at University College Dublin (UCD). Her research looks at issues within SLA such as identity and language learning in a migrant context. She is interested in quantitative and variationist approaches to SLA, particularly within the area of discourse-pragmatic variation and change. Alongside her research, she teaches French language and translation at UCD. She holds an MA in second language studies from UCD and a BA in French and German from the National University of Ireland, Galway.

Amanda Edmonds received her PhD from Indiana University and is a lecturer in Linguistics and French as a Foreign Language at the Université de Pau et des Pays de l'Adour, France. She is currently the director of the Master's program in French as a Foreign Language at the University of Pau, where she teaches courses on language pedagogy and second language acquisition. Her research in the field of second language acquisition focuses on the acquisition of a phraseological competence in an L2 and on the acquisition of variable structures, both in the acquisition of French and of English as a second language.

Britt Erman is associate professor of English at Stockholm University. Her past research includes pragmatics, discourse and conversation analysis in particular from a gender perspective, grammaticalisation, and formulaic language. She has published most of her work in the past on formulaic language addressing the processing of formulaic language, and in particular collocations in native and non-native written production. More recent publications include studies of lexical bundles in speech and in academic writing, L2 pragmatics, formulaic language and phraseology in immersed L2 users and constructions within construction grammar and cognitive linguistics. She is currently involved in the area of L2 acquisition in particular formulaic language, vocabulary and syntactic complexity among high-level learners of English, which is part of a large-scale project including several language departments at Stockholm University aimed at establishing ultimate attainment in highly advanced and immersed L2 users.

Gisela Granena is an assistant professor at the School of Languages at the Universitat Oberta de Catalunya in Barcelona. Prior to coming to Barcelona, she was a postdoctoral fellow at the Center for Advanced Study of Language at the University of Maryland. She received her PhD in second language acquisition from the University of Maryland. Her main research area is cognitive individual differences, specifically cognitive aptitudes for explicit and implicit learning in instructed and naturalistic second language learning settings, as well as the effects of early and late bilingualism on long-term achievement.

Anna Gudmundson is a post-doc researcher and teacher of Italian as a second language at Stockholm University. She finished her PhD in 2012 where she investigated the acquisition of grammatical gender and number in Italian by Swedish university students. She teaches second language acquisition, general linguistics, linguistic methodology and theory, and has supervised several undergraduate research projects. Anna has published papers on vocabulary acquisition and lexical profiling, and her post-doc studies focus on the multilingual mental lexicon using word associations and priming. She recently took part in the research program *High Level Proficiency in Second Language Use*.

Catherine Guesle-Coquelet has been a lecturer in Linguistics and French as a Foreign Language at the Université de Pau et des Pays de l'Adour, France, since 2007. Her doctoral thesis, defended in 2003 at the Université Michel de Montaigne-Bordeaux 3, examined address terms in French and provided suggestions as to how to help non-native speakers understand and master their use. Her research interests include the understanding of the environment in the learning of a second language, where 'environment' can refer to social, university, professional, cultural, *etc.* aspects.

Kate Hammer is a researcher at the University of London, UK, and recipient of the Academic Excellence Scholarship from the School of Social Sciences, History and Philosophy at Birkbeck. Her principal interests are in the interaction between language use in bilinguals, cognition and culture. Kate has reviewed a number of books and academic papers in the fields of SLA, bilingualism, acculturation, bilingual cognition and identity. Her current research project investigates shift in language dominance following migration, and specifically its chronology and intensity across domains belonging to inner speech, cognitive and communicative functions. She is also interested in the linguistic and sociocultural realities of people living in global cities and in current or former borderlands in Europe.

Margareta Lewis, PhD, is affiliated to the English Department at Stockholm University. She published her thesis within the area of L2 acquisition, in particular focusing on formulaic language in intermediate learners' written production. She is still involved in the area of L2 acquisition with a focus on formulaic language, vocabulary and syntactic complexity among high-level learners of English, which is part of a large-scale project including several language departments at Stockholm University aimed at establishing ultimate attainment in highly advanced and immersed L2 users. At present, Lewis holds a position as senior lecturer in L2 English within adult education at Åsö Upper Secondary School in Stockholm.

Fanny Forsberg Lundell is associate professor of French linguistics at Stockholm University. She was appointed research fellow in French at The Royal Swedish Academy of Letters, History and Antiquities in 2010. Besides publishing extensively on formulaic language in French and Spanish as L2s with a particular focus on high-level proficiency, she also works on pragmatics, conversation analysis and spoken language in general. Recently, her work includes psychological perspectives on high-level L2 attainment.

Vera Regan, Chevalier de l'ordre des Palmes Académiques, is professor of sociolinguistics at University College Dublin. She researches variation theory and second language acquisition; language, migration, identity; acquisition of French by speakers of Irish English; sociolinguistic competence and year abroad. She is a holder of two Fulbright Research Awards and has held visiting professorships at the University of Pennsylvania and the University of Ottawa. She has been president of the European Association for Second Language Research, president of the Association of French Language Studies and member, executive committee of Association of University Professors and Heads of French. She has also been director of Ireland Canada University Foundation. She is the series editor of *Language, Migration and Identity* (Peter Lang).

Cultural Migrants: Introducing a New Concept in SLA Research

Fanny Forsberg Lundell and Inge Bartning

Linking Second Language Acquisition Research to Migration Studies

Global migration has become a natural feature in today's world and about 3% of the world's population are international migrants (cf. DELMI, 2014). However, host countries are very unequally distributed with 10 countries (including USA, Canada, Germany and France) receiving half of the world's migrants. Although creating many opportunities for individuals, the rapidly increasing migration also constitutes one of the foremost current societal challenges, and scholars from the humanities and social sciences can contribute considerably to our understanding of this phenomenon, possibly pointing ways forward for multicultural societies. As pointed out in another recent volume on language and migration (Duchêne *et al.*, 2013: 6), 'migration studies in the social sciences rarely examine the central role of language and, similarly, socio- and applied linguistics have given much more time to education than to the workplace'. This takes us to the main starting point for this volume: language is a vital – if not one of the most vital – factor(s) in adult migration and deserves more attention in the current debate on migration and globalisation. Dustmann and van Soest (2002) conclude that oral second language skills allowing communication with members of the adopted country is 'probably the most important single alterable factor contributing to their social and economic integration' (2002: 473).

It is important to recognise that migration is not only due to economic and political forces, but it is also a much broader reality, with numerous people choosing to move to another country for various reasons, be they professional, emotional or lifestyle-oriented. Lundström (2014) studies *white migration* from a sociological point of view and states that the concept is almost to be considered as an oxymoron, since migrants are rarely thought of as white.

Increased mobility, for one reason or another, opens up a magnitude of new research avenues for second language acquisition (SLA) research. When mobility was limited, in the early days of SLA research, it was natural to turn to classroom settings for data collection. In the 1970s and 1980s, when international migration increased, researchers turned to groups of labour migrants, such as the ZISA project (e.g. Meisel et al., 1981) and ESF project (e.g. Klein & Perdue, 1997). One of the conclusions of the ESF project was that the communicative needs of these migrants did not trigger their second language acquisition beyond basic levels of communicative competence. Since the 1990s, we have again seen more focus on classroom learners, perhaps due to the fact that UG-inspired SLA has, to quite a large extent, been decoupled from societal concerns, which is also proposed by Young-Scholten (2013), who calls for a tighter link between SLA and adult migrant education. One of the main problems, according to Young-Scholten, is that generative SLA puts very little emphasis on non-linguistic variables. In addition she states that: 'Basic research need not involve searching for relevance – social or otherwise – and researchers will not direct their attention to a population of learners simply because their lives might be improved by participation in studies. Research must also be relevant to SLA theory.' (2013: 442) As can be concluded from the studies cited above, SLA researchers tend to focus on formal learners more than on naturalistic settings, and if they do study migrants, they tend to study low-educated, and economically unprivileged migrants.

Native-Likeness in Second Language Acquisition Research and the Contribution of Studying Cultural Migrants

In studies on native-likeness in second language acquisition, it is participants stemming from economic or political migration who are normally investigated (cf. Abrahamsson & Hyltenstam, 2009; DeKeyser, 2000; DeKeyser et al., 2010; Granena & Long, 2013). A short state-of-the-art review of this research is therefore presented in order to provide some background to the issue of the extent to which adult L2 learners can be expected to attain native-likeness.

The literature on the incidence of native-likeness has recently grown rapidly, as evidenced by research in the field, e.g. Abrahamsson (2012), Abrahamsson and Hyltenstam (2009), Birdsong (2007), Granena & Long (2013), Moyer (2004), Muñoz (2008) and Muñoz and Singleton (2007, 2011). Many of these studies have examined the Critical Period Hypothesis (Lenneberg, 1967) (CPH), concentrating on SLA in late learners, i.e. after puberty. According to the CPH, as is well known, it is not possible, on maturational grounds to acquire a second language at a native-like level for speakers who start their L2 acquisition after puberty (cf. Long, 2013, who uses the term 'sensitive period or periods').

As shown in Forsberg Lundell and Bartning (this volume), a survey of the state-of-the-art about the possibility for late L2 learners to become native-like gave divergent results. Researchers can be characterised along two strands of factors: 1. Those advocating the critical period hypothesis with the principal factor 'age of onset' as an answer to native-likeness, i.e. native-likeness is not possible if the L2 learner starts after puberty; and 2. Those who propose other factors than maturational constraints, e.g. social, psychological, linguistic, and language experience etc. and that native-likeness is possible. The following studies belong to the first group: Abrahamsson (2012, Spanish L1, Swedish L2, GJT=grammatical judgement tests), VOT=voice onset time), Abrahamsson and Hyltenstam (2009, Swedish L2, e.g. GJT, perceptive tests), DeKeyser (2000), DeKeyser *et al.* (2010), Granena & Long (2013) and Ioup *et al.* (1994, Arabic L2, GJT). In the second group we find Birdsong (e.g. 1992, 2003, 2007, French L2), Montrul and Slabakova (2003, Spanish L2, tense and aspect), Muñoz and Singleton (2011) and Kinsella and Singleton (2014, English L1, French L2).

As still more recent research demonstrates (Abrahamsson, 2012, Hyltenstam *et al.*, 2014) the age of onset factor ceases to be significant among learners after the age of 15 and onwards. As a matter of fact, variation in social, psychological and linguistic factors such as length of residence, opportunities to use the TL, motivation, language aptitude, and structural distance between L1 and L2 interact with the age factor and play more important roles the older the learner is. The following studies propose that ultimate attainment in an L2 may be more a function of the quantity and quality of language experience than simply of maturation: Kinsella and Singleton (2014: 4), Marinova-Todd (2003), Moyer (2004, 2013), Muñoz and Singleton (2007, 2011) and Piller (2002).

Muñoz and Singleton (2011) and Moyer (2013) claim that age is confounded with other factors and that it would be worthwhile taking a closer look at other favourable social and psychological factors for second language acquisition. In the case of economic and political migrants, it can be assumed that social and psychological circumstances are far from favourable in many cases, in terms of possibilities to integrate, affective dimensions and attitudes, to mention just a few factors. If we wish to examine the positive effect of social and psychological factors on second language acquisition and high-level achievement in particular, these populations are probably not the most suitable. In several sociological studies (e.g. Benson & O'Reilly, 2009; Lundström, 2014), the authors put forward the purposes and gains of studying the hitherto less studied privileged migrants. Lundström (2014: 7) concludes that in order to understand the power relations of domination, people with class, race and gender privileges must be investigated. In a similar vein, one could argue that in order to fully grasp the possibilities and limitations of SLA, research has to be carried out on populations which seem to be socially and psychologically advantaged for the task of acquiring a second language as adults.

The current volume focuses on this latter type of migrant, which we call *cultural migrant*. By *cultural migrants*, we refer to people who choose, out of their free will, to move permanently to another country and to learn the language. The culture of the target language country appeals to them and they make an active choice to live in this new culture (see below for a closer definition). Taking Schumann's acculturation model (1986) into account, these individuals would have optimal prerequisites for native-like attainment, since they have positive attitudes and affect towards the target language community. Furthermore, they are often well-educated and well integrated, leading to plenty of opportunities to practice the second language (L2), which in itself is an important dimension of L2 attainment (cf. DeKeyser, 2007). All in all, these migrants are socially and psychologically advantaged, and the study of various dimensions of their linguistic knowledge and production could contribute considerably to our understanding of the possibilities and limitations of L2 learning. However, it should be noted that being a cultural migrant (in sociological terms) does not automatically mean that high-level L2 proficiency is always achieved. Edmonds and Guesle-Coquelet (this volume) discuss variation within this migrant population. Such variation could, for example, be due to differences in degree of motivation and differences in type of motivation (intrinsic, extrinsic, see e.g. Deci & Ryan, 2000). It would definitely be relevant and interesting to study the diverse motivational orientations of cultural migrants in order to further our understanding of their L2 use. None of the studies included in the present volume work within an explicit motivational framework, but the reader will notice that aspects touching upon motivation, identification and integration are brought up in several chapters, mainly based on opinions expressed in interviews with the participants (see e.g. chapters by Granena and Forsberg Lundell & Bartning).

In sum, cultural migrants are not often studied in the SLA literature, perhaps because they are not perceived as typical immigrant groups and have not attracted the interest of researchers involved with second language acquisition and migration. It is thus our belief that the present volume will fill a gap in SLA studies concerning high-level proficiency. It is also hoped that it will be of interest to social scientists working within the area of migration studies, since the volume focuses on the inevitable relationship between language, culture and integration. Some of the questions which will be addressed in the present volume are: What characteristics do we find in terms of linguistic features in cultural migrants in different settings? Are cultural migrants different in their L2 behaviour from other types of migrants? Does studying cultural migrants add anything to the state-of-the-art in SLA theorising, specifically as regards adult native-like attainment? What are the implications for existing theoretical models, such as the Acculturation model?

Defining the Cultural Migrant

As far as we know, the term 'cultural migrant' has not been used to date in second language acquisition research. However, the term is to be found in the sociological work by Fujita (2009) who uses it to refer to 'young Japanese migrants who emigrate to New York and London to engage with the cultural sphere'. It becomes clear that there are slight differences in our use of the term. As described above, our focus is on individuals who migrate from one country to another for cultural purposes, using the word 'culture' in the sense of 'ideas, customs and social behavior of a society' and not culture as in 'the arts'. However, it cannot be denied that these two senses of the concept 'culture' sometimes intersect and that the cultural motivations of cultural migrants may be a blend of the two. In Forsberg Lundell and Bartning's (this volume) contribution, one of the participants state that she has chosen to live in Paris because she finds the cultural scene appealing, in addition to the fact that she comes from a francophile family and has always wanted to learn French. A humble guess would be that many of the individuals drawn to the world's larger cities are drawn for both aspects of the term 'cultural'. However, it should be noted that the focus of this volume lies on culture in the first sense and as such, Fujita's (2009) sense of the term and ours do not completely coincide.

Transnationalism vs Migration

As Diskin and Regan (this volume) point out, migration studies within the social sciences currently focus more on transnationalism than immigration. As they put it: 'Migration research has thus shifted from assimilationist and integrationist perspectives to studies of transnationalism. Within the context of the developed world, transnational migrants are highly mobile individuals with tenuous ties to traditional nation states - they may be re-defined as 'trans-destinational' (King-O'Riain, 2008: 219). They move through cultural spaces fluidly, and make calculated decisions on their next destination based on the economic and human capital there is to be gained.' Without a doubt, migration patterns have changed during the last decade and transnationalism is becoming increasingly common. Nevertheless, one should keep in mind that the rise of a new kind of migration does not erase the more traditional kind, i.e. people moving from one country to another to settle for undetermined periods of time, often 'for good'. Many of the participants in the studies collected in the current volume are individuals who have chosen a particular country, since that specific country and culture interest them, almost always accompanied with an interest in the standard language of the country in question. It should also be noted that they have lived for long periods of time, having migrated in the 1990s or early 2000s. They would probably not be described as 'highly mobile individuals' since they have typically only lived in one other country than their country of origin. This characterisation is especially true for the first three contributions in this volume. Gudmundson and Bardel, Forsberg Lundell and Bartning, and Edmonds and Guesle-Coquelet all investigate migrants that have chosen Italy or France.

In this volume it is hypothesised that the active choice of a specific destination, coupled with a pronounced interest in the destination's majority language, will affect late L2 attainment possibilities significantly. It is certainly not a coincidence that one of the most recent studies on late L2 attainment (Kinsella & Singleton, 2014) deals with adult Anglophone migrants in France. It should be noted that these above mentioned countries, especially France, are countries which have attracted cultural migrants even historically. Benson and O'Reilly (2009) and Benson (2012) have investigated British migrants in the south of France from a sociological point of view. They label these migrants 'lifestyle migrants', by which they mean: 'relatively affluent individuals of all ages, moving either part-time or full-time to places, that for various reasons signify, for the migrant, a better quality of life' (Benson & O'Reilly, 2009: 610). Furthermore, they divide their orientations into 'Residential tourism', 'The rural idyll' and 'Bourgeois Bohemians'. In addition, they claim that their studied population provides reasons such as 'getting out of the trap' and 'making a fresh start' for migration. It is easy to observe similarities between lifestyle migrants and cultural migrants. They clearly both constitute privileged groups in the developed world who migrate based on lifestyle choice, and cultural migrants could hypothetically be included as a subcategory of the broader category lifestyle migrants. Nevertheless, it seems to us that the motivations of 'our' cultural migrants and those of the lifestyle migrants are divergent. Lifestyle migrants, as they are described in Benson and O'Reilly (2009), have as their main motivation to search for a better life, not seldom preceded by a traumatic or stressful event, whereas cultural migrants are mainly driven to migrate by their interest in and fascination of another culture and language. Accordingly, one could say that cultural migrants have a narrower and more focussed motivation, and one that would also be more linked to second language learning motivation than in the case of lifestyle migrants.

The studies by Diskin and Regan, Hammer and Dewaele, and Granena take not only cultural migrants into account, but also include migrants with other motivations, and thus discern characteristics of the cultural migrant population.

The present volume thus brings together research focusing on the notion of cultural migrants from various points of view. The included studies are not based on a common research program, but rather on a common research topic area. It is hoped that bringing these studies together into one volume will enhance the study of cultural migrants. Below follows a summary of the contents of each chapter.

Focus on Cultural Migrants

Gudmundson and Bardel investigate lexical variation, lexical sophistication and vocabulary use in the oral production of Swedish cultural migrants. The first part is a cross-sectional study based on data from a selected group of Swedish L2 users of Italian who live or have lived in Italy, and a matched control group of native speakers of Italian. Two measures are used: lexical variation (as measured with Vocd) and lexical sophistication (as measured with the Lexical Oral Production Profile, LOPP*f*). The second part of the chapter presents a case study which characterises the longitudinal lexical development of a very advanced L2 user of Italian living in Italy. Besides the longitudinal development of Vocd and LOPP*f*, this part of the study offers a qualitative analysis aiming at categorising the words used by the informant, focusing mainly on the low-frequency words and the unique words, that is, words used only by this particular informant (and by none of the native controls). Results of the first part show that the L2 users have lower values for lexical variation than the native speakers but similar levels of lexical sophistication, measured in terms of proportion of advanced (i.e. low-frequency) words. Results from the second part seem to indicate a development as concerns Vocd and LOPP*f* over time. The informant reaches higher values than the native speakers as regards lexical sophistication, but for lexical variation she reaches the lower native speaker values. Furthermore, this particular learner has a higher number of unique words than any of the native speakers. The qualitative analysis shows that many of the words used by this particular cultural migrant are cognates between Italian and Swedish and words that are related to specific thematic vocabulary.

Forsberg Lundell and Bartning study typical *cultural migrants*, i.e. Swedes living in Paris, France. The authors have previously conducted several quantitative studies at a group level, and this study focuses on four individual profiles (three women, one man). All of them are highly advanced L2 users and have lived in France for at least 10 years. Using 10 different linguistic measures (spontaneous oral data and test data), the authors set out to investigate whether it is possible to become native-like as a late L2 learner and what linguistic measures are characteristic of the most successful learners. In addition, the study investigates the impact of language aptitude on degree of native-likeness. Besides investigating these questions quantitatively, a socio-biographic story for each participant also accompanies the analysis. One of the four participants can be regarded as native-like – she performs in a native-like way on 8 out of 10 measures.

The two measures for which she does not display native-likeness are problematised as less relevant for gauging native-likess, namely lexical richness and mean length of run. She is, furthermore, characterised by high scores on both oral and written measures. As regards language aptitude, although she has a high score, the least native-like speaker also does, so there does not seem to be an obvious link between aptitude and native-likeness. However, in spite of studying only four participants, the study shows a clear association between written test scores and language aptitude. So why is Hedda more native-like than the others? The most decisive sociobiographic factors in this case seem to be level of education and age of intensive exposure. Overall, the study shows encouraging results for late learners with native-likeness on many of the measures used.

Edmonds and Guesle-Coquelet examine reported usage and perceptions of the *tu/vous* distinction by a group of 30 Anglophone cultural migrants who have settled in the South-west of France with the intent of integrating into their adopted communities. The reported usage was captured by questionnaires and interviews and the participants were divided into two groups, well integrated and less integrated. The purpose of the study was to determine what obstacles continue to hamper the efforts of the two sub-groups. All of the Anglophones who participated in this project were considered high proficiency users of French with a length of residence between 5 and 20 years, and ages between 30 and 60 years old. The underlying assumption was that it is plausible to expect that non-native speakers who have chosen to settle in a French-speaking country and who have relatively easy access to native speakers should be in a favourable position to develop their sociolinguistic competence in general and the *tu/vous* distinction in particular. The results from this study suggest that being a cultural migrant, and thus having regular contact with native speakers, may in fact be sufficient for the appropriate reported use of the *tu/vous* distinction of sociolinguistic competence. Obstacles may, however, still remain, particularly for those cultural migrants who do not consider themselves to be well-integrated into their adopted community. The study also highlights the fact that the concept of cultural migrant encompasses not only a wide variety of socio-biographical profiles but that the attitudes towards the L2 in this population also are varied.

Erman and Lewis' study long-residency Swedish migrants in London that do not express cultural motives for migrating, but have come to cultural motives post-hoc, appreciating the *global* culture, which characterises London. Their study deals with two aspects of the English L2 lexicon, i.e. the L2 users' knowledge of formulaic language and their knowledge of words, as apparent in one multiword study, and one 'single word' study. On all the measurements presented, a matched group of native English speakers has been used as benchmarks. The overall aim of the two studies is to display similarities and differences in the spoken production of the Swedish non-natives (10) and the natives (10) in their use of multiword structures, and high-frequency and low-frequency words. The selection of the London Swedes (LS) met the following three criteria: (1) they had completed upper secondary studies in Sweden, entailing nine years of English, (2) they had had at least five years residency in the target country, and (3) at the time of testing they were residents of the TL country and used the L2 as a principal means of communication. Most of the participants also had experience of academic studies. The participants performed the following tasks: two types of dialogic tasks: a role play and a semi-structured interview, and one monologic task, an online retelling of a video clip (14.5 minutes). The main hypothesis of both studies was that the LS group, as a result of daily exposure to English at work as well as at home, would perform in a similar way to the native speakers in the role play and the interview, whereas the results from the retelling task performed under considerable time pressure would deviate from the native speakers. The results show that the LS group, in accordance with the hypothesis, was native-like on both types and tokens of single words and on multiwords in the role play, while the retelling task turned out to be more cognitively demanding. The results also show that it is with regard to types in both frequency ranges (1–2000 and 2000+) in the interview, and in the retelling task with regard to multi words structures (MWSs) that there is room for further development for the LS group. It was also observed that in the cognitively most demanding task, i.e. the retelling task, the proportion of cognates was significantly higher compared to the NS group. The area where the LS group diverged the most from the NS group was in the range of low-frequency words (i.e. the 2000+ range) in the interview and the retelling task.

Acculturation or 'Culture' as a Decisive Factor in SLA

The studies presented below differ from these above in that they do not focus exclusively on cultural migrants. Diskin and Regan include cultural migrants among other categories of migrants and the two subsequent chapters consider the effect of acculturation on L2 attainment.

Diskin and Regan examine the acquisition of discourse-pragmatic features by migrants in Ireland. It has earlier been shown that the degree to which a non-native speaker (NNS) feels integrated within a speech community correlates positively with the frequency of their use of discourse-pragmatic markers in the target language. This chapter follows on from these earlier studies by analysing discourse-pragmatic variables, and while it will not look at integration per se, it will take migration and specifically migratory experience as a context for second language acquisition. The data come from a corpus of sociolinguistic interviews recorded in Dublin. The participants are recently-arrived Polish and Chinese migrants and native Dubliners. In this sociolinguistic study the analysis expands on categories such as gender, age, length of residence (LOR), nationality and level of education. It uses migratory experience as the major factor/perspective on acquisition. The participants are divided into four groups: academic migrants, chain migrants, cultural migrants and economic migrants. The main research questions are the following: Does migratory experience affect SLA? Do migrants in Ireland mirror patterns of native speakers (NS) of Irish English in their choice and frequency of use of discourse-pragmatic markers? The division of participants by type of migrant showed that as far as quotatives (*like, say*) are concerned, there appeared to be examples of stance taking and identity work on the part of the economic and cultural migrants. The division by nationality showed that the Poles had a preference for 'you know', providing some evidence for L1 transfer. All the NNS followed the NS in their preference for 'you know' and 'you mean', illustrating that accommodation, especially when it is less socially marked, is happening at all levels of proficiency and length of residence. Finally, the avoidance of the 'Irish variable', clause-final *like*, by the NNS, shows a sensitivity to varietal variation and displays evidence of identity construction.

Hammer and Dewaele take Schumann's acculturation model as a starting point and are interested in the link between self-reported proficiency and acculturation. The population investigated consists of 149 migrants (L1 Polish and L2 English) who relocated to the UK in early adulthood. They are highly educated sequential bilinguals who have been resident in the UK for an average of eight years following migration. The independent variables analysed in the study are divided into three categories: (1) post-migration sociolinguistic aspects, namely, acculturation level and frequency of L2 use following migration; (2) possible temporal predictors of the L2 attainment, namely, age of onset, age at migration and length of domicile in the host country; and (3) socio-biographical variables, namely, context of L2 acquisition, education level, age, gender and motivation behind migration. Their results showed that acculturation level, as measured through a questionnaire, is strongly linked to self-reported L2 attainment.

Granena also chooses Schumann's acculturation model as a theoretical starting point when she investigates the role of socio-psychological factors in a population of Chinese L1 Spanish L2 learners. A population of 100 learners are included, separated in groups of early age of onset and late age of onset. The independent variables included were target language group identification and confidence/ease with the L2 learning task. These variables were operationalised by means of four questions, with answers given on a Likert scale. The dependent variables studied consisted of four different versions of a grammatical judgement test

(GJT), i.e. morphosyntactic intuition. The different versions include different timing (timed/untimed) and modality (auditory/visual tests) conditions. The author found that one of the socio-psychological dimensions – 'satisfaction with one's own pronunciation' – correlated significantly with the GJTs, especially the untimed ones, both in early and late starters. In addition, GJT scores were also related significantly to a question regarding self-perceived degree of native-likeness. This correlation was only significant in the group of early learners. However, a multiple regression analysis, showed very low predictive power for the included socio-psychological factors. Granena suggests that other socio-psychological factors than those investigated in the present study should be investigated, since the regression analysis indicated that neither age of onset nor length of residence could explain variation in ultimate outcomes. The author also stresses that phonology may be a more interesting measure for correlation with socio-psychological factors than morphosyntax.

In sum, the volume provides both linguistic and socio-psychological perspectives of cultural migrants' L2 use in different geographical settings. It is hoped that the study of this particular population will offer new insights for SLA theory, especially with regard to native-likeness. Migration is an increasing phenomenon in today's world and it gives SLA researchers possibilities to expand their empirical field. In the concluding chapter, the findings of the seven contributions will be discussed in the light of research on native-likeness and possible new research avenues will also be proposed.

References

Abrahamsson, N. (2012) Age of onset and nativelike L2 ultimate attainment of morphosyntactic and phonetic intuition. *Studies in Second Language Acquisition* 34 (2), 187–214.

Abrahamsson, N. and Hyltenstam, K. (2009) Age of L2 acquisition and degree of nativelikeness – Listener perception vs linguistic scrutiny. *Language Learning* 58 (3), 249–306.

Benson, M. (2012) How culturally significant imaginings are translated into lifestyle migration. *Journal of Ethnic and Migration Studies* 38 (10), 1681–1696.

Benson, M. and O'Reilly, K. (2009) Migration and the search for a better way of life: A critical exploration of lifestyle migration. *The Sociological Review* 57 (4), 608–625.

Birdsong, D. (1992) Ultimate attainment in second language acquisition. *Language* 68, 706–755.

Birdsong, D. (2003) Authenticité de prononciation en français L2 chez des apprenants tardifs anglophones: analyses segmentales et globales. *AILE* 18, 17–36.

Birdsong, D. (2007) Nativelike pronunciation among late learners of French as a second language. In S.-O. Bohn and M. Munro (eds) *Second Language Speech Learning: The Role of Language Experience in Speech Perception and Production* (pp. 99–116). Amsterdam: John Benjamins.

DeKeyser, R.M. (2000) The robustness of critical period effects in second language acquisition. *Studies in Second Language Acquisition* 22 (4), 499–533.

DeKeyser, R.M., Alfi-Shabtay, J. and Ravid, D. (2010) Crosslinguistic evidence for the nature of age effects in second language acquisition. *Applied Psycholinguistics* 31 (3), 413–438.
DELMI (Delegationen för migrationsstudier). Utkast till program och strategi. Bakgrundspapper till seminarium i Rosenbads konferenscenter, Stockholm. Thursday, 5 June 2014.
Deci, R.M. and Ryan, E.L. (2000) Self-determination theory and the facilitation of intrinsic motivation, social development, and well-being. *American Psychologist*, 55 (1), 68–78.
DeKeyser, R.M. (2000) The robustness of critical period effects in second language acquisition. *Studies in Second Language Acquisition* 22 (4), 499–533.
DeKeyser, R.M. (ed.) (2007) *Practice in a Second Language. Perspectives from Applied Linguistics and Cognitive Psychology*. New York: Cambridge University Press.
DeKeyser, R.M., Alfi-Shabtay, J. and Ravid, D. (2010) Crosslinguistic evidence for the nature of age effects in second language acquisition. *Applied Psycholinguistics* 31 (3), 413–438.
Duchêne, A., Moyer, M. and Roberts, C. (2013) Introduction: Recasting institutions and work in multilingual and transnational spaces. In A. Duchêne, M. Moyer and C. Roberts (eds) *Language, Migration and Social Inequalities. A Critical Sociolinguistic Perspective on Institutions and Work*. Bristol: Multilingual Matters.
Dustmann, C. and van Soest, A. (2002) Language and the earnings of immigrants. *Industrial and Labor Relations Review* 55 (3), 473–492.
Fujita, Y. (2009) *Cultural Migrants from Japan. Youth, Media, and Migration in New York and London*. Lanham: Lexington Books.
Granena, G. and Long, M. (2013) Age of onset, length of residence, language aptitude, and ultimate attainment in three linguistic domains. *Second Language Research* 29 (3), 311–343.
Hyltenstam, K., Bartning, I. and Fant, L. (eds) (2014) *Avancerad andraspråksanvändning. Slutrapport från ett forskningsprogram*. RJ:s Skriftserie 2. Stockholm: Makadam Förlag.
Ioup, G., Boustagui, E., Eltigi, M. and Mosette, M. (1994) Reexamining the critical period hypothesis. A case of successful adult second language acquisition. *Studies in Second Language Acquisition* 16 (1), 73–98.
King-O'Riain, C. (2008) Target earning/learning, settling or trampolining? Polish and Chinese immigrants in Ireland. *Irish Geography* 41 (2), 211–233.
Kinsella, C. and Singleton, D. (2014) Much more than age. *Applied Linguistics* 35 (4), 441–462.
Klein, W. and Perdue, C. (1997) The basic variety (or: Couldn't natural languages be much simpler?). *Second Language Research* 13 (4), 301–347.
Lenneberg, E.H. (1967) *Biological Foundations of Language*. New York: Wiley.
Long, M. (2013) Maturational constraints on child and adult SLA. In G. Granena and M. Long (eds) *Sensitive Periods, Language Aptitude, and Ultimate Attainment* (pp. 3–42). Amsterdam: John Benjamins.
Lundström, C. (2014) *White Migrations: Gender, Whiteness and Privilege in Transnational Migration*. Basingstoke: Palgrave MacMillan.
Marinova-Todd, S. (2003) Comprehensive analysis of ultimate attainment in adult second language acquisition. Unpublished doctoral dissertation. Harvard University.
Meisel, J, Clahsen, H. and Pienemann, M. (1981) On determining developmental stages in natural second language acquisition. *Studies in Second Language Acquisition* 3 (2), 109–135.
Montrul, S. and Slabakova, R. (2003) Competence similarities between native and near-native speakers: An investigation of the preterite/imperfect contrast in Spanish. *Studies in Second Language Acquisition* 25 (3), 351–398.

Moyer, A. (2004) *Age, Accent and Experience in Second Language Acquisition. An Integrated Approach to Critical Period Inquiry.* Clevedon: Multilingual Matters.
Moyer, A. (2013) *Foreign Accent: The Phenomenon of Non-native Speech.* Cambridge: Cambridge University Press.
Muñoz, C. (2008) Symmetries and asymmetries of age effects in naturalistic and instructed L2 learning. *Applied Linguistics* 29 (4), 578–596.
Muñoz, C. and Singleton, D. (2007) Foreign Accent in advanced learners: Two successful profiles. *EUROSLA Yearbook* 7, 171–191.
Muñoz, C. and Singleton, D. (2011) A critical review of age-related research on L2 ultimate attainment. *Language Teaching* 44 (1), 1–35.
Piller, I. (2002) Passing for a native speaker: Identity and success in second language learning. *Journal of Sociolinguistics* 6 (2), 179–206.
Schumann, J.H. (1986) Research on the acculturation model for second language acquisition. *Journal of Multilingual and Multicultural Development* 7 (5), 379–392.
Young-Scholten, M. (2013) Low-educated immigrants and the social relevance of second language acquisition research. *Second Language Research* 29 (4), 441–454.

Part 1

Focus on Cultural Migrants

1 Beyond Native-like? The Lexical Profile of a Cultural Migrant in Italy

Anna Gudmundson and Camilla Bardel

Introduction

In this study we analyse lexical variation and lexical sophistication in cross-sectional data from six Swedish L2 users of Italian, who regularly visit Italy or have lived in the country for long periods, but then moved back to Sweden and enrolled in courses in Italian at Stockholm University. The main focus of this chapter, however, is a longitudinal study of a very advanced learner of Italian, a young Swedish woman, Alva, who has chosen to live in Italy for personal reasons. Her level of oral proficiency is very high when it comes to grammar and pronunciation. As regards her vocabulary, there are no formal deviances from the target norm. Aspects of her vocabulary are compared, using lexical profiling data based on the tools Vocd and LOPP*f*, to that of native speakers of Italian, and in addition to the profiling data, we also carry out a qualitative analysis of her vocabulary, focusing mainly on the low-frequency words and on the words that differ between Alva and the native speakers. Analysing the words that are unique in Alva's production, that is, words that are not used in any of the native speakers' productions, allows us to see if, and in that case how, an advanced learner's vocabulary may differ from that of native speakers. A frequency-based perspective is adopted, according to which high-frequency words are assumed to be learnt earlier than low-frequency words (Cobb & Horst, 2004).

What characterises a cultural migrant from a sociolinguistic and a proficiency point of view? By the term cultural migrant, we mean someone who, for one reason or the other, is personally interested in the target language and culture, and therefore moves to, or spends a lot of time in, a country where the target language is spoken.

According to Forsberg Lundell and Bartning (this volume) cultural migrants are people who decide 'out of their free will, to move to another country permanently and learn another language. The culture of the target language country is highly appealing to them and they make an active choice to live in this new culture'. They are also, according to Forsberg Lundell and Bartning (this volume), often well integrated, with high degrees of education, something that leads to good chances to practice the L2. While the effect of practice in a second language is still an issue of debate (DeKeyser, 2007), it is assumed here that time spent in the TL country under the circumstances characterised by the motivation of someone who has chosen to live in a particular country may promote a high level of L2 attainment.

The informant Alva satisfies all the prerequisites of the above definition of a cultural migrant. In addition to her case, the other informants investigated in this study can be said to fulfil part of the definition. The main difference between them and Alva is that they have moved back to Sweden, their home country. The periods they have spent in Italy are in some cases also shorter than the time spent by Alva, in others longer. Characteristic for the whole group is that they all have high degrees of education, and they all have positive attitudes towards Italy and the Italian language, and during their stays in the country they were all immersed in the target language culture (see Tables 1.1 and 1.2 for detailed information about the informants). In Schumann's (1986) terms, the degree of acculturation can be assumed to be high in all the informants, and thus, as Schumann's acculturation model suggests, their chances of achieving high levels of L2 attainment are high: 'Learners will acquire the target language to the degree they acculturate to the target language group' (Schumann, 1986: 379).

As already mentioned, the particular linguistic aspect of interest in this study is vocabulary use. To our knowledge, the vocabulary of cultural migrants has not been much investigated (but see Forsberg-Lundell & Lindqvist, 2014). It seems reasonable to assume that someone living in the TL country has optimal chances to develop the L2 vocabulary, thanks to a rich input and many opportunities for practice in interaction.

The level of vocabulary richness in oral production can be measured with a number of different measures, ranging from the type-token ratio and more elaborated variants thereof (Daller *et al.*, 2003) to mere judgements made by language teachers (Tidball & Treffers-Daller, 2008). In this study, we will discuss the results obtained from two measures, the D measure, or Vocd (Malvern *et al.*, 2004), which measures lexical variation, and the Lexical Oral Production Profile (LOPP*f*), a recently developed instrument for measuring lexical sophistication in Italian oral production, by means of proportion of low-frequency words. The production of the learners is compared to frequency bands based on the 3000 most frequent words from target language corpora and the words that fall outside the 3000 most frequent words are the so-called offlist words. In some studies (e.g. Lindqvist *et al.*, 2011) the words that fall outside the 2000 most frequent words, i.e. band 3-words and offlist words, are considered advanced. Hence, LOPPf is an instrument used for measuring lexical sophistication defined as the proportion of low-frequency words in the total of words produced (Laufer & Nation, 1995). Lexical variation, or diversity, can be measured by the simple type/token ratio (TTR), a calculation of the number of types divided by the number of tokens in a text. However, it has been pointed out by many that a problem with TTR is its sensitivity to text length: 'The more words (tokens) a text has, the less likely it is that new words (types) will occur' (McCarthy & Jarvis, 2007: 460). The longer the text, the more often words are repeated, high-frequency words will be repeated more often, in comparison to low-frequency words, and this tendency will increase the longer the text is. A tentative solution to this problem is the D measure (for details see Lindqvist et al., 2013).

In this study, the lexical profiles of the L2 users are compared to those of native speakers. Because native speakers have varied lexical competence, particularly depending on their level of education and reading habits, data were gathered also from a group of L1 speakers who have an educational level that is similar to that of the Swedish informants. Being native-like in this study thus means reaching levels similar to those of native speakers with the same educational background.

In the qualitative analysis of Alva's production, we look into the longitudinal lexical development of this particular L2 user, focusing on the new lemmas that are added at the different times of measurement, starting from the lexical sophistication data. There will be a particular focus on the low-frequency words used by Alva and in a second step we will look at those low-frequency words that are used only by Alva and none of the Italian native speakers. Finally, we will see if there are any words that are used by all the native speakers, but not by Alva.

Data Collection

The data in this study comes from recordings of semi-guided interviews led by a native speaker of Italian contained in the InterIta corpus (see Bardel et al., 2012 for a brief description of the corpus). The topics of conversation are daily activities such as family life, hobbies, studies, job experiences, travelling and stays in Italy. The questions of the different interviews aim at inducing the L2 speakers to use different grammatical structures each time, but there is no systematic intention to elicit different vocabulary from time to time. Some of the recordings include a narration task, which induces the informants to use vocabulary of particular semantic fields. This, as well as other conditions, is the same for all informants, native speakers and non-native speakers.

Each of the six L2 users of this study have been immersed in the target language context for long periods, or they visit the target language country regularly and are then living in contexts where Italian families or friends are highly present (see Tables 1.1 and 1.2). All informants have studied Italian at Stockholm University or do study there at the time of the data collection. One of the learners, Alva, decided to move to Italy and to stay there, and she still lives there at the time of the fourth and last recording with her.

Alva started to learn Italian in a natural context at the age of 27, when she moved to Italy to stay with her Italian boyfriend, as she reports in the following extract from the first recording:

*ALV: sono fidanzata con [/] con un ragazzo di Biella.
I am engaged to a boy from Biella.
*PAO: quindi è per questo motivo che sei in Italia oppure?
so this is the reason for you being in Italy, or...?
*ALV: esatto sì.
exactly, yes.
*PAO: eh hm quindi mi pare di capire che abiti in Italia soltanto per motivi affettivi oppure ci sono anche altre ragioni?
eh so you live in Italy only for affective reasons, or are there also other motives?
*ALV: ma eh: no mi [/] mi sono trasferita soltanto per il fatto che lui abita lì e poi ovviamente anche sono [/] sono curiosa di [/] di imparare l'italiano +...
well eh no I moved there just because he lived there and obviously I am curious to learn Italian...
*ALV: di [/] di avere l' opportunità di [/] di vivere in un altro paese...
to get the opportunity to live in another country...
*ALV: ...una cosa che mi interessa molto.
... something that interests me a lot.
*ALV: ma la cosa che mi ha fatto eh trasferirmi lì è stato lui [=! ride].
but what really made me move there was him (laughs).

Alva works as an English teacher and as a designer. After a year in Italy, she enrolled in a web-based course of Italian at the University of Stockholm.

Table 1.1 Alva

Name	Age at the time of the first recording	Dates of recordings	Info
Alva	29	26.9. 2004 17.3. 2005 27.2. 2007 20.8. 2009	Has lived, and is still living, in Italy. She's married to an Italian and works in an Italian company.

Table 1.2 All learners

Name	Age at the time of the first recording	Info
Nina	25	Studies Italian at Stockholm University but goes to Italy every second year to visit her Italian family. Her mother is Italian, but Italian has never been used at home in Stockholm. When in Italy, she stays with her grandmother, who also speaks Swedish.
Frank	24	Has lived in Italy for eight months and goes there regularly. He's not currently living in Italy but would like to do so.
Nora	24	Has never lived in Italy but she goes there every year to visit her father who is Italian.
Ulla	37	Used to live in Italy as a child, and now visits the country regularly.
Kristina	38	Has lived in Italy for eight years but is now back in Sweden.

She was recorded four times during five years. The other learners of the study are presented in Table 1.2.

As the following extracts show, the learners have positive attitudes towards Italy, its culture and language. Frank, for instance, plans to go to the country and to work there:

*FRA: tz perché [/] eh: perché: eh penso forse di poter abitare e lavorare in Italia perché anche sto studiando economia # eh: a [/] # a me piacerebbe forse lavorare almeno un paio di anni all' estero.
tz because eh because I think that maybe I could live and work in Italy, because I also study economics eh I would like to work maybe at least a couple of years abroad.
*FRA: eh: hm l' Italia sarebbe proprio # eh il paese giusto per [/] per me eh.
eh hm Italy would be exactly the right country for me.

Nora says that Italian is the language she likes the best, because it gives her the liberty to express herself:

*PAO: c'è una lingua del cuore una lingua che ti <piace un po' di più> [>] rispetto alle altre?
is there any language that you prefer over the others?
*NOR: <ah ecco> [<].
ah, ok.
*NOR: va beh.
well.

*NOR: l' italiano sì perché mi dà una libertà di [/] di esprimermi molto eh +...
Italian yes because it gives me the liberty to express myself much eh...

Ulla, who used to live in Italy in her childhood, misses many aspects of the Italian lifestyle:

*PAO: e quando sei in Svezia che cosa ti manca dell' Italia?
and when you are in Sweden what do you miss about Italy?
*ULL: eh: il modo di vivere.
eh the lifestyle.
*ULL: il modo di pensare.
the way people think.
*ULL: eh ## il clima.
the climate.
*ULL: il mangiare.
the food.
*ULL: sono cose abbastanza importanti.
those are rather important things.

The control group

The control group is a group of six Italian native speakers recorded during their time as Erasmus students at the University of Stockholm. They were all between 21 and 25 years of age at the time of recording.

Research Questions

Previous studies (Bardel *et al.*, 2012; Lindqvist *et al.*, 2011) show that only very advanced L2 learners reach levels that are close to those of native speakers, when it comes to lexical sophistication in oral production.[1] Indeed, all native speakers cannot be expected to have the same degree of lexical richness or sophistication, but our previous studies have shown that the group of Erasmus students examined here all fall within a rather restricted range when it comes to lexical sophistication, as measured by LOPP*f*. This study investigates whether it is possible for an L2 learner who lives, or has lived in the country, more or less regularly, to achieve a native-like lexical profile as measured both by Vocd and LOPP*f*.

If so, what characterises the vocabulary of such an advanced L2 speaker, from a qualitative point of view? Are the words used by a cultural migrant the same as those used by native speakers? In order to investigate this, we will look, from a qualitative point of view, into the words used by Alva, focusing on the low-frequency words. We will also look at the words that are used only by Alva and none of the Italian native speakers, trying to categorise them. We think that this could be a way to understand what possibly makes a cultural migrant different from native speakers from a vocabulary perspective. For the same scope, we will see if there are any words that are used by all the native speakers, but not by Alva.

Results

The cross-sectional study

In this section, we aim at answering our first research question, regarding the possibility for a cultural migrant achieving a native-like lexical profile as concerns lexical sophistication and variation.

In Table 1.3, the results for the non-native speakers are shown, in both lexical variation (Vocd) and lexical sophistication (LOPPf).

As Table 1.3 shows, Kristina has the highest lexical variation and Alva has the highest lexical sophistication (i.e. proportion of low-frequency words) in the group.

In Table 1.4, the same measures are reported for the native speakers.

When comparing the two groups, one can see that the lexical variation is clearly higher in the native speakers' group (mean 123.74) than in the non-native speakers (mean 90.92). A Mann-Whitney U test reveals a statistically reliable difference as regards the Vocd value between the native speakers and the non-native speakers, with native speakers receiving higher scores than non-native speakers, $z=-2.40$, $p=0.016$.[2] Non-natives had an average rank of 4.00, while natives had an average rank of 9.00.

When it comes to lexical sophistication, the mean is only slightly higher in the native speakers (8.20) as compared with the non-natives (7.88). A Mann-Whitney U test failed to reveal a statistically reliable difference as regards the LOPPf value between the native speakers group and the non-native speaker group, $z=-0.962$, $p=0.336$. Non-natives had an average rank of 5.50, while natives had an average rank of 7.50.

Table 1.3 Results for the non-native speakers of Italian, rec. 1: Vocd and LOPPf

Name	Vocd	LOPPf
Alva	88.74	8.62
Kristina	114.73	8.13
Ulla	87.41	8.37
Nora	103.6	7.86
Frank	77.67	7.31
Nina	73.41	7.00
Mean	90.92	7.88
SD	15.66	0.62

Table 1.4 Results for the native speakers of Italian, rec. 1: Vocd and LOPP*f*

Name	Vocd	LOPP*f*
Tiziana	110.02	8.78
Franco	121.26	9.15
Natale	134.64	7.38
Flavio	156.8	8.17
Antonio	114.24	8.10
Riccardo	105.49	8.10
Mean	123.74	8.28
SD	19.12	0.62

This is illustrated in Figure 1.1 and Figure 1.2, where the native and the non-native speakers are represented in the same plots. The horizontal line indicates the point, above which all native speaker values fall:

The difference between native speakers and non-native speakers, when it comes to lexical variation, can be seen above. As can be noted, only the informant Kristina falls within the native-speaker range, while all the others are located below the horizontal line. As for lexical sophistication, however, there is practically no difference, as seen in Figure 1.2.

As can be seen from Figure 1.2, only two informants, Frank and Nina, fall below the native-speaker range, and it can be noted that the difference between Frank and Natale, the native speaker with the lowest LOPP*f*-value, is very small, 7.31 compared to 7.38.

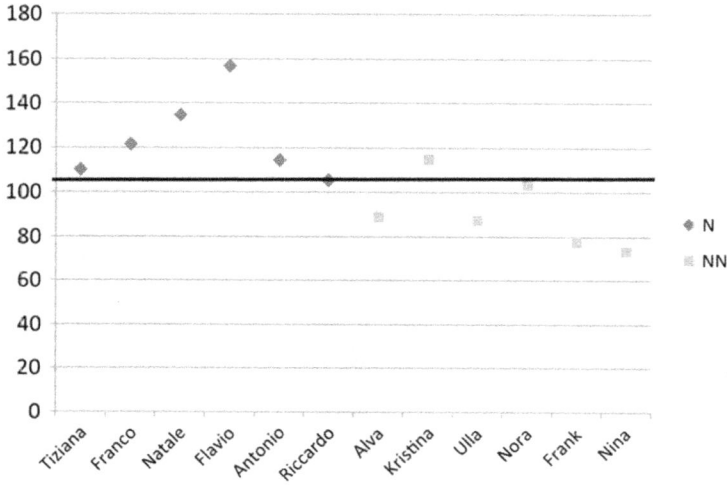

Figure 1.1 Lexical variation (Vocd), native speakers vs non-native speakers, rec 1

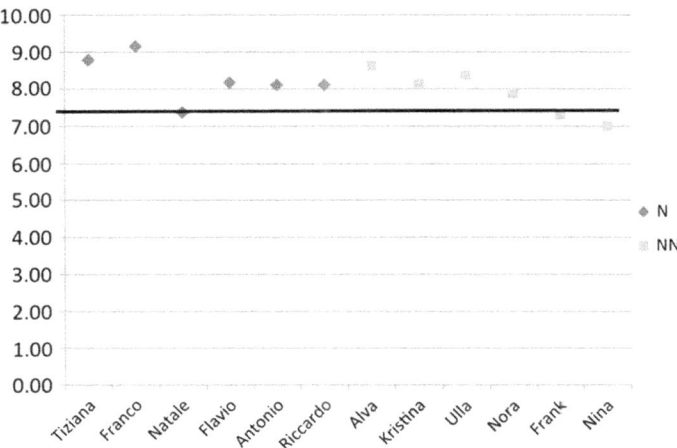

Figure 1.2 Lexical sophistication (LOPPf), native speakers vs non-native speakers, rec 1

In summary the results indicate that even though cultural migrants seem to reach a rather advanced level when it comes to lexical sophistication, they don't seem to vary their vocabulary as much as native speakers do. This could be interpreted as if they use many low-frequency words, but that those low-frequency words are repeated more often.

The case of Alva – quantitative results

In this section, a closer look will be taken at Alva and her longitudinal development in the four recordings, comparing her results to the results from three recordings with the native speakers.[3] Table 1.5 and Figure 1.3 show the Vocd values in the sequences of recordings of Alva and the native speakers.

Table 1.5 Lexical variation (Vocd), sequences of recordings of Alva and the native speakers

Name	Rec. 1	Rec. 2	Rec. 3	Rec. 4
Alva	88.74	103.9	111.84	114.09
Tiziana	110.02	127.78	128.74	
Franco	121.26	111.92	119.04	
Natale	134.64	130.8	124.24	
Flavio	156.8	137.56	140.45	
Antonio	114.24	118.76	128.8	
Riccardo	105.49	107.64	110.28	

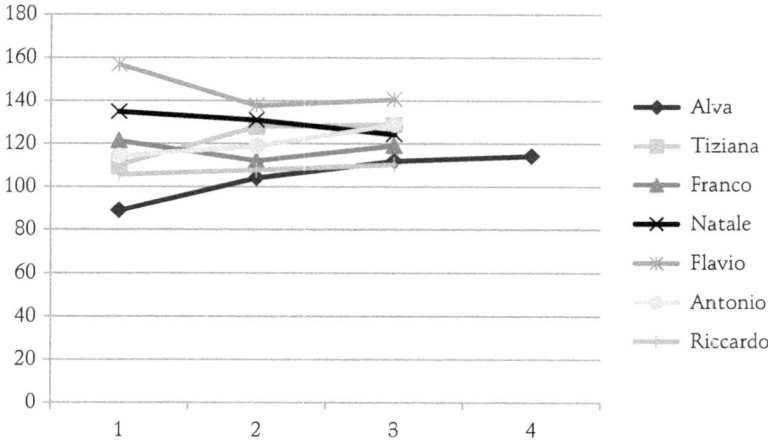

Figure 1.3 Lexical variation (Vocd), sequences of recordings of Alva and the native speakers

As can be seen in Figure 1.3, while the lexical profiles of the Italian native speakers seem to vary randomly in time 1, 2 and 3, the pattern shown in Alva's recordings could be interpreted as a development. Her profile is slightly lower in the first recording, and then in the lower range of the natives when measured by Vocd. Alva's development could of course also be interpreted as random variation. Since this is a case study, it is in fact impossible to say with certainty that her pattern differs from that of the native speakers (see e.g. Antonio, whose profile could also be interpreted as developmental). But considering the group of native speakers as a whole, it seems as though their pattern differs from that of Alva, which clearly points upwards. Furthermore, it doesn't seem plausible that the native speakers would develop the lexical sophistication of their L1 during their stay in Sweden. The same reasoning is valid for the results concerning lexical sophistication, which is shown in Table 1.6 and Figure 1.4.

Table 1.6 Lexical sophistication (LOPPf), sequences of recordings of Alva and the native speakers

Name	Rec. 1	Rec. 2	Rec. 3	Rec. 4
Alva	8.62	8.41	10.01	10.25
Tiziana	8.78	8.08	8.67	
Franco	9.15	8.78	6.77	
Natale	7.38	7.65	7.54	
Flavio	8.17	9.42	9.25	
Antonio	8.10	8.97	9.56	
Riccardo	8.10	6.90	8.71	

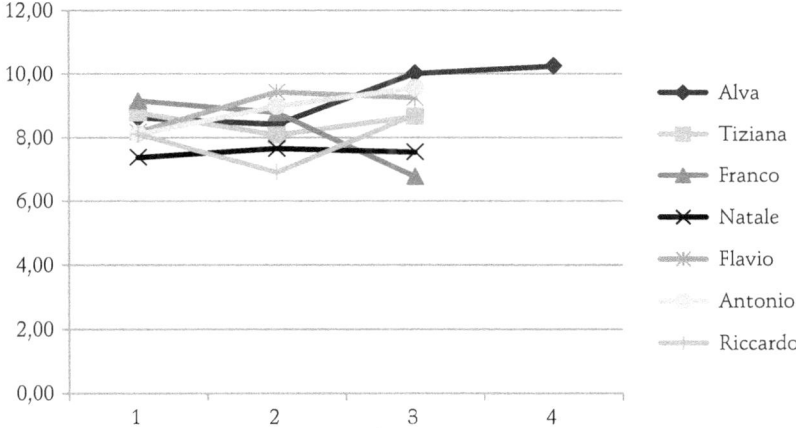

Figure 1.4 Lexical sophistication (LOPP*f*), sequences of recordings of Alva and the native speakers

As can be seen, in contrast with the Vocd value, when it comes to lexical sophistication, Alva is on par with the natives, scoring within the native speaker range already from her first recording. It is interesting to notice that her last recordings show even higher values than any of those reached by the native speakers.

In summary, the quantitative results related to the longitudinal development of Alva indicate that she has lower lexical variation than all the native speakers in her first recordings, and that she, in her last recordings, reaches the lower range of the natives (that is, she tends to repeat the same words to a higher extent than many of the native speakers). When it comes to lexical sophistication, the results are quite different: already in her first recordings Alva scores within the native speakers range, and in her last recordings she has a higher proportion of rare words in her speech than any of the native speakers.

Let us now turn to look at the vocabulary used by Alva from a qualitative point of view.

The case of Alva

We have seen that in the case of Alva, a learner whom we had the possibility to follow longitudinally during five years of her living in Italy, the lexical profile is not very different from that of the native speakers used as controls in this study. As for the proportion of low-frequency words, it was found to be higher in Alva's profile than in any of the native speakers. In order to understand how this can be the case, we will now look into the words used by Alva, more in detail, focusing mainly on the low-frequency words. We will also look at those low-frequency words that are used only by Alva and none of the Italian native speakers. Finally, we will see if there are any words that are used by all the native speakers, but not by Alva.

From a developmental point of view, it can be noted that new words from all the bands and the N (=Null) category continue to be added to Alva's vocabulary use throughout the four recordings. The whole picture of her vocabulary can be seen in Appendix 1. During the four recordings Alva uses a total of 914 different lemmas. During her first recording she uses 321 different lemmas. During recording 2 229 new lemmas are added, during recording 3, 229 new lemmas are added, and in the last recording 135 new lemmas are added.

Table 1.7 and Figure 1.5 show how the new lemmas that are added to Alva's vocabulary during the four recordings are distributed over the four bands. It can be seen that in recording 2, a total number of 229 lemmas are added to her vocabulary, and that 46.72% out of these new lemmas belong to band 1, 18.34% belong to band 2, 9.17% belong to band 3, and finally 25.76% belong to the offlist or Null (N) category. The overall pattern is best seen in Figure 1.5, where it can be noted that, even though the band 1 lemmas continue to constitute the biggest part of the new words that are added in all recordings, the proportion of band 1 lemmas that are added over time decreases radically, while the proportion of offlist lemmas increases the most.

Dividing the 914 lemmas used by Alva into those belonging to a closed word class, such as articles, prepositions, conjunctions and some adverbs, and those belonging to an open word class such as nouns, verbs and adjectives, we get the following results: 145 lemmas can be classified as belonging to the first class and 769 as belonging to the latter. As can be noticed in Table 1.8, the majority (91 out of 145) of the closed-class lemmas are used already in Alva's first recording, and rather few are added in the consecutive recordings. In the first recording we find band 1 prepositions like *a, con, di, tra, in, per* and *su*; band 1 pronouns, like *che, cui, io, lei, loro, questo, quello* and *ogni*; band 1 conjunctions, like *e, ma, o, però, mentre, perché* and *se*; band 1 adverbs such as *abbastanza, adesso, ancora, troppo, tanto, prima* and *neanche*. Alva also uses an offlist adverb, namely *occhei* (*ok*), which is

Table 1.7 The distribution of new lemmas that are added during the four recordings

Rec	band 1(n)	band 2(n)	band 3(n)	N(n)	Tot.	band 1 (%)	band 2 (%)	band 3 (%)	N (%)
1	227	33	14	47	321	70.72	10.28	4.36	14.64
2	107	42	21	59	229	46.72	18.34	9.17	25.76
3	98	39	19	73	229	42.79	17.03	8.30	31.88
4	56	24	6	49	135	41.48	17.78	4.44	36.30
Tot	488	138	60	228	914				

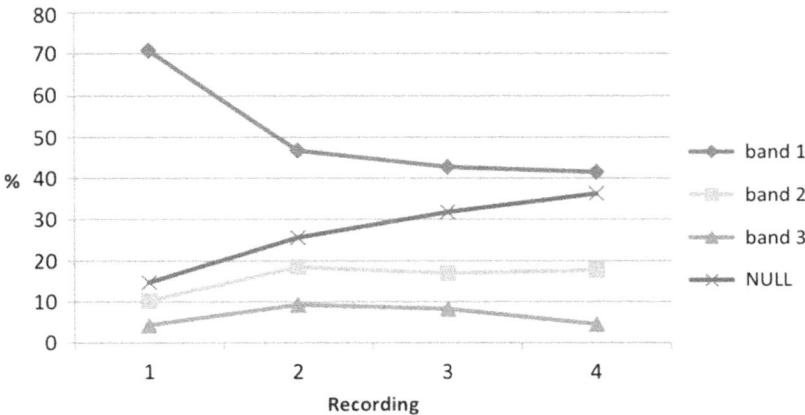

Figure 1.5 The distribution of new lemmas that are added during the four recordings

a rather common word in spoken Swedish, but less common in Italian. It could be classified as a cognate or as lexical transfer. In recording 2, five band 1 prepositions are added: *contro, davanti, dietro, indietro* and *verso*, and one band 2 preposition, *attorno*. Furthermore, six band 1 pronouns, *chi, egli, quale, quanto, stesso* and *ti* are added as well as two band 1 conjunctions, *infatti* and *mentre*, and one band 2 conjunction, *perciò*. Also five band 1 adverbs are added, e.g. *allora, anzi* and *vicino*, and one offlist adverb, *attorno*. In recording 3, four band 1 prepositions are added (*sopra, sotto, fra* and *dentro*) and four band 1 pronouns (*ne, noi, nostro* and *vostro*); one band 1 conjunction (*cioè*); nine band 1 adverbs, e.g. *circa, ecco, magari* and *ormai*, and one offlist adverb: *ovunque*. In recording 4 the following closed-class words are added: two prepositions, *durante* which is a band 1 preposition, and *entro*, which is a band 2 preposition; two pronouns, *alcuno* which is a band 1 pronoun, and *gli* which is an offlist pronoun; One band 1 adverb, *appena*, and one band 2 adverb, *talmente*. No conjunction is added in recording 4.

When it comes to the open word class lemmas, Table 1.8 below shows that the number of new lemmas added in the four recordings is continuously large compared to the closed word class lemmas, where the majority of the total number of lemmas used throughout the recordings, 91 out of 145 (62.76%), seem to be known already in recording 1. Thus new

Table 1.8 Distribution of open word class lemmas and closed-word class lemmas

Type of word	Rec. 1	Rec. 2	Rec. 3	Rec. 4	Tot.
Open word class	230	207	204	122	769
Closed word class	91	22	21	13	145
Tot.	321	229	229	135	914

words continue to be added regularly during Alva's stay in Italy. As could be seen in Table 1.7 above, the proportion of offlist words increases the most longitudinally, while the proportion of band 1 words decreases the most. We will therefore focus on the low-frequency offlist words used in the four recordings, trying to categorise them in the following categories: *cognates, thematic words* related to Alva's work and personal interests and *other* words. The *other* category is simply the words that do not fit in any of the other categories mentioned. In Bardel and Lindqvist (2011), it was found that a relatively high proportion of cognates and thematic words were used by intermediate and advanced Swedish learners of French and Italian L2. It seems reasonable to assume that Alva, although very advanced, might produce at least some such words.

Examples of the cognates[4] (with Swedish or English) found in Alva, among the offlist words, are the following:

Rec 1: *charme* (Sw. charm, Eng. charm), *giacca* (Sw. jacka, Eng. jacket), *umore* (Sw. humör, Eng. mood).

Rec 2: *ambulanza* (Sw. ambulans, Eng. ambulance), *animato* (Sw. animerad, Eng. animated), *autunno* (Sw. höst, Eng. autumn), *circo* (Sw. cirkus, Eng. circus), *combinazione* (Sw. kombination, Eng. combination), *confuso* (Sw. förvirrad, Eng. confused), *includere* (Sw. inkludera, Eng. include), *paranoia* (Sw. paranoia, Eng. paranoia), *picnic* (Sw. pick-nick, Eng. pic-nic), *scultura* (Sw. skulptur, Eng. sculpture), *umanistico* (Sw. humanistisk, Eng. humanistic).

Rec 3: *egoista* (Sw. egoist, Eng. egoist), *individualista* (Sw. individualist, Eng. individualist), *intensivo* (Sw. intensiv, Eng. intensive), *intolleranza* (Sw. intolerant, Eng. intolerant), *organizzato* (Sw. organiserad, Eng. organised), *pausa* (Sw. paus, Eng. pause), *scioccato* (Sw. chockad, Eng. shocked).

Rec 4: *assistente* (Sw. assistant, Eng. assistant), *biologico* (Sw. biologisk, Eng. biological), *ceramic* (Sw. keramik, Eng. ceramics), *contrasto* (Sw. contrast, Eng. contrast), *legittimo* (Sw. legitim, Eng. legitimate), *unico* (Sw. unik, Eng. unique).

These are mainly advanced cognates, in the sense that they differ morphologically from their Swedish/English cognates and/or they belong to academic genres (cf. Bardel & Lindqvist, 2011; Bardel *et al.*, 2012).

The few 'easy' or 'basic' cognates (i.e. cognates that have the same morphology and a 1–1 form-meaning relation) are *charme, design, designer, paranoia* and *picnic*. This indicates that cognates are not used by Alva as a lexical strategy, but that the cognates she uses are part of an advanced vocabulary, which might however be positively influenced by her knowledge of other languages.[5] It is important to notice that cognates are common also in the other frequency bands, and it would be interesting to investigate whether Swedish learners of Italian use a higher number of cognate words compared to native speakers of Italian, and maybe even more interesting, to analyse how Swedish learners of Italian perform compared to learners with a different L1 background.

Thematic words (In some cases they overlap with the cognate category) related to Alva's work and personal interests among the low-frequency lemmas are, for example, words related to Alva's work as a designer:

Rec 1: *cucire* (sew), *designer, sarta* (dressmaker), *sartoria* (tailor's shop), *tessile* (textile – adjective).
Rec 2: *abito* (dress), *design, dipingere* (to draw), *maglia* (knitwear).
Rec 3: *abbigliamento* (clothing), *attrezzatura* (equipment), *cartamodello* (paper pattern), *creativo* (creative), *esteticamente* (aesthetically).
Rec 4: *collezione* (collection), *modellista* (pattern maker), *stilista* (stylist).

Other thematic low-frequency lemmas are related to Alva's work as an English teacher or university student:

Rec 1: *laureare* (graduate), *madrelingua* (mother tongue).
Rec 3: *tesina* (BA thesis).
Rec 4: *pronuncia* (pronunciation).

General work-related vocabulary (maybe typical of the situation of the cultural migrant) are:

Rec 1: *gavetta (fare la gavetta)* (to gain experience; to cut one's teeth), *progettista* (designer), *stage* (internship).
Rec 2: *specializzare* (specialise), *specializzazione* (specialisation).
Rec 3: *licenziare* (dismiss).
Rec 4: *disoccupazione* (unemployment), *burocrazia* (bureaucracy).

There are also a few words related to sports and spare time activities:

Rec 1: *sciare* (ski).
Rec 2: *ginnastica* (physical training).
Rec 3: *immersioni subacquee* (diving), *sciistico* (related to skiing).

Another subcategory to that of thematic words is represented by words related to discourse about cultural differences between Sweden and Italy:

Rec 1: *svedese* (Swedish), *sottotitolo* (subtitles), *doppiato* (dubbed).
Rec 4: *betulla* (birch tree), *cesta* (basket), *corteccia* (bark), *nordico* (Nordic), *scandinavo* (Scandinavian).

Other words that might be seen as typical for the conceptual reality of Alva, i.e someone that is well integrated in Italian everyday life, are words that relate to family life and family members:

Rec 2: *convivere* (live together).
Rec 3: *nipotina* (grandchild), *sposato* (married), *suocera* (mother-in-law).

What is the *other* category? It is very vast and could be further classified, but this goes beyond the scope of this paper (for all the words, see Appendix 1).

Words used only by Alva. Table 1.9 shows how many words that are unique to the informant Alva and to the native speakers of this study.

As can be seen above, Alva uses the greatest number of unique words, which could in some way indicate that her vocabulary is different from that of the native speakers. By unique words, we refer to the words that are not present in any of the native speakers in this study (cf. last column of Appendix 1). Alva uses altogether 223 unique lemmas (types), and from these as many as 143 are offlist lemmas. A majority of her unique words are thus found in the offlist category. Many of her unique words are, in fact, the cognates and thematic words we saw earlier. Some of these words can be characterised as related to Alva's personal interests, such as *subacqueo* and *ginnastica* (related to diving, gymnastics), while others are typical for her work and career, like *dipingere* (to draw), *design, modello* and *sarta* (dressmaker), i.e. the kind of vocabulary someone working in the field of fashion and textile design in Italy has to know.

Finally, as shown in Table 1.10, there are a number of words that are used by all the native speakers, but not by Alva. This can be due to pure coincidence, but it is especially interesting to note that while the discourse marker *beh* (well) is used as many as 95 times by the Italian group, it is never used by Alva. This does not necessarily indicate that she has not yet grasped the sense of this particular expression, which seems to be used to varying extent and with different functions both in

Table 1.9 Number of unique lemmas

Informant	Unique lemmas (n)	Number of different lemmas (tot)	Unique lemmas (%)
Alva	223	914	24.40
Antonio	167	913	18.29
Flavio	149	918	16.23
Franco	136	943	14.42
Natale	80	821	9.74
Riccardo	121	834	14.51
Tiziana	129	924	13.96

Table 1.10 Lemmas used by all native speakers, but not by Alva

Lemma	Number of NS	Band	Occurrences
Beh	6	1	95
Bisognare	6	1	34
Costruire	6	1	11
Esame	6	1	28
Genitore	6	1	37
Madre	6	1	16
Positivo	6	1	23
Probabilmente	6	1	37
Rapporto	6	1	43
Scoprire	6	1	9
Senso	6	1	58
Servire	6	1	15
Stato	6	1	16

native speakers and very advanced L2 users of Italian, but the fact that she is not using it at all could also indicate that she has not yet reached a native-like level as far as interactional and/or metatextual competences are concerned (Pauletto & Bardel, submitted). It can also be noted that all these words are rather common in Italian, all being band 1 words, and are used often by all native speakers in this study. It is difficult to explain why these precise words are not used by Alva.

Conclusion

As has been shown in this study, an adult cultural migrant might well develop a vocabulary as advanced as that of a schooled native speaker when it comes to lexical sophistication, but inasmuch as lexical variation it seems more difficult, but not impossible, to reach native speaker levels. This was seen both in the cross-sectional study and in the longitudinal study of Alva. Thus, although very advanced L2 users tend to use many low-frequency words, they also seem to repeat the same words more often. High lexical sophistication values could be explained by the fact that they use a vocabulary that is, in some ways, different from that of the native speakers, maybe influenced by their mother tongue in the form of cognates. From that point of view, high values in lexical sophistication, especially when these values are higher than the natives', could therefore indicate a deviation from the native speaker norm when it comes to lexical choices. The proportion of low-frequency words found in the particular L2 user of this case study was higher than in any of the native speakers she was compared to.

The qualitative results showed that Alva used many cognates, something that could be interpreted as traces from other languages, although this interpretation has to be further investigated in a comparison to native speakers' use of cognates. The analysis also showed that a part of the informant Alva's low-frequency words and unique words was related to her career and family life in Italy, e.g. *sartoria, licenziare, progettista, nipotina* and *suocera* (tailor's shop, dismiss, designer, grandchild, mother-in-law). Maybe this kind of thematic vocabulary could be said to be typical for the situation of a cultural migrant, i.e. someone who is well integrated in Italian society by work or family. Among the low-frequency words used by Alva, there were a few that could be classified as typical for a Swedish person in an Italian context. Here we refer to words such as *svedese, corona, betulla, scandinavo* and *sottotitolo* (Swedish, crown, birch tree, Scandinavian, subtitles), i.e. words that appear in discussions about Sweden and differences between Sweden and Italy. It seems unlikely, even though speculative, that these words would arise in a conversation between an Italian and, for example, a German. However, some of these words, like *svedese* and *corona* (Swedish, crown), are also used by the Italian Erasmus students who spend a term in Stockholm – maybe not so surprising, as they are also cultural migrants in a sense.

The results from this study also suggest that the band 1 words are learnt relatively early (cf. Table 1.7), and the same thing is valid for the closed-class words such as pronouns and prepositions. A majority of these words are used by Alva already in her first recording. The results could be said to support functionalist theories of language acquisition (e.g. MacWhinney, 1987; Ellis, 2002) which focus on frequency effects when learning an L2 vocabulary.

Notes

(1) The proficiency level of these learners was measured independently from vocabulary use.
(2) The statistics were made with the IBM SPSS Statistics 21 software.
(3) The reason for recording the native speakers was not to study a development of their vocabulary, but merely to achieve a benchmark for the recordings of the L2 learners of the InterIta corpus, from which we have both single and multiple recordings (for a description of the InterIta corpus see www.isd.su.se/interita).
(4) Some of the cognates listed here differ more than others in spelling. This is the case of e.g. *giacca* and *scioccato*. Nevertheless, the pronunciation of these Italian words comes close to their Swedish and/or English counterparts.
(5) Such a positive influence from other languages is a hypothesis that might be tested in future work, although positive transfer at the lexical level is hard to isolate from general learning. In order to draw safe conclusions about the role of cognateness, the use of cognates in native speakers of Italian must also be examined.

References

Bardel, C. and Lindqvist, C. (2011) Developing a lexical profile for spoken French and Italian L2. The role of frequency, cognates and thematic vocabulary. In L. Roberts, G. Pallotti and C. Bettoni (eds) *EUROSLA Yearbook* (vol. 11, pp. 75–93). Amsterdam: John Benjamins.

Bardel, C., Gudmundson, A. and Lindqvist, C. (2012) Aspects of lexical sophistication in advanced learners' oral production: Vocabulary acquisition and use in L2 French and Italian. In N. Abrahamsson and K. Hyltenstam (eds) *High-Level L2 Acquisition, Learning and Use* (pp. 269–290). Thematic issue of *Studies in Second Language Acquisition* 34 (2).

Cobb, T. and Horst, M. (2004) Is there room for an academic wordlist in French? In P. Boogards and B. Laufer (eds) *Vocabulary in a Second Language: Selection, Acquisition, and Testing* (pp. 15–38). Amsterdam: John Benjamins.

Daller, H., Van Hout, R. and Treffers-Daller, J. (2003) Lexical richness in the spontaneous speech of bilinguals. *Applied Linguistics* 24 (2), 197–222.

DeKeyser, R.M. (ed.) (2007) *Practice in a Second Language. Perspectives from Applied Linguistics and Cognitive Psychology*. New York: Cambridge University Press.

Ellis, N.C. (2002) Frequency effects in language processing: A review with implications for theories of implicit and explicit language acquisition. *Studies in Second Language Acquisition* 24 (2), 143–188.

Forsberg Lundell, F. and Lindqvist, C. (2014) Vocabulary aspects of advanced L2 French: Do lexical formulaic sequences and lexical richness develop at the same rate? In C. Lindqvist and C. Bardel (eds) *The Acquisition of French as a Second Language* (pp. 75–94). Amsterdam: John Benjamins.

Laufer, B. and Nation, P. (1995) Vocabulary size and use: Lexical richness in L2 written production. *Applied Linguistics* 16 (3), 307–322.

Lindqvist, C., Bardel, C. and Gudmundson, A. (2011) Lexical richness in the advanced learner's oral production of French and Italian L2. *International Review of Applied Linguistics (IRAL)* 49 (3), 221–240.

Lindqvist, C., Gudmundson, A. and Bardel, C. (2013) A new approach to measuring lexical sophistication in L2 oral production. In C. Bardel, C. Lindqvist and B. Laufer (eds) *L2 Vocabulary Acquisition, Knowledge and Use. New Perspectives on Assessment and Corpus Analysis* (pp. 109–126). EUROSLA Monographs Series 2.

MacWhinney, B. (1987) *Mechanisms of Language Acquisition*. Hillsdale, NJ: Erlbaum.

McCarthy, P. and Jarvis, S. (2007) VocD: A theoretical and empirical evaluation. *Language Testing* 24 (4), 459–488.

Malvern, D.D., Richards, B.J., Chipere, N. and Durán, P. (2004) *Lexical Diversity and Language Development: Quantification and Assessment*. Houndmills, Hampshire: Palgrave Macmillan.

Pauletto, F. and Bardel, C. (submitted) *Be'-prefaced Turns in Italian: A Comparison Between Native and Non-native Speakers*.

Schumann, J.H. (1986) Research on the acculturation model for second language acquisition. *Journal of Multilingual and Multicultural Development* 7 (5), 379–392.

Tidball, F. and Treffers-Daller, J. (2008) Analysing lexical richness in French learner language: What frequency lists and teacher judgement can tell us about basic and advanced words. *Journal of French Language Studies* 18 (3), 299–313.

Appendix 1
Alva's vocabulary in order of appearance in the four recordings

Rec	Lemma	Band	Freq	Only by Alva
1	a	1	52	
1	abbastanza	1	7	
1	abitare	1	2	
1	adesso	1	5	
1	adulto	2	1	x
1	affittare	3	2	
1	ah	1	4	
1	aiutare	1	1	
1	albergo	2	3	x
1	almeno	1	1	
1	alto	1	1	
1	altro	1	7	
1	americano	1	1	
1	amica	2	1	
1	amico	1	1	
1	anche	1	18	
1	ancora	1	1	
1	andare	1	23	
1	anno	1	7	
1	anziano	1	1	
1	aperto	1	1	
1	appartamento	2	2	
1	arte	1	2	
1	autostrada	N	2	x
1	autostradale	N	1	x
1	avere	1	35	
1	avventura	N	1	
1	bambino	1	1	
1	base	1	1	
1	bastare	1	1	
1	bello	1	9	
1	bene	1	7	
1	bisogno	1	1	
1	cambiare	1	1	
1	capire	1	1	
1	casa	1	8	
1	casino	2	1	x

Rec	Lemma	Band	Freq	Only by Alva
1	catturare	N	1	x
1	centro	1	1	
1	cercare	1	3	
1	certo	1	5	
1	charme	N	1	x
1	che	1	37	
1	chiacchierone	N	1	
1	chiamare	1	3	
1	ci	1	14	
1	cinema	1	2	
1	città	1	5	
1	come	1	4	
1	comodo	2	3	
1	comprare	1	4	
1	comune	1	1	
1	comunicazione	1	1	
1	comunque	1	9	
1	con	1	8	
1	concentrare	2	3	
1	conoscere	1	2	
1	contento	1	1	
1	corona	N	2	
1	correre	2	1	
1	corso	1	1	
1	cosa	1	10	
1	così	1	11	
1	cucire	N	3	
1	cugino	2	1	
1	cui	1	1	
1	cultura	1	3	
1	curioso	3	1	
1	danese	N	1	x
1	dare	1	12	
1	designer	N	1	x
1	di	1	39	
1	difficile	1	4	
1	difficoltà	1	1	
1	diffidente	N	1	x
1	dire	1	8	
1	diventare	1	4	
1	diverso	1	1	

Rec	Lemma	Band	Freq	Only by Alva
1	domandare	2	1	
1	dopo	1	1	
1	doppiato	N	1	x
1	dovere	1	8	
1	e	1	33	
1	economico	1	1	
1	eh	1	109	
1	esatto	1	1	
1	esperienza	1	1	
1	essere	1	73	
1	fa	1	1	
1	fabbrica	2	1	
1	facile	1	1	
1	fare	1	16	
1	fatto	1	1	
1	fermare	1	1	
1	fidanzato	3	5	
1	fidare	3	1	
1	film	1	6	
1	fino	1	1	
1	forse	1	23	
1	forzato	N	1	x
1	francese	1	1	
1	fuori	1	1	
1	gavetta	N	1	x
1	già	1	2	
1	giacca	N	1	x
1	giornale	1	2	
1	giorno	1	3	
1	giovane	1	1	
1	giù	1	1	
1	grammatica	3	1	x
1	grande	1	3	
1	guardare	1	5	
1	idea	1	1	
1	il	1	102	
1	imparare	1	4	
1	in	1	41	
1	incontrare	1	1	
1	individualità	N	1	x
1	industria	2	1	

Rec	Lemma	Band	Freq	Only by Alva
1	inglese	1	11	
1	insegnante	1	1	
1	insegnare	1	3	
1	insieme	1	3	
1	interessare	1	2	
1	interessato	2	1	
1	intero	1	1	
1	invece	1	2	
1	io	1	11	
1	italiana	N	2	
1	italiano	1	10	
1	laureare	N	1	
1	lavorare	1	9	
1	lavoro	1	4	
1	leggere	1	9	
1	lei	1	2	x
1	lento	3	1	x
1	lezione	1	1	
1	lì	1	8	
1	libro	1	3	
1	lingua	1	4	
1	livello	1	2	
1	lo	1	9	
1	loro	1	3	
1	lui	1	11	
1	luogo	1	1	
1	ma	1	45	
1	macchina	1	2	
1	madrelingua	N	1	x
1	mah	1	2	
1	mai	1	2	
1	male	1	1	
1	mamma	1	2	
1	mancare	1	4	
1	mare	1	1	
1	me	1	6	
1	media	2	1	
1	meglio	1	1	
1	meno	1	2	
1	mente	2	1	
1	mese	1	7	

Rec	Lemma	Band	Freq	Only by Alva
1	mettere	1	3	
1	mezzo	1	2	
1	mh	1	8	
1	mi	1	30	
1	migliorare	2	2	
1	mio	1	11	
1	moda	2	1	x
1	modo	1	1	
1	molto	1	21	
1	montagna	2	1	
1	monumento	3	1	
1	neanche	1	1	
1	nessuno	1	1	
1	niente	1	2	
1	no	1	14	
1	non	1	50	
1	normalmente	2	2	
1	notare	1	2	
1	novembre	2	1	
1	o	1	5	
1	occasione	1	1	
1	occhei	N	1	
1	ogni	1	6	
1	opinione	1	1	
1	opportunità	2	1	
1	oppure	1	5	
1	ora	1	3	
1	originale	3	2	
1	ovviamente	1	3	
1	paese	1	4	
1	pagare	1	2	
1	parlare	1	8	
1	parola	1	2	
1	parte	1	1	
1	paura	1	2	
1	pensare	1	3	
1	pensione	2	1	x
1	per	1	11	
1	perché	1	17	
1	perdere	1	1	

Rec	Lemma	Band	Freq	Only by Alva
1	però	1	1	
1	perso	N	1	x
1	persona	1	9	
1	pessimista	N	1	x
1	piacere	1	12	
1	piccolo	1	2	
1	più	1	15	
1	poco	1	26	
1	poi	1	14	
1	possibilità	1	1	
1	posto	1	4	
1	potere	1	5	
1	preferibilmente	N	1	x
1	preferire	2	3	
1	pregiudizio	N	1	
1	prima	1	3	
1	principiante	N	1	
1	privato	1	1	
1	professione	3	1	
1	progettista	N	1	x
1	progetto	1	1	
1	programmare	N	1	
1	proprio	1	3	
1	protetto	N	1	x
1	pubblicità	2	1	x
1	pullman	N	1	
1	qua	1	2	
1	qualche	1	5	
1	qualcosa	1	2	
1	qualcuno	1	2	
1	quando	1	7	
1	quasi	1	6	
1	quello	1	10	
1	questo	1	3	
1	qui	1	1	
1	quindi	1	1	
1	ragazzo	1	1	
1	ragione	1	1	
1	rendere	1	1	
1	ricco	2	1	

Rec	Lemma	Band	Freq	Only by Alva
1	ricordo	1	1	x
1	ridicolo	N	1	x
1	rilassante	N	1	
1	rispetto	1	1	
1	rivista	2	1	x
1	romanzo	1	1	
1	rovinare	3	1	
1	rovinato	N	1	x
1	sapere	1	19	
1	sarta	N	1	x
1	sartoria	N	1	x
1	scarso	N	2	
1	scegliere	1	2	
1	scelta	1	1	
1	sciare	N	1	
1	scuola	1	6	
1	se	1	7	
1	secondo	1	2	
1	seguire	1	1	
1	sempre	1	8	
1	sentire	1	9	
1	senza	1	1	
1	settimana	1	2	
1	sì	1	64	
1	siccome	1	2	
1	situazione	1	1	
1	sogno	2	1	
1	solo	1	1	
1	soltanto	1	1	
1	soprattutto	1	6	
1	sostenere	2	1	
1	sottotitolo	N	2	x
1	spagnolo	2	2	
1	spazio	1	1	
1	spesso	1	1	
1	sporco	3	1	
1	sport	2	1	
1	stage	N	1	x
1	standard	3	1	x
1	stare	1	1	

Rec	Lemma	Band	Freq	Only by Alva
1	strano	1	2	
1	studente	1	1	
1	studiare	1	2	
1	su	1	6	
1	sud	1	1	
1	suo	1	2	
1	svedese	N	4	
1	tanto	1	18	
1	telefono	1	1	
1	tenda	3	1	x
1	tessile	N	1	x
1	timido	N	1	
1	tipico	2	1	
1	tornare	1	4	
1	tra	1	2	
1	trasferire	3	2	
1	traslocare	N	1	x
1	trattare	1	1	
1	treno	1	2	
1	troppo	1	1	
1	trovare	1	7	
1	tu	1	1	
1	tuo	1	1	
1	tutto	1	8	
1	uno	N	75	
1	usare	1	1	
1	vacanza	2	2	
1	vecchio	1	1	
1	vedere	1	8	
1	veloce	2	1	
1	venire	1	7	
1	vergognare	N	1	x
1	vestito	1	2	
1	viaggiare	N	7	
1	viaggio	1	2	
1	vivere	1	10	
1	viziato	N	1	
1	voce	1	2	
1	volere	1	9	
1	volta	1	3	

Rec	Lemma	Band	Freq	Only by Alva
1	zulù	N	1	x
2	abitante	N	1	
2	abito	N	1	
2	accontentare	N	1	x
2	agosto	2	1	
2	albero	2	3	
2	allora	1	2	
2	ambiente	1	1	
2	ambito	2	1	
2	ambulanza	N	1	
2	andata	N	1	
2	animato	N	1	x
2	annoiare	N	1	x
2	anzi	1	1	
2	aprire	1	2	x
2	aria	2	1	
2	arrabbiare	2	2	
2	arrivare	1	1	
2	asilo	N	1	
2	attivo	N	1	
2	attorno	N	3	
2	autunno	N	1	
2	avanti	1	1	
2	azienda	1	1	
2	biglietto	1	3	
2	borsa	1	1	
2	buffo	N	1	x
2	buono	1	1	
2	busta	3	1	
2	buttare	1	1	
2	calare	3	1	x
2	camminare	1	1	
2	campagna	1	1	
2	campanello	N	1	
2	carino	2	3	
2	carriera	3	1	
2	carta	1	1	
2	cartone	2	1	
2	casalinga	3	1	
2	caso	1	1	

Rec	Lemma	Band	Freq	Only by Alva
2	cerotto	N	1	
2	chi	1	1	
2	chilometro	2	1	
2	chiudere	1	1	
2	chiuso	2	1	
2	cieco	N	1	x
2	circo	N	1	x
2	collana	N	1	
2	collegare	2	1	
2	colorato	3	1	x
2	coltello	N	2	
2	combinazione	N	1	x
2	completamente	1	1	
2	confusione	3	1	
2	confuso	N	1	x
2	conoscenza	1	1	
2	continuare	1	3	
2	contro	1	1	
2	convivere	N	1	
2	coprire	2	1	
2	creare	1	1	
2	credito	N	1	x
2	crescere	1	1	
2	curare	2	1	
2	davanti	1	2	
2	design	N	2	x
2	dietro	1	1	
2	differenza	1	1	
2	dimenticare	1	1	
2	dipendere	1	1	
2	dipingere	N	1	x
2	disegnare	3	1	x
2	dispiacere	1	1	
2	distanza	2	1	
2	dito	3	1	
2	divano	2	1	
2	divertente	2	1	
2	donna	1	2	
2	eccetera	1	2	
2	egli	1	2	

Rec	Lemma	Band	Freq	Only by Alva
2	elementare	2	1	
2	entrare	1	2	
2	erba	3	1	x
2	esempio	1	2	
2	estero	2	2	
2	faccia	2	1	
2	febbraio	2	1	
2	figlio	1	5	
2	filosofia	2	6	
2	fine	1	7	
2	forte	1	2	
2	furbo	3	1	
2	futuro	1	3	
2	gennaio	1	1	
2	ginnastica	N	1	x
2	giocare	1	1	
2	giro	1	2	
2	giusto	1	1	
2	grazie	1	1	
2	gridare	N	1	x
2	grigio	2	1	x
2	guidare	2	1	
2	ignorante	N	1	x
2	immaginare	1	1	
2	immagine	1	1	
2	immondizia	N	1	x
2	importante	1	4	
2	improvviso	3	1	x
2	incidente	2	1	
2	includere	N	1	x
2	indietro	1	1	
2	infatti	1	2	
2	iniziare	1	2	
2	interesse	1	1	
2	intervistare	N	1	
2	irlandese	N	1	x
2	ladro	N	1	
2	lanciare	2	3	
2	lasciare	1	3	
2	legno	2	1	

Rec	Lemma	Band	Freq	Only by Alva
2	lettera	1	2	
2	letteratura	2	1	
2	libero	1	1	
2	liceo	2	2	
2	maglia	N	1	
2	mandare	1	1	
2	mano	1	1	
2	marito	1	1	
2	matematica	2	1	
2	materia	1	4	
2	medio	1	2	
2	mentalità	3	3	
2	mentre	1	4	
2	mezzanotte	3	1	
2	misto	2	1	
2	momento	1	2	
2	mordere	N	1	
2	motivo	1	2	
2	muovere	1	1	
2	natura	2	3	
2	nido	N	1	
2	nome	1	1	
2	nuovo	1	1	
2	occhio	1	1	
2	padre	1	2	
2	paranoia	N	1	x
2	pasticcio	N	1	x
2	perciò	2	7	x
2	periodo	1	2	
2	perla	3	1	x
2	permettere	1	1	
2	personaggio	1	1	
2	pezzo	1	1	
2	picco	N	1	x
2	picnic	N	1	x
2	piede	1	1	
2	pigro	N	1	
2	politica	1	2	
2	portare	1	1	
2	postino	N	1	

Rec	Lemma	Band	Freq	Only by Alva
2	prendere	1	4	
2	pressione	3	1	x
2	promessa	N	1	x
2	protezione	N	1	
2	pubblico	1	1	
2	quale	1	1	
2	quanto	1	2	
2	ragazza	1	3	
2	realizzare	1	1	
2	ricercare	3	1	x
2	riguardare	1	2	
2	riservato	N	1	
2	riuscire	1	1	
2	rompere	1	1	
2	rubare	N	1	
2	sabbia	N	1	x
2	sbagliare	1	1	
2	scienza	2	2	
2	scultura	N	1	x
2	sembrare	1	3	
2	sera	1	2	
2	sfogare	N	1	x
2	sicuro	1	2	
2	sigaretta	3	1	
2	signora	1	2	
2	signore	1	8	
2	simile	2	1	
2	simpatico	1	1	
2	sinceramente	2	1	
2	smettere	2	1	
2	soddisfatto	N	2	
2	soluzione	2	1	x
2	sorpreso	N	1	
2	sostanza	2	1	
2	specializzare	N	1	
2	specializzazione	N	1	
2	spiegare	1	1	
2	stesso	1	4	
2	storia	1	6	
2	straniero	2	1	

Rec	Lemma	Band	Freq	Only by Alva
2	studio	1	3	
2	stufare	N	1	x
2	succedere	1	2	
2	sudafricano	N	1	x
2	suonare	2	1	
2	superficiale	N	1	
2	supplenza	3	1	x
2	teatro	1	3	
2	telegiornale	N	2	
2	televisione	1	4	
2	teoretico	N	1	x
2	tessuto	3	1	x
2	ti	1	1	
2	tradizione	2	1	
2	traffico	3	1	
2	tramite	2	1	
2	ultimo	1	1	
2	umanistico	N	2	x
2	umano	1	1	
2	unico	1	1	
2	università	1	3	
2	uomo	1	4	
2	urlare	N	2	x
2	vero	1	3	
2	verso	1	1	
2	via	1	2	
2	vicino	1	2	
2	voglia	1	1	
2	volare	3	1	
2	vuoto	2	2	
3	abbigliamento	N	1	
3	accogliente	N	1	x
3	accordo	1	1	
3	acqua	1	1	
3	aeroporto	3	2	x
3	aiuto	2	1	
3	alzare	1	2	
3	ascoltare	1	1	
3	attimo	1	1	
3	attrezzatura	N	1	x

Rec	Lemma	Band	Freq	Only by Alva
3	avvicinare	2	1	
3	baciare	N	1	
3	bagaglio	N	1	x
3	bagno	2	1	x
3	bambina	2	1	x
3	bara	N	2	x
3	barella	N	2	x
3	basso	1	1	
3	bendato	N	1	x
3	bere	2	1	
3	bravo	1	1	
3	caldo	1	1	
3	calmare	N	1	x
3	cane	1	2	x
3	capo	1	2	
3	cappello	N	1	
3	caricare	2	1	
3	carne	1	1	x
3	caro	1	2	x
3	cartamodello	N	2	x
3	cattivo	2	1	x
3	cenare	N	3	
3	centrale	1	2	
3	chiave	2	1	
3	chiedere	1	1	
3	cibo	3	3	
3	cioè	1	3	
3	circa	1	1	
3	colazione	2	1	
3	colpo	2	2	x
3	comportare	2	1	
3	concludere	2	1	x
3	conosciuto	N	1	x
3	contare	1	1	
3	coppia	2	1	
3	costare	1	1	
3	creativo	N	1	x
3	cucinare	N	2	
3	davvero	1	3	
3	decisione	2	1	

Rec	Lemma	Band	Freq	Only by Alva
3	dedicare	2	1	
3	dentro	1	1	
3	dibattito	1	1	x
3	dimostrare	1	2	x
3	disponibile	2	1	
3	disturbare	3	3	x
3	ditta	2	1	x
3	domani	1	2	
3	dormire	1	1	
3	durare	1	1	
3	ecco	1	2	
3	egoista	N	1	x
3	energia	2	1	
3	estate	2	1	
3	esterno	1	1	
3	esteticamente	N	1	x
3	euro	2	2	
3	facilmente	N	1	
3	famiglia	1	2	
3	fattore	2	1	
3	felice	2	1	
3	feria	N	1	x
3	ferire	N	2	x
3	festa	1	2	
3	fianco	2	1	
3	filmino	N	3	
3	finire	1	4	
3	fortunato	3	1	
3	fra	1	1	
3	freddo	1	1	
3	gamba	2	1	x
3	genere	1	1	
3	gente	1	2	
3	gentile	3	1	
3	gettare	3	1	x
3	giapponese	3	1	x
3	ginocchio	3	1	x
3	gioco	1	1	
3	giovedì	1	1	x
3	giugno	1	1	

Part 1: Focus on Cultural Migrants

Rec	Lemma	Band	Freq	Only by Alva
3	grado	1	2	
3	imbrogliare	N	1	x
3	immersione	N	1	x
3	incluso	N	1	x
3	incorporare	N	1	x
3	individualista	N	1	x
3	insomma	1	2	
3	intensivo	N	1	
3	interessante	1	1	
3	Internet	N	1	
3	intolleranza	N	1	x
3	isola	N	1	
3	la	1	1	
3	libanese	N	1	x
3	licenziare	N	1	x
3	lunatico	N	1	x
3	lungo	1	2	
3	magari	1	31	
3	maggiore	1	1	
3	maleducazione	N	1	x
3	mangiare	1	6	
3	mansarda	N	1	x
3	manuale	N	1	
3	marzo	2	1	
3	matrimonio	2	2	
3	mattina	1	1	
3	mestiere	3	2	x
3	mezzora	N	1	x
3	migliore	1	1	
3	minuto	1	4	
3	modellistica	N	1	x
3	modello	1	1	x
3	modernità	N	1	x
3	moderno	2	1	
3	mondo	1	1	
3	morto	2	1	x
3	moto	2	2	
3	musica	1	1	
3	nascere	1	1	
3	nascondere	2	1	

Beyond Native-like? The Lexical Profile of a Cultural Migrant in Italy 53

Rec	Lemma	Band	Freq	Only by Alva
3	ne	1	2	
3	neve	3	2	
3	nevicare	N	2	
3	nipotina	N	1	x
3	noi	1	5	
3	nord	1	1	
3	nostro	1	2	
3	nozze	N	1	x
3	occhiale	N	1	
3	offesa	N	1	x
3	offrire	1	1	
3	opera	1	1	
3	organizzato	N	1	x
3	ormai	1	1	
3	ovunque	N	1	
3	paio	1	2	
3	palloncino	N	3	
3	papà	1	2	
3	parco	2	1	
3	parete	3	2	
3	partire	1	5	
3	passatempo	N	1	x
3	passeggiata	N	1	
3	pausa	N	4	x
3	pettinare	N	1	x
3	piacevole	N	1	
3	piano	1	2	
3	pigiama	N	1	
3	piovere	3	1	x
3	piscina	3	1	x
3	piuttosto	1	4	
3	pochettino	N	2	x
3	possibile	1	1	
3	pranzo	2	1	
3	pratico	1	1	
3	preferito	N	1	x
3	prenotare	2	2	
3	preparare	1	1	
3	prezzo	1	1	
3	problema	1	1	

54   Part 1: Focus on Cultural Migrants

Rec	Lemma	Band	Freq	Only by Alva
3	prossimo	1	1	
3	provare	1	3	
3	regolato	N	1	x
3	ricordare	1	1	
3	ridere	1	1	
3	rifiuto	N	1	
3	rigido	N	1	
3	rimanere	1	2	
3	rispondere	1	1	
3	ritardo	3	1	
3	sacco	1	1	
3	scalo	N	1	x
3	scena	2	1	
3	sciarpa	N	1	x
3	sciistico	N	1	x
3	scioccato	N	1	x
3	scorso	1	2	
3	scrivere	1	2	
3	sedere	2	1	
3	selvaggio	N	1	
3	sicuramente	1	4	
3	slittare	N	1	x
3	sobbalzare	N	1	x
3	sognare	3	1	
3	sopra	1	1	
3	sorella	1	1	
3	sotto	1	1	
3	specie	1	2	
3	spettacolo	2	2	x
3	sporcizia	3	1	x
3	sposato	N	1	
3	stanco	3	1	x
3	stazione	1	2	x
3	strada	1	1	
3	straordinario	2	1	
3	subacqueo	N	1	x
3	subito	1	3	
3	suocera	N	1	x
3	tagliare	1	1	
3	tardi	1	1	

Rec	Lemma	Band	Freq	Only by Alva
3	tassa	3	1	
3	tempo	1	5	
3	tenere	1	1	
3	terra	1	1	
3	tesina	N	1	
3	testa	1	1	
3	tipo	1	1	
3	totale	2	1	
3	triste	N	1	
3	umore	N	1	x
3	una	N	1	x
3	uscire	1	4	
3	vario	1	1	
3	velocemente	3	1	x
3	venditore	N	1	
3	veramente	1	7	
3	vestire	2	1	x
3	vita	1	1	
3	vostro	1	1	x
4	accadere	2	1	
4	accettare	1	2	
4	alcuno	1	2	
4	appena	1	1	
4	aprile	2	1	
4	arredamento	N	1	x
4	aspettare	1	2	
4	assistente	N	1	x
4	assumere	1	1	x
4	autunnale	N	1	x
4	betulla	N	1	x
4	biologico	N	1	
4	breve	1	3	
4	burocrazia	N	1	
4	campo	1	2	
4	cap	N	1	x
4	ceramica	N	1	x
4	cerimonia	N	2	x
4	cesta	N	1	x
4	chiacchierare	N	1	x
4	chiaro	1	1	

Rec	Lemma	Band	Freq	Only by Alva
4	cinquantina	N	1	x
4	collezione	N	1	x
4	collina	N	1	
4	compiere	2	1	
4	comunale	1	1	x
4	comunicare	1	2	
4	confine	2	1	
4	consigliere	1	1	x
4	contrasto	N	1	
4	contratto	1	2	x
4	corteccia	N	1	x
4	credere	1	1	
4	crisi	1	3	x
4	cuore	1	1	x
4	d'accordo	N	1	x
4	definire	1	1	
4	dici	N	5	x
4	disoccupazione	N	1	x
4	distribuire	N	1	x
4	divertimento	3	1	
4	domenica	1	1	
4	durante	1	2	
4	ed	N	3	x
4	ehm	N	1	x
4	entro	2	1	
4	eseguire	N	1	x
4	europeo	1	1	
4	familiare	2	1	
4	favore	1	2	
4	fenomeno	1	1	
4	fico	N	1	x
4	fiera	2	1	x
4	finanziario	2	1	x
4	foto	2	1	x
4	frase	1	1	
4	fratello	1	2	
4	giornata	1	3	
4	gli	N	1	x
4	grosso	1	1	
4	guadagnare	2	1	

Rec	Lemma	Band	Freq	Only by Alva
4	incerto	N	1	x
4	indipendente	3	1	
4	infanzia	N	2	x
4	informazione	1	2	
4	laboratorio	1	1	
4	largo	2	1	x
4	lato	1	2	
4	legato	2	1	
4	legittimo	N	1	x
4	limite	1	1	
4	linea	1	3	
4	locale	1	1	
4	lontano	1	1	
4	lunghissimo	N	1	x
4	massimo	1	1	
4	menti	N	1	x
4	mezzogiorno	2	1	
4	mhm	N	2	x
4	modellista	N	4	x
4	motivato	N	1	x
4	negozio	2	4	
4	nordico	N	1	
4	notte	1	2	
4	occupare	1	2	
4	oggetto	1	1	
4	oggi	1	3	
4	oh	1	2	
4	ordinato	N	1	
4	ordine	1	1	
4	ospitare	3	1	
4	ottimista	N	1	x
4	ottimo	2	1	
4	ottobre	2	1	x
4	parente	2	2	
4	parere	1	5	
4	pari	2	1	
4	passare	1	2	
4	pelle	2	1	x
4	piatto	1	1	
4	preoccupato	N	1	

Rec	Lemma	Band	Freq	Only by Alva
4	prodotto	1	3	
4	produrre	1	2	x
4	produzione	1	1	x
4	pronuncia	N	1	
4	proposta	1	1	x
4	realtà	1	1	
4	recessione	N	1	x
4	restituire	3	1	x
4	resto	1	1	
4	ricercato	N	1	
4	richiedere	1	1	x
4	ricominciare	2	1	x
4	rinnovare	N	1	x
4	risposta	1	1	
4	ristorante	2	1	
4	rivolgere	N	1	x
4	rosso	1	1	x
4	sacrificio	2	1	
4	scadere	N	1	
4	scandinavo	N	1	
4	sessantina	N	1	x
4	settore	1	1	x
4	spedire	3	1	x
4	sperare	1	1	
4	sposare	1	2	
4	stilista	N	3	x
4	storto	N	1	x
4	sviluppare	2	1	
4	talmente	2	1	
4	tecnico	1	2	
4	tz	N	3	x
4	unica	N	1	
4	vendere	1	3	
4	zio	3	1	

2 Successful Profiles in High-level L2 French – 'c'est un choix de vie'[1]

Fanny Forsberg Lundell and
Inge Bartning

Introduction: Aim and Rationale

In the last decade, the interest in late adult L2 learners'/users' performance has grown immensely (Abrahamsson & Hyltenstam, 2009; Bartning *et al.*, 2012; Birdsong, 2007; Granena & Long, 2013; Muñoz, 2008; Muñoz & Singleton, 2007, 2011). Researchers want to know if it is possible to reach native-like attainment even in adults' L2. Many studies have focused on the age issue, demonstrating that the possibility to become native-like varies enormously from quite high rates of native-likeness [see Birdsong (1992, 2003) (French L2 pronunciation); Montrul & Slabakova (2003) (Spanish L2 tense and aspect)] through moderate rates [Birdsong (2007) (French L2, pronunciation)] to low rates [Coppieters (1987) (French grammar through GJT), Ioup *et al.* (1994) (Arabic L2, GJT), Abrahamsson and Hyltenstam (2009) (Swedish L2, a large number of tests, esp. GJT, grammatical intuition, perceptive tests); Granena (2013a) (Spanish L2, GJT, written, auditory)]. What is striking in this overview is the lack of research on lexis at different levels of ultimate attainment. Thanks to Laufer & Waldman (2011), Lindqvist *et al.* (2011) and Forsberg Lundell *et al.* (2014) and onward, lexical richness and formulaic language is now one of the important measures of high-level proficiency.

Other aspects in this field are, on the one hand, so-called 'late' features focusing on what fragile zones remain at these very high levels (e.g. Bartning *et al.*, 2012), and on the other, successful profiles focusing on favourable factors, e.g. social and psychological that contribute to success in L2 showing that it is sometimes possible to attain native-likeness in a L2 (Kinsella & Singleton, 2014; Moyer, 2004; Muñoz & Singleton, 2007, 2011; Piller, 2002).

In Forsberg Lundell *et al.* (2014), we examined different criteria for identifying high-level proficiency at a group level (advanced to highly advanced, near-natives vs natives). In the present paper we think it is time to take a closer look at the individual level in order to explore the intriguing questions about characteristics of high-level proficiency and the possibility to reach ultimate attainment (cf. Abrahamsson & Hyltenstam, 2009).

The aim of this chapter is two-fold: (1) to contribute to the debate on ultimate attainment, (2) to identify linguistic and psychological measures that are relevant to users of high-level proficiency, and look for relationships between the two types of measures in order to explain individual variation in L2 attainment.

In order to explore these issues, four L2 user profiles will be examined in detail by means of ten linguistic measures (spoken and written data) and a test of language aptitude.

Earlier Studies

In the first of a series of publications on high-level proficiency, Bartning *et al.* (2009) identified resources and obstacles in high- level users of oral L2 French. It was found that besides morphosyntax, formulaic sequences and information structure were some of the most interesting phenomena for highly proficient learners. Then, in the second publication, Forsberg Lundell *et al.* (2014), added three more measures, that is perceived native-likeness (via a listener test, cf. Abrahamsson & Hyltenstam, 2009), lexical richness and fluency. In order to differentiate between speakers from different advanced levels, and to identify candidates for a near-native level, the listener test was used. In this test the productions of four groups of NNS (30) and NS (10) speakers were evaluated by 10 NS. The judges were asked whether the speakers were native or not. On the basis of these tests – where the criterion for passing as a native was the judgement of six out of 10 judges – the speakers were placed into two groups: those who 'passed as natives' and those who did not. The results showed among other things that 10 NNS out of the three NNS groups (N=30) passed as natives, as did all the NS (N=10). The individual spoken productions of the whole cohort were then analysed according to the five measures mentioned above, i.e. morphosyntax, formulaic sequences, information structure, lexical richness and fluency.

The results of the listener tests, together with those of our five linguistic tests from Forsberg Lundell *et al.* (2014), also permitted us to classify the learners at new advanced/very advanced learner stages; the highest group, the near-natives, were learners who passed as natives and who also scored highest on the other five tests (stage 8). The two other stages were the advanced stage (originally stage 6 of Bartning & Schlyter's (2004) scale), and, finally, the highly proficient stage (stage 7), both stages with learners demonstrating 'late features' but who did not pass as natives. As we stated in Forsberg Lundell et al. (2014: 20), the vast majority of advanced L2 users are probably to be found within the category of highly proficient L2 users. The measures that were successful in defining the highly proficient users (stage 7) were fluency, lexical richness and formulaic sequences. It is interesting to see that around 30% of these 'late' learners from our 2014 study succeeded in passing as native speakers when, according to the listener test, the corresponding percentage in Abrahamsson and Hyltenstam (2009) was 19%.

In the present study there is new data from the same informants as above. However, this time a psychological test is also included in order to see if there are individuals who succeed in all tests and if there are psychological factors that reveal the most successful individuals. The results of the three studies in Bartning et al. (2009, 2012) and Forsberg Lundell et al. (2014) focused on results at group levels, whereas the present paper will focus on the individual level, thus on a deeper analysis of each individual profile.

Research Questions and Hypotheses

(1) Do speakers within the population of the present study reach native-likeness in their L2?
Hypothesis 1: According to the results from the PASS test, it is possible for some late adult learners to become native-like. However, Abrahamsson and Hyltenstam (2009) show that it is practically impossible to become native-like 'across the board', that is on a large variety of measures, especially phonetic and grammatical intuition. We hypothesise that speakers who pass as natives will perform within the native speaker range on more measures than speakers who do not pass as natives, but no speakers will perform within the native speaker range on all measures.

(2) What linguistic features characterise the most successful profiles?
Hypothesis 2: Based on Forsberg Lundell et al. (2014), we expect that formulaic sequences, morphosyntax and lexical richness in spoken production will be the most relevant features for the characterisation of L2 high-level achievement.

(3) Does language aptitude (LA) have an impact on L2 success?
Hypothesis 3: Based on Abrahamsson and Hyltenstam (2008) and Granena (2013a, 2013b), it is hypothesised that language aptitude will have an impact on L2 success. However, given that Granena (2013a, 2013b) found a difference according to test modality, it is hypothesised that aptitude effects will be more pronounced for written test data than for spontaneous spoken data.

Data and Method

The data used in the current study has already been presented for group comparisons in several publications, but they have never been presented all together. The measures included have been chosen since they have all been identified, in earlier studies, as relevant for the study of high-level L2 use. Given the restricted length of the present chapter, it is not possible to present each measure in great detail, and we therefore refer to Forsberg Lundell *et al.* (2014) for the spoken data, to Forsberg Lundell and Lindqvist (2013) for the linguistic written tests and to Forsberg Lundell and Sandgren (2013) for the grammatical judgment test and the psychological tests. After our presentation of the participants, a short description of each measure will be provided below.

The participants

Four informants at high-level proficiency are being examined. Three of them (Hedda, Saga, Mimmi) come from a group with French as a Second Language that consists of 10 Swedish-speaking advanced L2 users of 25–30 years old. Most of them work in French settings and have a French partner; a few are finishing their French university degrees. They were between 18 and 19 when they arrived in France after secondary school. This group is called French as a Second Language (FSL) Junior.

The fourth informant, Patrick, comes from a group called FSL Seniors, which consists of 10 Swedish-speaking adults who after high school have lived in France for 15–30 years. They are 45–60 years old (called French as a Second Language Seniors), have French partners and bilingual children, and all work in bilingual settings (Swedish-French), as opposed to the Juniors, who work in entirely French settings. The members of this group came to France at the age of 21–24.

Two of the informants, Hedda and Patrick, pass as native speakers according to the pass-as-a-native test (see 'The pass-as-a-native test' below), whereas the other two, Mimmi and Saga, do not pass as native speakers (detailed information about productions and meta-data of all informants of the InterFra corpus is to be found at the website www.fraita. su.se/english/interfra and in Bartning, 2014). The following background data were elicited by questionnaires and interviews (see Table 2.1).

The participants as cultural migrants

In contrast to economic and political migrants, there is another category of migrants, which we call cultural migrants (see Introduction, this volume). By cultural migrants we refer to people who decide, out of their free will, to move to another country permanently and learn the

Successful Profiles in High-level L2 French – 'c'est un choix de vie' 63

Table 2.1 Specification of the four informants' biodata

Informant	Year of birth	Length of French studies	LOR (years)	Education	Profession	French partner/ children	Other lgs	Age of onset
Hedda	1978	5 years	10	PhD in computer Science	Software developer	Yes / 3 children: 6 months, 3 and 6 years	English, some German	13
Mimi	1972	7 months	18	Master of dance, BA in theatre	Teacher of dance, choreographer	Yes /1 son of 3.5 years	Italian, Greek, German, Portuguese, Spanish, Catalan, English	20
Patrick	1963	5.5 years	20	Economist university	Sales manager	Yes /No	Italian, (father, bilingual) English, German, Spanish	16
Saga	1978	2.5 years	13	Master of cultural exchanges, DEUG of cultural mediation, Art history	PR manager	Yes /No	English, German	16

language of this country. The culture of the target language country is highly appealing to them and they make an active choice to live in this new culture. These individuals would have access to optimal prerequisites for native-like attainment since they have positive attitudes and affect towards the TL country. Furthermore, they are often well educated and well integrated, leading to optimal opportunities to practice the L2, which in itself is an important dimension of L2 attainment (DeKeyser, 2007; Regan, 2013; Singleton *et al.*, 2013). This group has not often been studied in SLA for several reasons, including, among other things, that they are hard to find, that they do not tend to live in communities, etc. Many of these characteristics coincide with the profiles of our four participants (see Table 2.1, above, and section Socio-biographic profiles, below).

Linguistic Tests: Spoken Data

All measures are based on the analysis of semi-structured interviews with topics such as studies, family, life stories, leisure life, work, etc. Below follows a presentation of the six measures analysed for spoken production.

The pass-as-a-native test

Inspired by a test designed by Abrahamsson and Hyltenstam (2009), we asked 10 NS judges to evaluate the 20 informants mentioned above (FSL Juniors and Seniors) and the 10 NS with respect to native-likeness (cf. Forsberg Lundell *et al.*, 2014). The judges were encouraged to listen to the extracts of 20–30 seconds from the informants' interviews. The native judges were asked to choose between the following options: (a) this person has French as her/his mother tongue, and she/he comes from the Paris region; (b) this person has French as her/his mother tongue and she/he does not come from the Paris region; (c) this person does not have French as her/his mother tongue. The judges also were asked to evaluate the certainty of their answers on a scale from 1 to 3 and they were not allowed to listen to the extracts again. Our definition of the PASS criterion is a person judged as a native by at least 6 out of the 10 native judges.

The native judges were all from the Paris region. They were recruited by a French research assistant and some of the criteria were: 23–40 years, not linguists, no knowledge of Swedish. They had all completed post-secondary education and worked in the education system, in business or as technicians.

Lexical formulaic sequences/100 words

The present study makes use of Erman and Warren's (2000) original categorisation of formulaic sequences (henceforth: FS), a model based on the phraseological tradition. Formulaic sequences can be classified into Lexical and Qualifier FSs according to our model, but we will only focus on Lexical FSs, since they have turned out to be the most interesting for the study of high-level L2 use (cf. Forsberg, 2008). Lexical FSs incorporate at least one content word. They denote actions (such as *faire la fête* 'to party'), states (*avoir peur* 'to be scared') and entities (*chef d'entreprise* 'company leader'). The criterion *restricted exchangeability* (Erman & Warren, 2000) was used for identification. In order for a sequence to qualify as formulaic, an exchange of one of the words for a synonymous word must always result in a change of meaning or a loss of idiomaticity (Erman & Warren, 2000: 32). In addition, for a sequence to be considered as formulaic, it has to appear at least twice as frequently on Google as any of the modified versions, in order to provide some sort of measure of native-like preference. For a problematisation on the identification of formulaic sequences, see Granger and Pacquot (2008) and Forsberg (2010).

Morphosyntax

The selection of morphosyntactic features, that is non-target-like morphosyntactic forms in the VP and the NP, draws on results from earlier overviews of late-acquired features in SLA research and on our own work (see Bartning, 2009, 2012, 2014; Labeau & Myles, 2009).

The features chosen for this study are the following:

(1) The verb phrase:
   a. Subject–verb agreement in simple and complex utterances: non-target-like forms of 3rd person plural in the present tense (*il y a des voleurs qui *vient la nuit*).
   b. Forms of tense, mode and aspect: a broad category of simplification patterns or deviant rules in the tense system: *passé composé* instead of pluperfect forms, *imparfait* instead of *passé composé* in past tense contexts; problems with auxiliaries (Ayoun, 2013; Bartning *et al.*, 2012; Hyltenstam, 1992; Lardiere, 2007).
(2) The noun phrase:
   c. Gender agreement and gender assignment of determiners: **un image très romantique*; and gender agreement on adjectives in different positions (*une *petit ville*), and anaphoric pronouns *il* instead of *elle*. Gender agreement and assignment is one of the most difficult features in high-level L2 French, as shown by several studies: Frenck-Mestre *et al.* (2009), Holmes and Segui (2006), Franceschina (2005), Ågren *et al.* (2012) and Bartning *et al.* (2012).

The measure used here is the number of non-target-like morphosyntactic forms per 100 words.

Lexical richness

The method used to measure lexical richness in French L2 is the Lexical Oral Production Profile (LOPP), which is presented in Lindqvist *et al.* (2011). It is a frequency-based measure, which is inspired by the Lexical Frequency Profile (Laufer & Nation, 1995). While the Lexical Frequency Profile is developed for written language, the LOPP method is extended to spoken language. The method consists of dividing a speaker's words into different frequency bands: Band 1, Band 2, Band 3 and Off-list. The frequency bands were created on the basis of the Corpaix corpus (Véronis, 2011, http://sites.univ-provence.fr/veronis; see Forsberg Lundell *et al.*, 2014). The list contains word forms. The profile is seen as the proportions of lemmas in the different frequency bands, e.g. Band 1: 95%, Band 2: 2%, Band 3: 1%, Off-list: 2%. The general assumption is that a relatively high proportion of low-frequency words is indicative of a rich vocabulary (cf. Laufer & Nation, 1995).

Fluency: Speaking rate and mean length of run

The present study focuses on temporal variables of two kinds, and uses the following measures: (a) the speech rate and (b) the mean length of run (see Forsberg *et al.*, 2014). These variables are defined as follows: (a) The speech rate is calculated by dividing the number of words by the time needed to produce the speech sample in question (including silent and filled pauses); (b) the second measure, the mean length of run, corresponds to the mean number of words between two silent pauses – a silent pause being defined as exceeding 25 milliseconds (see e.g. Towell *et al.*, 1996).

Linguistic Tests: Written Test Data

The four measures studied through written tests were the following.

Grammaticality judgment test

The written grammaticality judgment test was elaborated by Forsberg Lundell and Bartning (cf. Bartning, 2012). The test was originally based on Bylund's (2008) GJT for Spanish, and grammatical features tested include subject–verb agreement in complex syntax, NP agreement, anaphors, verb constructions and TMA. All in all, the test included 46 items. It should be noted that both the VP and NP agreement sentences include deviances in silent morphology, which would not be audible in an auditory GJ-test. These probably tap into metalinguistic awareness more than any mental grammar. Here are some examples of the sentences:

(1) * *Les élèves croyaient que le sapin <u>avaient</u> (avait) comme crigine la mythologie allemande.* (The pupils thought that the Christmas tree had German mythology as an origin.)
(2) *L'inspecteur pensait que l'avion n'était plus suffisamment performant.* (The inspector thought that the aircraft was no longer airworthy.)

This individual test was, like the other linguistic tests, untimed. However, there was a maximum amount of time for all the written tests.

Productive collocation test

Productive collocation knowledge is probably one of the most difficult challenges for the L2 learner (Schmitt, 2012). Forsberg Lundell and Lindqvist (2013) created a test on productive collocation knowledge in French, based on Gyllstad (2007) for the procedure for choosing test items and on Mizrahi and Laufer (2010).

The following sentences illustrate sample items:

(1) *L'ONU est fermement résolue à **r(endre)___ justice** aux victimes du génocide.* (The United Nations are determined to d(o)__ justice to the victims of the genocide.)
(2) *Si les petites entreprises **é(prouvent)_____ des difficultés** à embaucher, c'est aussi parce qu'elles disposent de moyens qui sont moindres.* (If small companies h(ave)__ problems in hiring, it's also because they have access to smaller budgets.)

In contrast to Mizrahi and Laufer (2010), who provided the two first letters in each word, only one letter was given in the gap, in order to avoid ceiling effects. Even though this meant that a possible alternative collocating verb was occasionally provided, it was decided, for practical reasons, to only judge as correct answers the most frequent collocating verbs, i.e. only one correct answer for each sentence.

Receptive deep knowledge test

The deep knowledge test was based on Bogaards' (2000) *The Euralex French Tests*, which were developed for very advanced learners of French L2. The test contains a certain number of word pairs, and the informant's task is to indicate whether there is any obvious relation between the words in the word pair, e.g. *gâchis* ('waste') and *gaspiller* ('to waste'), *éplucheur* ('peeler') and *pomme de terre* ('potato'). The original test contained 70 items (word pairs) and the relationships were of four types: semantic (hyponymy, synonymy, antonymy), fixed expressions (compound nouns, collocations), selection restrictions (verbs/nouns, free associations) and cultural aspects.

There were also some dummy items where there was no obvious relationship between the words. As we developed a collocation test as part of the test battery (see above), we wanted to avoid testing collocations in this deep knowledge test (although there is, of course, a difference between productive and receptive knowledge). Thus all items that elicited collocation knowledge were removed from the test, which resulted in a final test containing 30 items. According to Bogaards (2000: 509), the test has proved to be a good predictor of language proficiency.

The C-test

The C-test is a fill-in-the gap test. The test begins with a complete sentence, after which the second half of every second word has been deleted. The texts used for the present study were developed by Tidball & Treffers-Daller (2007). The informants were given six short texts, each containing 20 gaps. The C-test has proved to be a useful discriminator for proficiency levels, as it is a vocabulary test that measures general proficiency (Tidball & Treffers-Daller, 2007). Below is an extract from one of the texts.

Example: *Les vaches folles*

Selon une récente enquête, 45% des Français auraient diminué ou cessé de manger de la viande de boeuf depuis le début de la crise de la vache folle. Ils s(e)_____ tournent ve(rs)_____ les vian(des)_____ blanches e(t)_____ la nourr(iture)_____ végétale. (They turn to white meats and vegetarian food.)

A Psychological Test

Language aptitude

Language learning aptitude is generally defined as a largely innate and relatively fixed talent for learning languages (for discussion, see Abrahamsson & Hyltenstam, 2008; Granena, 2013a, 2013b). As Abrahamsson and Hyltenstam state (p. 485), language aptitude (LA) is an individual factor that varies considerably within normal populations and has been found to be relatively independent of other factors (see e.g. Dörnyei & Skehan, 2003). First, aptitude tests were developed as diagnostic tools to predict success in instructed and formal settings. Krashen (1981) suggested that LA is a good predictor of success in explicit learning. Later studies, however, suggest that LA may play a decisive role in naturalistic SLA, thus in implicit learning, see e.g. DeKeyser (2000).

The aptitude test that we use is the LLAMA test (Meara, 2005), described e.g. in Granena (2013a, 2013b). The LLAMA test was also used by Abrahamsson and Hyltenstam (2008). Theoretically, it builds on the same assumptions as the MLAT test (The Modern Language Aptitude test), the most notable difference, according to Meara, being its user-friendliness. The test is intended to measure four different components of language aptitude (to date), which also explains why the results of each subtest are accounted for individually. The four components are as follows: LLAMA B (vocabulary learning), LLAMA D (phonetic memory), LLAMA E (sound–symbol correspondence) and LLAMA F (grammatical inference). All the subtests are based on nonsense languages or rare languages, which are most likely unknown to the test takers (see Granena, 2013a). The tests are downloadable and supplied by Meara and his colleagues. It should be noted that Meara (2005) insists on the preliminary quality of the test and that it should not be used in high-stakes situations. All our tests were administered on computer by a research assistant in France.

Results

Table 2.2 shows the individual results for each informant according to the 10 measures.

Difference between PASS and NON-PASS Profiles

The results of Table 2.2 show that at least one of the PASS profiles (either Hedda or Patrick depending on the measure) generally has higher scores on the oral measures than the NON-PASS profiles. This is interesting, since there seems to be a relationship between passing as a native speaker and mastery of linguistic features in oral production. However, it should be noted that there is variation between the two PASS profiles. Whereas Hedda scores highest on formulaic language and morphosyntax, Patrick scores highest on lexical richness and the two fluency measures. However, he scores fairly high on the two other spoken measures as well. It could be assumed that Patrick scores higher than Hedda on lexical richness and fluency, since he has resided for double the number of years in France and is also considerably older. One can assume that at least lexical richness would be associated with exposure, and experience with different domains and accumulated professional experience. The two measures they have in common for high scores are the following: quantity of formulaic sequences and (quasi) absence of morphosyntactic errors, which corroborates results on group level found in Bartning *et al.* (2009) and Forsberg Lundell *et al.* (2014).

Regarding the written test data, it is quite clear that Hedda is the most successful participant. In addition, she has the highest score of all participants on the collocation test and even scores higher than the NS participants. If collocations are to be considered a good yardstick of native-like proficiency, Hedda certainly reaches this when it comes to productive knowledge, which, according to Schmitt (2012), is more

Table 2.2 Test results

Language data	Hedda	Patrick	Mimmi	Saga	NNS average	Max	NS average	NS range
Spoken data								
LFS/100 words	4.3	3.5	3.2	2.5	3.4	n.a.	3.9	3.2–5.5
MSD/100 words	0	0.0002	0.002	0.005	0.3	n.a.	0	0–0.0006
Pass as a native (% of raters)	90%	70%	20%	30%	38%	100%	99%	90–100%
Lexical richness	3.8%	6%	7%	4.4%		n.a.	7.26	6.4–8%
Speaking rate	2.2	5.2	2	2.9	2.8	n.a.	2.94	2.1–3.5
MLR	3.2	12.7	5.8	9.6	9.2	n.a.	9.22	4.2–13.3
Written Test data								
GJ test	40	34	38	42	38.3	46	42	40–46
Collocation	46	25	37	25	29.2	46	35.2	26–43
Receptive deep knowledge	26	26	27	24	23.9	30	28.3	25–30
C-test	119	97	110	110	106.7	120	112.4	110–115
Total score test data	231	182	212	201		242		
Total no of measures in NS range	8/10	6/10	7/10	4/10				
Language aptitude					Average	Max		
LLAMA B	85	65	60	95	54	100	n.a.	n.a.
LLAMA D	50	50	55	45	37	100	n.a.	n.a.
LLAMA E	100	0	100	90	78.5	100	n.a.	n.a.
LLAMA F	80	80	70	90	64.6	100	n.a.	n.a.
	315	195	285	320		400	n.a.	n.a.

Note: LFS=Lexical Formulaic Sequences, MSD=Morphosyntactic Deviances, MLR=Mean Length of Run.

difficult than receptive knowledge. The only test for which she does not score within the NS range is the receptive deep knowledge test. However, Patrick does not have results within the NS range on the tests, except for the receptive deep knowledge test, where he scores within the native speaker range. It can consequently be concluded that passing does not, in a clear-cut manner, seem to be related to results on written linguistic tests.

The Impact of Language Aptitude on Spoken and Written Data

The results of the language aptitude test show that one PASS profile, Hedda, and one NON-PASS profile, Saga, have the highest scores on this test, which implies that there is no obvious connection between the language aptitude test and passing as a native speaker. The same conclusion can be drawn regarding the connection between the oral data measures and the results on the aptitude test. However, it is easier to observe a correspondence between the written test data results and the results of the aptitude tests. Patrick, with the lowest score on the aptitude tests, also has the lowest score on the written linguistic tests, whereas Hedda scores high on both. Most of the research done on language aptitude in ultimate attainment includes test data and not spontaneous spoken production (cf. Abrahamsson & Hyltenstam, 2008; DeKeyser et al., 2010; Granena, 2013b). It could possibly be assumed that the kind of aptitude that is measured through the LLAMA test shares variance with the kind of knowledge that the linguistic tests tap into. This finding is in line with Granena (2013b), who shows that aptitude only correlates with an untimed grammatical judgment test, where participants can rely on their analytical ability, but it does not correlate with auditory timed GJTs. It is also reminiscent of Österberg's (2008) study, where correlations were found between high school grades in Spanish and aptitude, but not between measures of spoken production and aptitude. It is fairly well known that written test results are important for teachers when marking their students. One could assume that there is a correlation between the general aptitude for test taking and language aptitude. Hedda seems to possess this kind of aptitude, besides her oral skills, whereas Patrick only has an excellent oral mastery.

Summary of Results

We will now summarise the results in relation to our research questions and hypotheses. Our first question concerns the possibility of attaining native-likeness in late L2 acquisition. The results table shows that it is indeed possible to become native-like on a large number of measures, since the score of the four speakers studied within the native speaker range was 8 out of 10 (Hedda), 6 out of 10 (Patrick), 7 out of 10 (Mimi) and 4 out of 10 (Saga). However, there were no non-native speaker scores within the native speaker range across the board, which confirms our first hypothesis. In addition, it should also be added that there is no measure for which none of the non-native participants scored within the native speaker range. The most difficult aspect in terms of scoring within the native speaker range, for our non-native speakers, is the pass-as-a-native test.

Our second question concerns the characteristics of the passing profiles as compared to the non-passing profiles. It was found that passing is related to higher scores on oral measures, a larger quantity of formulaic sequences and an absence of morphosyntactic errors in spoken language, but it does not seem related to lexical richness. Furthermore, it was found that passing is not necessarily related to high scores on the written tests. Our second hypothesis is thus only partly confirmed.

Finally, our third research question examines whether language aptitude has an impact on L2 success. Our answer would be both no and yes in this respect. Language aptitude does not seem related to passing, except for the fact that our two passing profiles have a high score on the LLAMA D test (phonetic memory). However, language aptitude does seem related to results on the written tests. It is suggested that the written tests probably tap into metalinguistic knowledge, which would correlate more with language aptitude measured by the LLAMA test, as suggested by Granena (2013a, 2013b).

Socio-biographical profiles

The PASS profiles
Hedda
Linguistic evaluation

Hedda performs within the native speaker range on 8 out of 10 measures. 90% of the judges perceived her to be a French native speaker, and 70% perceived her to be a native Parisian speaker (see sections Lexical formulaic sequences/100 words and The-pass-as-a-native test above). This makes her the only participant receiving a score within the native speaker range. She clearly constitutes what Muñoz and Singleton (2007) would label a 'successful profile'. Her results are stable, regardless of data collection mode: she scores highly on both oral and written measures.

Language aptitude

Hedda scores highly on the LLAMA aptitude test (315/400).

Language background

Hedda was raised in a Swedish-speaking family and reports to have studied the following foreign languages: English (nine years), French (five years), and German (two years). She is not a particularly multilingual L2 user and does not report a particular interest in any foreign language besides French.

Education and professional occupation

Hedda moved to France at the relatively early age of 17 as an exchange student during a year in upper secondary school (the French *lycée*). She did not live in Paris at that time, but in a small city in South West France. Having finished her upper secondary studies, she studied two years of Engineering Physics at a technical university in Sweden, completed with a third year in Paris at a technical university and finished her master's degree, spending six months in the US and six months in Sweden. During a year at a French university, she met her husband. She started PhD studies in Sweden in Industrial Maths and after two years (one of which was spent in France) she switched to a French technical institute and completed her PhD in computer science there. She has not studied French formally, besides her upper secondary school studies. The last time we recorded data from her she had successfully completed her PhD and was working as a software developer.

LOR

Hedda has lived a total of 10 years in France.

Personal situation and attitudes towards France

Hedda is married to a Frenchman she met during her university studies. They have three children together and live in a suburb in the outskirts of Paris. She is originally from Gothenburg, Sweden (the second-largest city in Sweden) but claims no urge to go back there. If she were to move back to Sweden, she says it would be to Stockholm, Sweden's largest city and its capital. This would also be the preference of her husband, for both professional and social reasons. However, she does not rule out moving to yet another country, for example the United States. It seems, then, that she is open-minded regarding where to live. In general, she appears to have a positive and uncomplicated attitude towards life. Despite commenting upon gender inequality as a cultural difference between France and Sweden, she is not distressed by this difference. Throughout her interview she appeared to be a well-adjusted person who made the free decision to live in France. She not only enjoys living in France, she has created a meaningful life there with an advanced occupation and a family. In other words, her life in France does not seem limited by the fact that she is not French. Her social and linguistic adaptation seems to have been accomplished without great emotional strain or personal sacrifice. Her successful life in France, however, does not express itself through an overt passion for the country. Hedda followed the path she began during her upper secondary education, which opened the door for her to continue living in France. Her satisfaction with her life in France seems general and not particularly tied to locality.

Patrick
Linguistic evaluation

Patrick does not score well on the written measures, but does score well on the oral measures. He scores within the native speaker range on 6 out of 10 measures, five of them being oral. He has very high scores on lexical richness and fluency, which is understandable, due to the fact that he has lived in France for 20 years. He scores below average on all tests, except for the receptive deep knowledge test, which also includes items of cultural knowledge, and thus draws heavily on the experience the informant has with both language and culture.

Language aptitude

Patrick received a low score on the language aptitude tests. He misunderstood one of the tests, which resulted in a score of zero.

Language background

Patrick was raised in a bilingual household. His mother is Swedish and his father is Italian. Besides Swedish and Italian, he claims knowledge of English, German and Spanish. He studied French for two years in upper secondary school, but decided to go to France at the age of 20 to learn French. He claims his French surname inspired the move. He took a language course in Aix-en-Provence, enjoyed living there and stayed for almost two years working as an au pair, bartender and administrative assistant. Back in Sweden, he studied French at university for one year, among other disciplines.

Education and professional occupation

Patrick received a degree in economics from a Swedish university. After graduating, he worked in tourism in the South of France, Spain and Turkey. Finally, he moved to Paris permanently in 1992, where he got a job at a large tourism agency. He still works within the field of tourism, leading the divisions of sales and marketing. He uses both French and Swedish on a daily basis and English and Spanish on a frequent basis.

LOR
20 years.

Personal situation and attitudes towards France

Patrick has lived in Paris for 18 years. He has had the same French partner for 10 years and they have no children. Being a true Francophile, Patrick claims in his interview to feel more at home in France than in Sweden. He expresses his preference for what he calls the 'French way', which, he explains, involves gestures and body language. Having lived most of his adult life in France, he sometimes finds it difficult to adjust in Sweden. He is a true cultural migrant in that he prefers his experience of the French mentality and lifestyle.

The NON-PASS profiles
Mimmi
Linguistic evaluation

Mimmi's results are close to the NNS averages on many of the measures, except for the collocation and word association tests. She does slightly better on the written tests than on the oral measures, which matches her non-passing result. The only oral measure for which she scores above average is lexical richness, which is probably due to the fact that she uses a highly specialised vocabulary when she speaks about her profession, which impacts the figures. The 18 years she has lived in France should also be taken into account as a contributive factor to her lexical richness. She scores within the native speaker range on 7 out of 10 measures.

Language aptitude

Mimmi scores well on the language aptitude test, but her score is not excellent.

Language background

Mimmi has a very multilingual background. She was raised bilingually by her Swedish mother and German father. Her father was not consistent in using German at home, but she continued to develop her German by studying the language at school. In addition, she studied English, like all Swedes, for nine years. She also took a short Greek language course in Athens, which was inspired by the summer holidays her family spent in Greece, where she made Greek friends. After finishing her upper secondary studies, she studied Italian for a year in Italy. Her partner, who was born in France, is of Spanish/Catalan descent and she claims knowledge of Spanish and Catalan. Finally, she also knows Portuguese. Her knowledge of French was acquired in France, through a language course of one semester that she took when arriving in Paris at age 20 and then through her university studies (see below). However, she mentions that both her parents knew French and were Francophiles, so the French language was present during her childhood. Mimmi qualifies as a polyglot.

LOR
   18 years.

Education and professional occupation
   Mimmi is a professional dancer, dance teacher and choreographer. She also writes for a dance journal.
   She has received all her education in France. Besides dance studies, she also holds two degrees from university: a bachelor's in theatre studies and a master's in dance studies.

Personal situation and attitudes towards France
   Mimmi has lived, for many years, with a Paris-born man of Spanish/Catalan descent and they have one child. The family life is trilingual, with each parent speaking the mother tongue to the child and the parents communicating in French. Mimmi says that she decided early in life that she did not want to live in Stockholm, and that Paris was a natural choice, since she wanted to learn French and wanted to live in a big city where she could develop her interest in dancing. It is clear by her interview that she has no intention of moving back to Sweden. If she moved from Paris, it would be to her husband's native country, Spain. She particularly appreciates the cultural scene in Paris, mentioning places where dancers and musicians meet to dance and jam. When asked about cultural differences, especially those concerning relationships between men and women, she says that differences exist, but they do not bother her, since she has made the choice to live in Paris: *'c'est un choix de vie'*. This type of utterance reveals a character of both agency and determination. Finally, it is worth noting that her communication in French extends to even her immediate family. Mimmi has a half-sister who has lived in France long enough to experience an attrition of her Swedish. Not only does Mimmi speak French with her sister, but when their father, a Francophile, visits, they all three communicate in French. This shows that not even her immediate family possesses a typical monolingual, monolithic identity, but that different languages and cultures are a very natural part of their lives. Through Mimmi's interview one gets a sense of the relative ease with which she chose to live in France. Her background and descriptions suggest that this 'choice of life' occurred naturally.

Saga
Linguistic evaluation
   Saga scores close to the NS average on the oral tests, but above average on two of the written tests. This seems to align with her results of non-passing on the listener evaluation. She has the lowest total score in the group, scoring within the native speaker range on 4 out of 10 measures.

Language aptitude

Saga scores highly on the LLAMA aptitude test (315/400). (She shares the highest score with Hedda.)

Language background

Saga studied English, German and French. She studied French for the last two years in upper secondary school. After completing her upper secondary studies, she wanted to travel, but did not know where to go. By chance, she followed a friend to France, where she studied French for a year at the Sorbonne. She became fond of France and claims an appreciation of its architecture and aesthetic values. Besides her interest in French, she has not mentioned a desire to deepen her knowledge of the languages she has studied in the past, or to acquire a new language.

LOR

13 years.

Education and professional occupation

Saga spent a year in France, where she met her future partner. She returned to Sweden to study Art history, but returned to Paris after a year. There she studied intercultural mediation and management at a French university. She currently works in a bilingual environment (French/Swedish), in a public relations job promoting Swedish culture.

Personal situation and attitudes towards France

Saga lives with the same partner she met at the beginning of her stay in France. They do not have children. She seems very satisfied with her life in France and says that she particularly appreciates the cultural values she finds typical of France: architecture, design and French cuisine. Nevertheless, she also speaks of values and lifestyle, claiming that French people are more tolerant than Swedish people and that they are more forgiving regarding people's weaknesses. She appreciates what she characterises as the more chaotic and spontaneous lifestyle of Paris. Saga seems to take pleasure in what Paris has to offer and enjoys taking part in cultural activities. Saga could be considered the prototypical cultural migrant, because she has chosen to live in her preferred environment.

Discussion

The present study has shown that all four participants, who are all Swedish L1 French L2 late learners, perform within the native speaker range on numerous measures of L2 production. With a native speaker baseline as a norm, all of them qualify as 'successful' in their L2. However, they do not all demonstrate equal levels of success. With respect to the measures investigated in the present study, it is clear that Hedda is the most successful profile. On 8 out of 10 measures, she scores within the native speaker range and, interestingly enough, the measures for which she does not perform within the native speaker range may in fact be questioned as measures of native-likeness, viz. mean length of run and lexical richness. Fluency measures are known to be highly related to L1 fluency (cf. De Jong *et al.*, 2013) and mean length of run might be a measure that reflects personal speech style more than nativeness. Lexical richness has been a useful measure in distinguishing between different proficiency groups, though its usefulness as a yardstick, at very advanced levels, is questionable since it is highly tied to the communicative situation at hand and the speaking preferences of the individual. Disregarding these two measures, Hedda could be considered a native-like speaker in Abrahamsson and Hyltenstam's (2009) terms; that is she performs as a native speaker on all relevant measures, although she is not a French native speaker. It is therefore clear that the measures included gauge oral and written production and not sound perception, as some of the tests in Abrahamsson and Hyltenstam's (2009) study. It is important to point out that, regarding productive capacity in an L2, native-like speakers are, in fact, possible to find among cultural migrants, which is supported by Hedda's results.

The question then arises: Why is Hedda's the most successful profile? What factors may be decisive in determining her success? In examining the factors discussed in the profiles section, it can be seen that she began learning French at a younger age than the other participants (she began at 13, which is still past the purported critical period). However, her age of significant exposure is also lower than the others. She came to France as an exchange student at 17, spending a critical year of personal development in full French immersion. With respect to language aptitude, she scores highly, but so does Saga, and she is the least successful profile in terms of linguistic resources. Therefore, aptitude does not come across as the only explanatory factor in the present study. It is more likely that her exceptional educational background plays a more important role. Hedda holds a PhD from a well-reputed technical research centre in France, where high demands are often placed upon her French. It should also be noted that she does not operate in a bilingual environment. Her relationship status is consistent with the others, who also have French partners. The most apparent difference is that she has three children, which leads to even more interaction with French society, through school and daycare contacts.

Summing Up

In summary, the present study suggests that native-like performance is indeed possible for a large number of productive competencies in L2 acquisition. This is not to deny the existence of sensitive periods of language learning, especially with regards to phonetic production and perception, but it is important to emphasise the possibilities of late-onset language learning. Furthermore, it suggests the complexity of determining second language success. Abrahamsson and Hyltenstam (2008) propose that language aptitude is a determining factor for late L2 success, but at the same time, they reveal that their highest-scoring participants had also engaged intensively with language. Our study, although small in scale, suggests that while language aptitude may play a part in L2 success, it seems more linked to performance on written tests than to spontaneous production data. We have found convincing reasons to believe that the level and extent of interactions, that is quality and quantity of L2 use (cf. Moyer, 2004; Muñoz & Singleton, 2011), constitutes a more adequate explanation, especially if we look at all four participants. Obviously, our perception of quantity and quality of L2 acquisition is impressionistic in this case. Hedda interacts mainly in French, both professionally and personally. Patrick has a long LOR in France, and an important professional position, which demands that he can impose himself verbally. He uses several languages at work, however. Mimmi also has a long LOR in France, but her job as a dance teacher and choreographer is not necessarily a job that puts high demands on her speaking skills. Saga has a slightly longer LOR in France than Hedda, and while language use is important for her PR job, the nature of her job allows for the daily use of Swedish, which may influence her lower scores, especially with respect to speaking skills. One could thus imagine that L2 use and input are decisive factors, but for these to 'happen', some prerequisites in terms of aptitude and personality factors (cf. Forsberg Lundell & Sandgren, 2013; open-mindedness and cultural empathy) may be necessary. Kormos (2013: 147) goes so far as to suggest that affective and conative factors may actually be more important than cognitive aptitude for L2 success, since it may be crucial for the right social circumstances to be created, which are needed for quantity and quality of input to take place. Some individual factors can thus be considered as prerequisites and then L2 use and input as determining factors. Further studies investigating the intricate relationship between social-psychological variables and selected linguistic measures, such as formulaic sequences, are warranted. This is especially the case regarding longitudinal studies, which would shed more light on the effect of individual differences and L2 use in the process of language learning.

Note

(1) This research was funded by The Bank of Sweden Tercentenary Foundation, grant number M2005–459:1–RJ.

References

Abrahamsson, N. and Hyltenstam, K. (2008) The robustness of aptitude effects in near-native second language acquisition. *Studies in Second Language Acquisition* 30 (4), 481–509.
Abrahamsson, N. and Hyltenstam, K. (2009) Age of L2 acquisition and degree of nativelikeness – Listener perception vs linguistic scrutiny. *Language Learning* 58 (3), 249–306.
Agren, M., Granfeldt, J. and Schlyter, S. (2012) The growth of complexity and accuracy in L2 French. Past observations and recent applications of developmental stages. In A. Housen, F. Kuiken and I. Vedder (eds) *Dimensions of L2 Performance and Proficiency. Complexity, Accuracy and Fluency in SLA* (pp. 95–119). Amsterdam: Benjamins.
Ayoun, D. (2013) *The Second Language Acquisition of French Tense, Aspect, Mood and Modality*. Amsterdam: John Benjamins.
Bartning, I. (2009) The advanced learner variety: 10 years later. In E. Labeau and F. Myles (eds) *The Advanced Learner Variety: The Case of French* (pp. 11–41). Bern: Peter Lang.
Bartning, I. (2012) High-level proficiency in second language use. Morpho-syntax and discourse. In S. Benazzo, M. Hickmann and M. Watorek (eds) *Comparative Perspectives to Language Acquisition: A Tribute to Clive Perdue* (pp. 170–187). Bristol: Multilingual Matters.
Bartning, I. (2014) Synthèse retrospective et nouvelles perspectives développementales. In C. Lindqvist and C. Bardel (eds) *The Acquisition of French as a Second Language. New Developmental Perspectives* (pp. 7–28). Amsterdam: John Benjamins.
Bartning, I. and Schlyter, S. (2004) Itinéraires acquisitionnels et stades de développement en français L2. *Journal of French language Studies* 14 (3), 281–299.
Bartning, I, Forsberg, F. and Hancock, V. (2009) Resources and obstacles in very advanced L2 French. Formulaic language, information structure and morphosyntax. In L. Roberts, G.D. Véronique, A. Nilsson and M. Tellier (eds) *EUROSLA Yearbook 9* (pp. 185–211). Amsterdam: John Benjamins.
Bartning, I., Forsberg Lundell, F. and Hancock, V. (2012) On the role of linguistic contextual factors for morphosyntactic stabilisation in high-level L2 French. *Studies in Second language Acquisition* 34 (2), 243–267.
Birdsong, D. (1992) Ultimate attainment in second language acquisition. *Language* 68, 706–755.
Birdsong, D. (2003) Authenticité de prononciation en français L2 chez des apprenants tardifs anglophones: analyses segmentales et globales. *AILE* 18, 17–36.
Birdsong, D. (2007) Nativelike pronunciation among late learners of French as a second language. In S.-O. Bohn and M. Munro (eds) *Second Language Speech Learning: The Role of Language Experience in Speech Perception and Production* (pp. 99–116). Amsterdam: John Benjamins.
Bogaards, P. (2000) Testing L2 vocabulary knowledge at a high level: The case of the Euralex French Tests. *Applied Linguistics* 21 (4), 490–516.
Bylund, E. (2008) Conceptualización de eventos en español y en sueco. Estudios sobre hablantes monolingües y bilingües. Tesis doctoral. Departamento de español, portugués y estudios latinoamericanos. Universidad de Estocolmo.
Coppieters, R. (1987) Competence differences between native and non-native speakers. *Language* 63, 544–573.
DeKeyser, R.M. (2000) The robustness of critical period effects in second language acquisition. *Studies in Second Language Acquisition* 22 (4), 499–533.
DeKeyser, R.M. (ed.) (2007) *Practice in a Second Language: Perspectives from Applied Linguistics and Cognitive Psychology*. Cambridge: Cambridge University Press.
DeKeyser, R.M. (2003) Implicit and explicit learning. In C. Doughty and M. Long (eds) *The Handbook of Second Language Acquisition* (pp. 313–345). Oxford: Blackwell.
DeKeyser, R.M., Alfi-Shabtay, J. and Ravid, D. (2010) Crosslinguistic evidence for the nature of age effects in second language acquisition. *Applied Psycholinguistics* 31 (3), 413–438.
De Jong, N., Steinel, M.P., Florijn, A., Schoonen, R. and Hulstijn, J. (2013) Linguistic skills and speaking fluency in a second language. *Applied Psycholinguistics* 5, 893–916.

Dörnyei, Z. and Skehan, P. (2003) Individual differences in second language learning. In C. Doughty and M. Long (eds) *The Handbook of Second Language Acquisition* (pp. 589–630). Oxford: Blackwell.

Erman, B. and Warren, B. (2000) The idiom principle and the open choice principle. *Text* 20 (1), 29–62.

Forsberg, F. (2008) *Le langage préfabriqué – formes, fonctions et fréquences en français parlé L2 et L1*. Bern: Peter Lang.

Forsberg, F. (2010) Using conventional sequences in L2 French. *IRAL* 48 (1), 25–50.

Forsberg Lundell, F. and Lindqvist, C. (2012) Vocabulary development in advanced L2 French – Do formulaic sequences and lexical richness develop at the same rate? *LIA: Language, Interaction and Acquisition* 3 (1), 73–92.

Forsberg Lundell, F. and Lindqvist, C. (2013) Lexical aspects in very advanced L2 French. *Canadian Modern Language Review* 70 (1), 28–49.

Forsberg Lundell, F, Bartning, I., Engel, H, Gudmundsson, A, Hancock, V. and Lindqvist, C. (2014) Beyond advanced stages in high-level spoken L2 French. *Journal of French Language Studies* 24 (2), 1–26.

Forsberg Lundell, F. and Sandgren, M. (2013) High-level proficiency in late L2 acquisition – Relationships between collocational production, language aptitude and personality. In G. Granena and M. Long. *Sensitive Periods, Language Aptitude and Ultimate L2 Attainment* (pp. 231–259). Amsterdam: John Benjamins.

Franceschina, F. (2005) *Fossilized Second Language Grammars. The Acquisition of Grammatical Gender*. Amsterdam: John Benjamins.

Frenck-Mestre, C.M., Foucart, A., Carrasco, H. and Herschenson, J. (2009) Processing grammatical gender in French as a first and second language. In L. Roberts, D. Wronique, A. Nilsson and M. Tellier (eds) *EUROSLA Yearbook 9* (pp. 76–106). Amsterdam: John Benjamins.

Granena, G. (2013a) Cognitive aptitudes for second language learning and the LLAMA aptitude test. In G. Granena and M. Long (eds) *Sensitive Periods, Language Aptitude and Ultimate L2 Attainment* (pp. 105–129). Amsterdam: John Benjamins.

Granena, G. (2013b) Reexamining the robustness of aptitude in second language acquisition. In G. Granena and M. Long (eds) *Sensitive Periods, Language Aptitude and Ultimate L2 Attainment* (pp. 179–205). Amsterdam: John Benjamins.

Granena, G. and Long, M. (2013) *Sensitive Periods, Language Aptitude and Ultimate L2 Attainment*. Amsterdam: John Benjamins.

Granger, S. and Paquot, M. (2008) Disentangling the phraseological web. In S. Granger and F. Meunier (eds) *Phraseology: An Interdisciplinary Perspective* (pp. 27–49). Amsterdam: John Benjamins.

Gyllstad, H. (2007) Testing English collocations. Developing receptive tests for use with advanced Swedish learners. Doctoral Dissertation, Lund University.

Holmes, V. and Segui, J. (2006) Assigning grammatical gender during word production. *Journal of Psycholinguistic Research* 35 (1), 5–30.

Hyltenstam, K. (1992) Non-native features of near-native speakers: on the ultimate attainment of childhood L2 learners. In R.J. Harris (ed.) *Cognitive Processing in Bilinguals* (pp. 351–368). Amsterdam: North-Holland.

Ioup, G., Boustagui, E., Eltigi, M. and Mosette, M. (1994) Reexamining the critical period hypothesis. A case of successful adult second language acquisition. *Studies in Second Language Acquisition* 16, 73–98.

Kinsella, C. and Singleton, D. (2014) Much more than age. In *Applied Linguistics 2014* (pp. 1–23). Oxford: Oxford University Press.

Kormos, J. (2013) New conceptualisations of language aptitude in second language attainment. In G. Granena and M. Long (eds) *Sensitive Periods, Language Aptitude, and Ultimate L2 Attainment* (pp. 132–152). Amsterdam: John Benjamins.

Krashen, S.D. (1981) *Second Language Acquisition and Second language Learning*. Oxford: Pergamon.
Labeau, E. and Myles, F. (eds) (2009) *The Advanced Learner Varieties: The Case of French*. Bern: Peter Lang.
Lardiere, D. (2000) Mapping features to forms in SLA. In J. Archibald (ed.) *Second Language Acquisition and Linguistic Theory* (pp. 102–129). Oxford: Blackwell.
Lardiere, D. (2007) *Ultimate Attainment in Second Language Acquisition. A Case Study*. Mahwaw, NJ: Erlbaum.
Laufer, B. and Nation, P. (1995) Vocabulary size and use: Lexical richness in L2 written production. *Applied Linguistics* 16 (3), 307–322.
Laufer, B. and Waldmann, T. (2011) Verb – Noun collocations in second language writing. A corpus analysis of learners' English. *Language Learning* 61 (2), 647–672.
Lindqvist, C., Bardel, C. and Gudmundson, A. (2011) Lexical richness in the advanced learner's oral production of French and Italian L2. *IRAL* 49 (3), 221–240.
Meara, P. (2005) *LLAMA Language Aptitude Tests*. Swansea, UK: Lognostics.
Mizrahi, E. and Laufer, B. (2010) Lexical competence of highly advanced L2 users: Is their collocation knowledge as good as their productive vocabulary size? Paper presented at Eurosla 20, Reggio Emilia, Italy.
Montrul, S. and Slabakova, R. (2003) Competence similarities between native and near-native speakers: An investigation of the preterite/imperfect contrast in Spanish. *Studies in Second Language Acquisition* 25 (3), 351–398.
Moyer, A. (2004) *Age, Accent and Experience in Second Language Acquisition. An Integrated Approach to Critical Period Inquiry*. Clevedon: Multilingual Matters.
Muñoz, C. (2008) Symmetries and asymmetries of age effects in naturalistic and instructed L2 learning. *Applied Linguistics* 29 (4), 578–596.
Muñoz, C. and Singleton, D. (2007) Foreign accent in advanced learners, two successful profiles. In *EUROSLA Yearbook 7* (pp. 171–191). Amsterdam: John Benjamins.
Muñoz, C. and Singleton, D. (2011) A critical review of age-related research on L2 ultimate attainment. *Language Teaching* 44 (1), 1–35.
Österberg, R. (2008) Motivación, aptitud y dessarrollo estructural. Un estudio sobre la actuación lingüística en aprendientes suecos de español L2. Doctoral thesis. Department of Spanish, Portugues and Latinamerican studies. Stockholm University.
Piller, I. (2002) Passing for a native speaker: Identity and success in second language learning. *Journal of Sociolinguistics* 6 (2), 179–206.
Regan, V. (2013) The bookseller and the basketball player: Tales from the French Polonia. In D. Singleton, V. Regan and E. Debaene (eds) *Linguistic and Cultural Acquisition in a Migrant Community* (pp. 28–48). Bristol: Multilingual Matters.
Schmitt, N. (2012) Size and depth of vocabulary – A review. Paper presented at AAAL 2012, Boston, MA, USA.
Singleton, D., Regan, V. and Debaene, E. (eds) (2013) *Linguistic and Cultural Acquisition in a Migrant Community*. Bristol: Multilingual Matters.
Tidball, F. and Treffers-Daller, J. (2008) Analysing lexical richness in French learner language: What frequency lists and teacher judgement can tell us about basic and advanced words. *Journal of French Language Studies* 18 (3), 299–313.
Towell, R., Hawkins, R. and Bazergui, N. (1996) The development of fluency in advanced learners of French. *Applied Linguistics* 17 (1), 84–119.
Treffers-Daller, J. (2009) Language dominance and lexical diversity: how bilinguals and L2 learners differ in their knowledge and use of French lexical and functional items. In B. Richards, D. Malvern, P. Meara, J. Milton and J. Treffers-Daller (eds) *Vocabulary Studies in First and Second Language Acquisition* (pp. 74–90). Basingstoke: Palgrave Macmillan.
Véronis, J. (2011) *Fréquences des mots en français parlé*. http://sites.univprovence.fr/veronis/data/freq-oral.txt.

3 Reported Use and Perception of *tu* and *vous* Among Less Integrated and Highly Integrated Anglophone Cultural Migrants in France

Amanda Edmonds and
Catherine Guesle-Coquelet

In the 19 February 2000 issue of *The International Herald Tribune*, Mary Blume published an article entitled 'Mastering the unmasterable: A French puzzle'. For Blume, as for many others, the unmasterable puzzle refers to the second person pronominal address system in French: *tu* (T) versus *vous* (V). Blume began her article with this comment: 'With some effort and application, foreigners can learn to tie a scarf like a French woman or to chew wine like a French man. But they cannot hope to master the intricacies of the *tu* and *vous* forms of address, because the French can't either' (Blume, 2000). Blume's observation echoes findings from the fields of second language (L2) acquisition and sociolinguistics. We know, for example, that L2 learners often experience difficulty in mastering the differences between T/V, but also that native speakers (NS) experience hesitation, anxiety and worry related to these terms of address. That said, the sources of difficulties for natives and non-natives are not exactly the same. Whereas non-native speakers (NNS) may experience trouble related to their linguistic competence (e.g. manipulating the T/V verbal forms) or with sociolinguistic competence (e.g. determining which pronoun to use with whom and in which situation), hesitations on the part of NSs result from the interpersonal nature of these forms, insofar as the choice between T and V necessarily brings into play questions of personal and social identity in a given situation. As summed up by Dewaele and Planchenault (2006: 147), 'in interactions in French, the choice between *tu* and *vous* is a perilous socio-cultural exercise.'[1]

Numerous authors in the field of L2 acquisition have taken an interest in pronominal terms of address and, in particular, in how the sociolinguistic knowledge necessary for their appropriate use may be best addressed within a classroom setting. For French, studies have been conducted in immersion settings (Lyster, 1994; Lyster & Rebuffot, 2002), as well as among university classroom learners (Belz & Kinginger, 2002; Liddicoat, 2006; Planchenault, 2009; van Compernolle, 2010), identifying various practices that aim to allow for learners to apprehend the social – in addition to the purely linguistic – aspects of the T/V distinction. Most of these authors have concluded that 'learning to use these forms and to understand their meanings is as much a function of language socialization as of language acquisition' (Belz & Kinginger, 2002: 208). With respect to the development of sociolinguistic competence more generally, Dewaele (2004a) states that '[o]nly a prolonged and regular contact with NS of the TL [target language] seems to have a noticeable effect' (p. 314). If Dewaele is correct, this would imply that mastery of the sociolinguistic dimension of the T/V distinction requires contact with NSs, as NNS-NNS interactions – such as are common in language classrooms – do not entail the same social and communicative risks as do interactions with NSs (van Compernolle et al., 2011, make this point with respect to online NNS-NNS chat discussions). This position finds support in Belz and Kinginger's (2002) study of NS-NNS telecollaborative interactions, in which they found that relatively negative social consequences (which took the form of overt corrections or questioning by the NS) in response to inappropriate pronoun choice on the part of the NNS can lead to development of sociolinguistic competence.

It thus seems plausible to expect that NNSs who have chosen to settle in a French-speaking country and who have relatively easy access to NSs should be in a favourable position in terms of the development of sociolinguistic competence in general and the T/V distinction in particular. This presumption is the starting point of our research project, in which we set out to examine reported usage and perceptions of T/V by a group of 30 Anglophone cultural migrants who had settled in the Southwest of France. Whereas previous research suggests that contact with NSs may be necessary for sociolinguistic development, we seek to determine whether this contact is sufficient. The present chapter will focus on the reported usage and perceptions of T/V from two subgroups of our cultural migrants chosen because their self-assessed integration scores were located on the extremes of our sample. In other words, the purpose of this study was to determine what, if any, stumbling blocks continue to hamper the efforts of a group of less integrated and a group of highly integrated cultural migrants in mastering what Blume called the unmasterable: *tu* versus *vous*.

Tutoiement and *Vouvoiement*

NS French

The dynamic relationship between T and V across time has been extensively documented (see Coffen, 2002; Guesle-Coquelet, 2009; Maley, 1972). Since the 1960s, this relationship has often been interpreted with reference to Brown and Gilman's (1960) now classic article. Their analysis, which concerned several European languages, suggested that pronouns of address originally encoded a power difference (resulting in numerous asymmetrical address situations, wherein one interlocutor uses T while the other uses V), but that modern systems are now encoded primarily along the dimension of solidarity and, as a result, most interactions are symmetrical (i.e., in a given interaction, both interlocutors use either T or V). If this model has been criticised as being too simplistic (Morford, 1997; Peeters, 2004), it forms the starting point of much research on T/V in French. Following the publication of Brown and Gilman (1960), numerous researchers undertook fieldwork in order to explore perceived usage of the two pronouns of address (e.g. Bustin-Lekeu, 1973; Gardner-Chloros, 1991; Guesle-Coquelet, 2009; Morford, 1997; Schoch, 1978; Warren, 2009). These studies were based on questionnaires, one-on-one interviews, and/or focus groups in a variety of contexts in France.[2] To take but one example, Guesle-Coquelet (2009) used the questionnaires designed by Gardner-Chloros and Schoch as a starting point and set out to examine T/V use in three different situations: with family and friends, at work, and in everyday life. Her 36-item questionnaire was completed by a total of 96 people residing in urban centres in France, with 70% of her respondents living in the Southwest (57% in Pau and 13% in Bordeaux).[3] The results from her study echo those found in previous work, namely the importance of (a) relative hierarchy between the two speakers, (b) whether the interlocutor is known or not, and (c) age (of the speaker and of the person spoken to).

The general conclusion reached by Guesle-Coquelet (2009) is that variables such as age, hierarchy and familiarity, among others, guide behaviour with respect to terms of address, thus creating a norm generally respected by the community under investigation, but this norm is rather flexible, as the different variables that come into play can pull speakers in opposing directions. Morford (1997) analysed the different factors influencing T/V use with respect to what she called first- and second-order indexicality, which are essential to understanding the socio-cultural dimension of T/V. Morford explains that first-order indexicality refers to 'characteristics of the immediate context, as they concern the relationship (degree of deference and/or intimacy) between speaker and addressee and/or the nature of the circumstances (degree of formality and/or publicness)' (Morford, 1997: 29). Second-order indexicality, on the other hand, concerns 'beliefs about who uses what kinds of forms in what particular ways' (1997: 16), which associates T/V use with 'enduring social attributes of individual speakers (primarily, refinement, status, and political orientation)' (1997: 30). The interplay of these two levels of indexicality results in a complex system capable of generating multiple significations. According to Kinginger and Farrell (2004: 24), 'it is obvious that address form competence [...] cannot be acquired as a set of straightforward rules.'

NNS French

Several L2 researchers interested in the acquisition of sociolinguistic competence, defined by Lyster (1994) as 'the ability to recognize and produce contextually appropriate language, including sensitivity to differences in variety and register' (1994: 266), have examined both the actual and reported use of T/V by NNSs of French, with the vast majority of studies concentrating on university learners. Research investigating actual usage include Dewaele (2002, 2004b) and van Compernolle et al. (2011).[2] In Dewaele's two studies, university students who were native and non-native speakers of French participated in dyadic conversations. Dewaele found that NNSs used more V than did the NSs, a result that parallels findings on other aspects of sociolinguistic competence showing that learners in formal education settings tend to overuse formal variants (see Rehner & Mougeon, 2003). Dewaele also noted that the frequency of French use (outside of the classroom) was a significant predictor of T use in the dyadic conversations. More specifically, NNSs who reported using more French overall also used more T during the experiment. In his 2004 article, Dewaele draws attention to the fact that some of the NNSs show variable use of T/V within the same interview and with the same interlocutor. Variable use of T/V was specifically investigated by van Compernolle et al. (2011) using online interactions among NNSs enrolled in first, second or third semester French courses at an American university. Using a variationist approach, the authors found evidence that linguistic structure, instructional level and supra-word constructions (i.e. formulaic language) significantly influenced the use of T versus V in their corpus.

In addition to actual use, several studies have investigated reported use, relying on either questionnaires (e.g. Dewaele, 2004b; Dewaele & Planchenault, 2006) or interviews (Kinginger & Farrell, 2004) for data collection. Results on reported use resemble in large part those found for actual use. For example, in Dewaele (2004b), the author found that NNSs reported using more V than did a group of NSs from a similar population, and that NNSs who used French more often outside of the classroom tended to report using T with greater frequency. Kinginger and Farrell (2004) were interested in both reported use (in six interpersonal situations) and in the rationale behind the address form selected. Their study focused on the development of metapragmatic awareness of the French T/V system during a study abroad experience (their NNS participants completed an individual interview before going abroad and after returning). The authors analysed the responses provided by eight of the participants and found evidence of development presumably linked to interactions engaged in while abroad. The authors concluded that the data do in fact show changes in the learners' awareness of the T/V system, particularly in the domain of authentic age-peer relationships not normally experienced in classroom foreign language learning. In nearly every case examined, the participants' direct or indirect access to participation in social encounters involving age-peers seems to have impressed upon them the genuine significance of the T/V system while simultaneously offering insights into the socio-cultural concepts underlying the indexicality of address form choice (Kinginger & Farrell, 2004: 38).

Cultural Migrants and the T/V Distinction: The Current Study

Overall, the various L2 studies reviewed have pointed to the importance of contact with NSs in the development of sociolinguistic competence for NNSs, including the T/V distinction, and certain studies have shown that such contact does in fact lead to improved sociolinguistic competence. That said, the existing research has been carried out almost exclusively with university learners of French who have limited contact with NSs. We know little about the sociolinguistic competence of cultural migrants in France, that is, those NNSs who have chosen out of their own free will and because of a lifestyle choice to move to France on a permanent basis. If interaction with NSs is indeed a crucial and perhaps necessary part of the equation, we might expect that cultural migrants have overcome the difficulties documented for NNSs in general (i.e. overuse of V, variable use of T/V in the same situation, etc.) to arrive at a profile that resembles what has been reported for the NSs around whom they live. Our research project sets out to address this issue by looking at the reported use and perceptions of T/V of a group of 30 Anglophone cultural migrants settled in the Southwest of France (the Aquitaine and Midi-Pyrénées regions). All of these participants completed a questionnaire and 13 of the 30 agreed to take part in a face-to-face interview. For the current article, we will be reporting on responses provided by a subset of 10 participants who differ in terms of their self-reported integration in France, thus allowing us to investigate the impact of this variable on one aspect of sociolinguistic competence (the T/V distinction).

Questionnaire

In order to examine aspects of both first- and second-level indexicality (Morford, 1997), we chose to administer a questionnaire to our cultural migrants in which they were asked to provide information on their use and perceptions of terms of address in French. The questionnaire used in the current project was taken from Guesle-Coquelet (2009) with some slight adaptations. The decision to use a questionnaire that has already been administered to a large group of individuals residing in France (of which the majority were living in the region where the current project was undertaken) allows us to draw comparisons between our group of cultural migrants and results from a larger sample of individuals who make up the community in which they live. The questionnaire we administered included two parts: a background questionnaire (21 questions) and a questionnaire on terms of address[5] (31 questions) in the contexts of family/friends, work, and everyday life. All questions were asked in French, although some participants chose to respond in English.

The seven-question background section from Guesle-Coquelet's (2009) original questionnaire was considerably expanded for the current project. On both the original and L2 versions, participants were asked to provide their name, gender, age bracket (20–29, 30–34, 35–39,[6] 40–49, 50–59, >60), number of children and their ages, profession and native language. In addition, NNSs were asked to provide their nationality and to respond to a series of questions aimed at evaluating their reason(s) for settling in France (questions 1–2), their history with and estimated use of the French language (questions 3–10), and their feelings of integration in their adopted country (11–13). For the full background portion of the questionnaire, see Appendix A. The second part of the questionnaire targeted the reported use and perception of address terms. In this case, little was changed from Guesle-Coquelet's (2009) original questionnaire, although five questions were removed because they were irrelevant for NNSs who had not grown up in a Francophone environment. The full questionnaire is available in Appendix B.

Interview

Interviews were conducted with a subset of participants and were undertaken in order to provide additional information on three main issues: integration in the target language community, reported use of T/V and one's status as a foreigner living abroad. In each face-to-face interview, we addressed the following questions:

(1a) **Integration in the target language community**
Do you consider yourself to be integrated? Since when? How do you know?

What is still missing?
Can you give an example of something that you didn't understand for a long time and that you finally understood?
What is still difficult for you in terms of the French language?

(1b) **Reported use of T/V**
What were your problems when you first arrived?
Can you give an example of a blunder?
If you have in-laws, how did T/V work with them?
How do address terms work in your work environment?
Do you have experiences with alternations between T/V with the same person?
What is still hard to understand?

(1c) **Status as a foreigner living abroad**
How do you feel as a foreigner living abroad?
Have you used your status as a foreigner as an excuse?
What have you learned about your own culture?

In addition to discussing these questions, the interviews were the occasion to talk about responses given in the questionnaire that were unclear or surprising. The interviews were semi-guided and conducted in French, although certain interviewees also used English to respond to some questions.

Procedure

Participants were contacted via email and those who responded reported spending between 20 and 45 minutes completing the questionnaire. Each participant was also asked whether they would be willing to participate in a face-to-face interview. Thirteen of the 30 participants accepted our invitation, and interviews lasted between 30 and 60 minutes. All interviews were audio recorded using Quicktime player.

Participants: A Population of Cultural Migrants

The participants in our research project can be identified as Anglophone cultural migrants in France. We chose to work solely with Anglophones for three reasons. First, as English does not have multiple forms of second-person pronominal address, the T/V distinction in French is widely considered difficult – both linguistically and socio-pragmatically – for English speakers (e.g. Dewaele, 2004b: 398; Lyster, 1994: 283). Second, the vast majority of research carried out on the acquisition of the T/V distinction by NNSs has concerned English-speaking university students, thus offering an interesting point of comparison for the current project. Finally, the Southwest of France, where this study was carried out, has a large Anglophone population (see Huart, 2012).

The concept of *cultural migrant* is the main thread tying together the different contributions to this volume. The two co-editors have defined cultural migrant in the following way: 'people who decide, out of their free will, to move to another country permanently and learn the language of that country' (Forsberg Lundell & Bartning, this volume), in opposition to those who have left their native country for economic and/or political reasons (see Noiriel, 2002: 10, for three types of factors responsible for emigration: economic factors, factors linked to social and cultural reasons, and political factors). In order to respect this definition, only Anglophones having chosen to settle in France out of their own free will were asked to participate in the study. All had been living in France for at least five years and had the intention of settling there permanently. In what follows, we will use the responses to the background portion of our questionnaire to characterise our population of 30 cultural migrants in a more detailed manner. We will then examine more closely the subset of 10 individuals studied in the current article.

The responses provided to the 21 background questions revealed a wide variety of socio-biographical profiles. As can be seen in Table 3.1, the age of our respondents varies from 30 to more than 60, with approximately one third of our participants ($n=9$) being in their 30s, one third in their 40s ($n=11$) and one third older than 50 ($n=10$). Lengths of residence vary widely, with the newest arrivals (three participants) having settled in France in 2009, whereas four of our participants have been in France since the 1970s. Finally, using the Common European Framework for Languages, all of our participants estimate their overall level of French to be at least intermediate (B1, $n=6$), and most consider themselves advanced (B2, $n=8$) or near-native (C, $n=16$). The group includes 8 men and 22 women with various professional activities, although language-related fields clearly predominate: there are 2 translators and 16 individuals who report teaching English in various contexts, ranging from private language centres to at University level. Finally, our group of 30 Anglophone cultural migrants covers five nationalities: Dutch (born to Anglophone parents, $n=1$), Irish ($n=1$), Australian ($n=2$), American ($n=7$) and British ($n=19$). Five of these

Table 3.1 Length of residence, overall proficiency in French and age of participants

	Length of residence								
	5–10 years			11–20 years			>20 years		
Age	B1	B2	C	B1	B2	C	B1	B2	C
30–34	1		1			1			
35–39	1	1	1		1	2			
40–49	2		1	3	2			1	2
50–59	1				1	1	1	1	
>60						2			3

participants have obtained dual French nationality and one other mentioned being in the process of completing the paperwork.

In addition to collecting these socio-biographical details, our background questionnaire also sought to gather information concerning each individual's self-reported integration in their adopted country. *Integration* can of course be defined in a variety of ways. For example, Benson (2010: 55), in her study of British lifestyle migrants to the Lot, defines integration as 'the degree of interaction between the local French and the incoming British population.' In our study, participants were asked to situate their level of integration in social and in professional life on a scale from 1 (negative) to 5 (positive). Responses ranged from 2 to 5, with the majority of responses falling between 4 and 5. This result suggests that the status of cultural migrant often correlates with a strong sense of integration, but that there are exceptions (cf. Benson, 2010; Smallwood, 2007). For the remainder of this article, we will take a closer look at two sub-groups of five participants each, whose scores of self-assessed integration situate them on the two extremes of our group of 30 cultural migrants. Given the strongly social and interpersonal nature of second-person address, we hypothesise that there will be a difference in pronominal address form reported use and perception on the basis of self-assessed integration in the host society.

In order to constitute these two groups, we identified the five individuals with the lowest integration scores in both social and work environments; for these participants, whom we will refer to as less integrated, all self-assessed integration scores were 2 or 3 on a scale from 1 to 5. We then identified all participants who had rated their social and professional integration to be 4.5 or 5. Sixteen participants exhibited such scores. Of these participants, we selected five whose lengths of residence, ages and self-assessed proficiency in French were most similar to the group of less integrated cultural migrants. These individuals will be referred to as our highly integrated group. The profiles of this subset of 10 participants are provided in Table 3.2. As can be seen in this table, the socio-biographical details of the less and of the highly integrated cultural migrants are similar. In terms of age, two participants are in their 30s, two are in their 40s, and one is older than 50. In both groups, lengths of residence range from 5 to 13 years and the three levels of self-assessed French proficiency found in our sample are represented. Each group includes one man and four women and a variety of nationalities. Finally, each group includes two individuals whose profession entails teaching English (one English literature professor, two English teachers providing language classes at university, and one English teacher employed by a private language centre), one person who does not work and two people exercising other professions.

Table 3.2 Socio-biographical details for the subset of 10 participants

Participants	Age	Length of residence (years)	Proficiency	Gender	Profession	Nationality	Integration scores Social	Work
Less integrated								
Participant 5	>60	13	C	M	English professor	UK	2	2
Participant 24	30–34	7	B1	F	Post-doc	USA	2	3
Participant 14*	35–39	5	B1	F	Psychotherapist	UK	3	2
Participant 17	40–49	6	B1	F	English teacher (private language centre)	UK	3	2
Participant 19	40–49	12	B2	F	—	USA	3	—
Highly integrated								
Participant 4*	35–39	13	C	M	Studies program coordinator	USA	4.5	4.5
Participant 27	50–59	9	B1	F	Studies program coordinator	Dutch	4.5	4.5
Participant 16	40–49	5	B1	F	—	Irish	5	—
Participant 13*	40–49	13	B2	F	English teacher (university)	UK	5	5
Participant 26	35–39	5	C	F	English teacher (university)	USA	5	5

Note: *=participant who completed a follow-up face-to-face interview.

Data Analysis

Two types of analyses were carried out. The first analysis concerns the questions on reported use of address terms with family and friends and in everyday life. Although the questionnaire also examined address term use in professional settings, unfortunately only 4 of the 10 cultural migrants responded to these questions and so they will not be taken into account in our analysis. Our findings will be compared with results obtained in Guesle-Coquelet (2009) on the same questions but with NSs of French. The second analysis will be qualitative in nature and will concentrate on three of the eight open-ended questions included in our questionnaire. These questions aimed to discern how these cultural migrants perceive the T/V distinction. In both analyses, reference will be made when relevant to the interviews conducted with three of the individuals in this sub-sample (P4, P13, and P14). All comments cited, whether from the questionnaires or the interviews, are reproduced exactly as they were written or pronounced.

Results: Reported Usage of T/V

Beginning with responses to questions targeting family and friends, we find that the two groups of cultural migrants behave rather similarly to the individuals reported on in Guesle-Coquelet (2009). In examining our 10 NNSs' reported use of T/V with family (spouse, children, in-laws), we see that when French is the language used, reciprocal T is categorically employed. Although the same tendencies were reported in Guesle-Coquelet (2009: 225) with spouses and children, the results were not categorical: 97% of respondents reported using T-T with spouses, whereas 95% reported using reciprocal T with their offspring.[7] It is with respect to in-laws that our NNSs differ most clearly from the NSs. As has been reported by other authors (e.g. Gardner-Chloros, 1991), pronominal address forms used with in-laws show considerable variety in native French, an observation that finds support in Guesle-Coquelet's data: Only 29% of men and 6% of women reported using reciprocal T with their in-laws, whereas 13% of men and 28% of women used reciprocal V. The largest proportion of respondents (36% of men, 45% of women) reported addressing their in-laws with V but receiving T in return. This clearly contrasts with the 100% T-T use reported by our 10 cultural migrants. That said, in the interviews conducted with three of the cultural migrants in this subset, we find one example of variation between T and V precisely in the context of address forms used with in-laws. This was the case for P14 (less integrated group), who has been in the Southwest of France for five years and who is married to a French man. This participant normally uses T with her mother-in-law.

(2) P14 : *Et quelques fois le vous sort avant que / même avec ma belle-mère de temps en temps je dis vous / et elle me dit pourquoi tu me dis ça / désolée c'est pas...*
'And sometimes *vous* comes out before / even with my mother-in-law every once in a while I say *vous* / and she says to me why do you say that to me / sorry it's not...'
Q : *Est-ce que vous pensez que ça correspond à une situation particulière / ou bien c'est pas du tout contrôlé / à votre avis*
'Do you think that it corresponds to a particular situation / or perhaps it's not at all controlled / in your opinion'
P14 : *XXX // je pense que si j'ai beaucoup de contacts avec les gens c'est plus facile / mais s'il y a un laps de temps / je le j'oublie je perds l'habitude*
'XXX // I think that if I have a lot of contact with people it's easier / but if there is a lapse of time / I it I forgot I lose the habit'
Q : *Vous ne vous souvenez plus de ce que vous disiez avant*
'You no longer remember which pronoun you used before'
P14 : *Oui / mais c'est pas / c'est pas que je j'ai la question dans ma tête de est-ce que c'est tu ou vous / c'est juste ça sort*
'Yes / but it's not / it's not that I I have the question in my head of do I say *tu* or *vous* / It's just that it comes out'

Of the three interviews conducted with this subset of participants, this type of comment was only found in the interview with P14, who is also the only participant with a self-assessed proficiency level of B1 to have completed a face-to-face interview. It is likely that her lower level of French mastery is in part responsible for her difficulty with control over these two pronouns (*c'est juste ça sort*). This comment is similar to what was reported in studies cited earlier with respect to variation between T/V with classroom learners of French (Dewaele, 2004b; van Compernolle *et al.*, 2011).

As concerns friends, our 10 NNSs all declare that they use a reciprocal T with all of their Francophone friends. However, as with her mother-in-law, P14 reports during her interview varying (but not on purpose) between T and V with the same friend.

(3) P14: *Le même avec les amis d'A,* [her husband] *de temps en temps je dis vous et ils me regardent quoi?*
'The same thing with the friends of A. [her husband] every once in a while I say *vous* and they look at me what?'

Although Guesle-Coquelet also found that reciprocal T was the most common form of pronominal address between friends, her results are more nuanced, as 20% of her participants indicated that they used V with at least some of their friends. An association between T and friendship or friendliness is prevalent in our cultural migrant data, as will be seen in the section on perceptions.

When meeting someone for the first time, the reported use data from the two groups of NNSs were similar to those provided by the NSs in Guesle-Coquelet (2009). In both sets of data, responses are rather evenly split between V and *it depends*. During our interview, P13 (highly integrated group) provided her definition of address behaviour when meeting someone for the first time:

(4) P13: *Je pense que c'est plus correct à dire vous au départ. Adresser quelqu'un: bonjour Monsieur, comment allez-vous?*
'I think that it's more correct to say *vous* at the beginning. Address someone: hello sir, how do you do?'

For those natives and non-natives who responded *it depends*, the factor most frequently cited was the age of the interlocutor. In a related but apparently more complicated situation – that of being introduced to a friend of a friend (with whom the speaker uses T) – the responses from our two groups of cultural migrants once again resemble those found by Guesle-Coquelet. For the natives and the non-natives, a wide variety of responses is found, including *it depends, I wait to see how the person addresses me, spontaneous T (with first name or without)* and *spontaneous V (with first name or with Monsieur/Madame/Mademoiselle)*. P4 (highly integrated group) discussed this very situation in our face-to-face interview in response to the question concerning in which situations he continues to hesitate between T and V:

(5) P4: *Uniquement si par exemple je suis avec un ami qui me présente à quelqu'un d'autre et je vois qu'ils sont très amis. Mais souvent ça dépend du contexte, si c'est un contexte dé- contexte décontracté, on si on a presque le même âge, je peux dire tu de suite. Mais, en cas de doute ou si la personne est plus âgée, ou si c'est, si je vois par exemple que c'est un collègue de cette personne, même s'ils se tutoient, je vais dire vous. Si je vois que c'est un ami ou le frère, quelque chose comme ça, je vais peut-être dire tu.*
'Only if for example I am with a friend who introduces me to someone else and I see that they're good friends. But often it depends on the context, if it's a relaxed context, we if we are almost the same age, I can say *tu* right away. But, if I have a doubt, or if the person is older, or if it's if I see for example that it's a colleague of this person, even if they say *tu* to each other, I'm going to say *vous*. If I see that it's a friend or the brother, something like that, I am going to maybe say *tu*.'

Whereas P4 has a good grasp on the numerous factors that come into play in this highly complex situation (age, situation, hierarchy, familiarity), this is not the case for all participants. This is evident in the following written comment provided by P14 (less integrated group) on her questionnaire, where we see that her original reading of the friend-of-a-friend situation concentrated solely on the fact that she was meeting a new person which, for her, meant that V was appropriate:

(6) P14: *I once used vous with the friend of a friend the same age as me and he thought it was very funny, so generally I try and wait to see how they address me*

Taken together, the responses to the questions concerning address form behaviour with family and friends and in everyday life reveal that the 10 cultural migrants do not differ greatly from the NSs studied by Guesle-Coquelet (2009). As opposed to university learners whose reported use was found to clearly differ from that of NSs in Dewaele (2004b), it appears that these cultural migrants have succeeded in apprehending the norm in their adopted community. The few differences that do emerge point to a more categorical behaviour on the part of the cultural migrants. This was the case for address forms used with family (and especially in-laws) and with friends. Importantly, no differences between the less and the highly integrated cultural migrants emerged, suggesting that reported T/V use may not vary as a function of self-assessed integration.

Results: Perceptions of the T/V Distinction

In this second part of the analysis, we will concentrate on how our two groups of cultural migrants perceive the T/V distinction, by examining the responses provided to three sets of questions on the written questionnaire:

(7) Are there situations in which you hesitate between *tu* and *vous*? Which situations? Are there times when you hesitate to make the T/V distinction? Can you give examples and explain how you get around the problem? (question 24)
Do you think that it is desirable to abandon the *tu/vous* distinction, as was done in English? Why or why not? (question 29)[8]
What do *tutoiement* and *vouvoiement* mean for you personally? (question 28)

The comments and examples provided by our 10 cultural migrants concerning situations in which they hesitate are reproduced in Table 3.3. These responses, which are reproduced exactly as the participants wrote them, are telling, and reveal clear differences between the less integrated and the highly integrated cultural migrants. Four of the five less integrated

Table 3.3 Do you hesitate between T and V?

Less integrated	Highly integrated
Oui. *Avec les artisans (par ex: au moment d'une rénovation de maison.) J'ai tendance a les tutoyer mais eux restent hésitants.* (P5) **'Yes.** With craftsmen (for example, when renovating a house). I tend to use *tu* with them, but I hesitate'	*Parfois, je ne me rappelle plus si j'ai déjà tutoyé quelqu'un ou pas, donc j'attends de voir si la personne en face me tutoie ou me vouvoie* (P4) 'Sometimes, I no longer remember if I've already used *tu* with someone or not, so I wait to see if the person uses *tu* or *vous* with me'
I'm not sure how to address parents of my daughter's classmates. I try to steer things towards the plural '*vous*', i.e. by talking about the child + parent group, to avoid the problem. **I'm also unsure** with people like my hairdresser whom I see regularly but have a somewhat professional relationship with. So far, we've kept to '*vous*'. (P24)	*Si je ne suis pas sure je vouvoie* (P27) 'If I'm not sure, I use *vous*'
	peut-être quelqu'un plus âgé (P13) 'maybe someone older'
	Non (P16) 'No'
sometimes unsure with older relatives of my husband or relatives I don't know very well, when I first arrived in France I would '*vouvoient*' everyone, until my husband's mum said to *tutoyer* family, but **still sometimes unsure** with relatives I don't know well. Sometimes when I first meet friends of friends **I'm not sure**, I once used *vous* with the friend of a friend the same age as me and he thought it was very funny, so generally I try and wait to see how they address me. (P14)	*A Pau, tous mes voisins se tutoient automatiquement (il y a un esprit de quartier, beaucoup d'entraide, etc). On a récemment acheté une maison à la campagne et on a de suite fait la connaissance des voisins les plus proches, des agriculteurs un peu plus âgés que nous, et j'étais surprise d'observer que mon mari continuait à les vouvoyer même après une certaine familiarité s'est établie, plusieurs visites réciproques, une journée entière ou ils nous ont aidé avec leur tracteurs, etc. Bref, mon mari n'a pas su me dire pourquoi ils se vousoient (et depuis on se*

(Continued)

Table 3.3 (Continued)

Less integrated	Highly integrated
Often!! *I think that the French use vous with me, when I would use 'tu', because I seem to have 'known' them a while. I think my lack of French, makes them use 'vous' with me, as we can't talk sufficiently well together!* (P17)	*tutoie avec un autre voisin, mais toujours « vous » avec les autres qu'on connaît pourtant mieux). Pour ne pas me tromper (je suis consciente de faire un effort pour les vousvoyer), surtout quand la discussion vire aux petites plaisanteries, je contourne le problème en m'adressant toujours au groupe ou en posant des questions généralisées (faut-il, peut-on, etc).* (P26)
Je n'hesite pas. (P19) 'I don't hesitate'	'In Pau, all of my neighbors use *tu* automatically (there is a real neighborhood spirit, lots of support, etc). We recently bought a house in the countryside and met the neighbors that live closest to us, farmers who are little bit older than we are, and I was surprised to observe that my husband continued to use *vous* with them, even after a certain familiarity had been established, several reciprocal visits, a whole day during which they helped us with their tractors, etc. Anyway, my husband wasn't able to tell me why they used *vous* with each other (and since then, we began to use *tu* with another neighbor, but we've stayed with *vous* for the first, and yet we know them better). In order to not make a mistake (I am conscious of making an effort to use *vous* with them), especially when the discussion goes towards joking, I get around the problem by always addressing the group and asking general questions (Is it necessary, Can we, etc)'

Note: All responses have been reproduced exactly as provided by the respondents on the written questionnaire. Original responses are in italics, our translations between quotation marks.

individuals make clear reference to a frequent sense of uncertainty (see bolded expressions), revealing an overall insecurity and perhaps even anxiety (see P24, P14, and P17). The only mentions of uncertainty among the highly integrated individuals are formulated differently – *si je ne suis pas sure* (P27) and *parfois je ne me rappelle plus* (P4) – highlighting the occasional and momentary nature of such situations for this group. Moreover, the highly integrated cultural migrants tend to concentrate on strategies that they have elaborated, giving the sense that they have accepted and perhaps come to terms with this aspect of the French language.

In response to the question of whether the T/V distinction should be abandoned, here again, we see clear distinctions between the two groups of cultural migrants (Table 3.4). Within the highly integrated group, only one individual argues for the giving up the T/V distinction, citing the more complicated verbal morphology associated with V. The responses given by the other highly integrated participants suggest acceptance of the T/V distinction as part of the French language, with participants 4 and 13 pinpointing functions that can be fulfilled by V. From the less integrated cultural migrants, on the other hand, the response to the question of whether the distinction should be abandoned is a resounding 'yes' on the part of four of the five. Reasons varied, with two participants referring to the fact that such a change would simplify the system, whereas P17 suggests that the result would be more equality within relationships. It would seem, then, that at least for this participant, the T/V distinction is felt to create inequality.

The final question that we will examine asked participants to define what *tutoiement* and *vouvoiement* means for them personally (Table 3.5).

The definitions provided suggest rather different perceptions of T/V on the basis of self-assessed integration. On the one hand, T is often defined with reference to the idea of friendship or friendliness, especially – but not exclusively – by the less integrated cultural migrants. This perhaps explains why we found that our participants exclusively use T with their Francophone friends. The comment provided by P17 (less integrated group) on the questionnaire with respect to *tutoiement* is particularly revealing:

(6) P17: *Makes me feel that people don't really see me as a friend (or potential) friend if they don't use tu*

Vouvoiement, on the other hand, receives a rather different treatment. Whereas the three highly integrated participants who responded all summed up *vouvoiement* with one word – respect – the less integrated cultural migrants tend to describe *vouvoiement* as something negative: unnecessarily formal (P17) and a barrier (P19, see Table 3.5).

Table 3.4 Should the T/V distinction be abandoned?

Response	Less integrated	Highly integrated
Yes	*Oui. Etant jeune j'appelais mes seniors 'Sir' (pour les mecs, bien entendu.) J'avais du mal à m'en débarrasser etw je ne veut pas, aujourd'hui, faire marche arrière.* (P5) 'Yes. As a young man I called my elders 'Sir' (for guys, of course). I had trouble getting rid of the habit, today I don't want to backpedal' *Personally yes I think it would be. I think it would be less complicated.* (P14) *Yes, so that there is more equality within relationships.* (P17) *Oui. Parce que c'est plus simple* (P19) 'Yes. Because it's simpler'	*OUI parce que c'est compliqué pour les verbes* (P16) 'YES because it's complicated for the verbs'
No		*Non, cela permet de garder un peu de distance et de montrer du respect à quelqu'un de plus âgé par exemple* (P4) 'No, it allows us to keep some distance and to show respect to someone who is older, for example' *Ce n'est pas nécessaire, nous sommes tous le même.* (P27) 'It's not necessary, we are all equal' Respect (P13)

Other	*I don't feel comfortable passing a judgement on this. I guess I would feel like I were trying to impose my culture on the French if I said yes.* (P24)	
	Je pense qu'il y a d'autres expressions à abandonner en priorité pour faire évoluer la société et faire face aux problèmes liés à la hiérarchisation des milieux. (P26) 'I think that there are other expressions that should be abandoned first in order to make society move forward and face problems linked to the hierarchical organisation of milieus'	

Note: All responses have been reproduced exactly as provided by the respondents on the written questionnaire. Original responses are in italics, our translations between quotation marks.

Table 3.5 Definitions of *tutoiement* and *vouvoiement*

Address form	Less integrated	Highly integrated
Tutoiement	*a more relaxed context* (P24)	*Moins de distance, plus de familiarité* (P4) 'Less distance, more familiarity'
	less formal, more friendly, relaxed (P14)	
	Makes me feel that people don't really see me as a friend (or potential) friend if they don't use tu (P17)	*des amis* (P16) 'friends'
	D'etre informal et proche (P19) 'To be informal and close'	
Vouvoiement	*can infer respect as well as distance* (P14)	*Respect* (P4, P13, P16)
	something unnecessarily formal, that distances people from each other (P17)	
	Un barrier professionelle ou par politesse (P19) 'A professional barrier or by politeness'	

Note: All responses have been reproduced exactly as provided by the respondents on the written questionnaire. Original responses are in italics, our translations between quotation marks.

In sum, the perceptions of the T/V distinction expressed in the open-ended questions indicate that the less integrated cultural migrants show more insecurity, which may be linked to deficits in linguistic competence (i.e. difficulties with conjugation of T vs. V forms) and/or in sociolinguistic competence (i.e. when to use which form and with whom). In our background questionnaire, we asked participants whether obstacles remained to their integration in France. Whereas four of the five less integrated individuals responded affirmatively (three cited social difficulties, whereas linguistic and cultural difficulties were highlighted by two respondents each), only one participant from the highly integrated group answered yes (identifying linguistic difficulties as the problem). In addition, the less integrated individuals tend to display more negative attitudes concerning the T/V distinction, both in their definitions of *vouvoiement* and in their arguments for the abandonment of the distinction altogether.

Cultural Migrants and the T/V Distinction

To conclude, we return to the question of what link can be identified between social and professional integration and the more or less advanced mastery of the system of address forms in French. As was seen in our analysis, the two groups of cultural migrants were not found to differ from each other in their reported usage of T/V in the contexts of everyday life and with family and friends. Moreover, unlike previous research (e.g. Dewaele, 2004b), the non-native responses resembled those provided by NSs to the same questions. Interestingly, however, our participants showed more homogeneity in their responses than did the NS population from Guesle-Coquelet (2009). We hypothesise that this may reflect the NNSs' pursuit of clear-cut rules for a system that defies such cut-and-dry categorisations.

If the two groups of cultural migrants did not differ in terms of reported usage, it became clear that the difference in self-assessed integration identified in our background questionnaire manifests itself in how our participants perceive these two pronouns. In particular, we found that the responses provided by the less integrated cultural migrants to three open-ended questions showed traces of more uncertainty, insecurity and negative attitudes with respect to the second-person pronominal system when compared to the responses provided by the highly integrated group. Certain responses from our less integrated cultural migrants suggest that they have a tendency to interpret the T/V distinction along a single dimension (such as equal vs unequal status or friendliness vs distance), not seeming to always understand the interplay between these different variables (and others as well) in expressing social deixis. Our highly integrated cultural migrants, on the other hand, were found to be more at ease with the complicated interplay of different factors in the expression of social deixis. Like NSs, there are situations in which they hesitate or are unsure, but this is simply taken to be part of the game. Their responses to our open-ended questions reveal little emotion – positive or negative – concerning the T/V distinction, unlike what the same questions evoked from our less integrated cultural migrants.

When taken together, the results from this study suggest that being a cultural migrant (and, thus, having regular contact with NSs) may in fact be sufficient for the appropriate (reported) use of this one aspect of sociolinguistic competence, but that stumbling blocks may still remain with respect to the perception and interpretation of these two pronouns, particularly for those cultural migrants who do not consider themselves to be well integrated into their adopted community. In addition to contributing to research on the T/V distinction in non-native populations, our findings allow us to highlight the fact that the concept of *cultural migrant* encompasses not only a wide variety of sociobiographical profiles, but that the perceptions of the L2 in this population are also varied, and that the factor of integration analysed here may very well be an important one to take into consideration in future research.

Notes

(1) '[d]ans les interactions en français, le choix du pronom d'adresse est un exercice socioculturel périlleux' (our translation).
(2) Although we limit our discussion to Hexagonal French, it should be noted that there has also been work done in other Francophone areas (see Lambert & Tucker, 1976).
(3) Seventy-eight were NSs, whereas 18 reported a L1 other than French. These 18 participants had been living in France since their childhood. In the remainder of this article, we will refer to Guesle-Coquelet's participants as NSs, for ease of presentation.
(4) Note that we have not mentioned here those studies that have looked at actual usage in order to draw conclusions related to pedagogy. Several of these studies are mentioned in the introduction.
(5) The questionnaire addressed both terms of address such as *Monsieur* and *Madame* and T/V. In this study, we will limit our comments to the results concerning T/V.
(6) It has been suggested that important changes (marriage, childbirth, etc.) that may influence behaviour with respect to T/V tend to occur in one's thirties, meaning that T/V often changes across this decade (see *La Lettre de l'INED* (Institut National d'Etudes Démographiques), février 2014, http://www.ined.fr/fr/ressources_documentation/focus_sur/age_pacs_mariage/.
(7) In modern day France, the use of V between parents and children is a marginal phenomenon. It can be either symmetrical or asymmetrical and results from a particular family history.
(8) This question was included in Guesle-Coquelet's (2009) study and was adapted from question 4 from Gardner-Chloros (1991).

References

Belz, J. and Kinginger, C. (2002) The cross-linguistic development of address form use in telecollaborative language learning: Two case studies. *Canadian Modern Language Review* 59 (2), 189–214.
Benson, M.C. (2010) The context and trajectory of lifestyle migration: The case of the British residents of Southwest France. *European Societies* 12 (1), 45–64.
Blume, M. (2000) Mastering the unmasterable: A French puzzle. *The International Herald Tribune*, 19 February 2000.
Brown, R. and Gilman, A. (1960) The pronouns of power and solidarity. In T.A. Sebeok (ed.) *Style in Language* (pp. 253–276). Cambridge: MIT Press.
Bustin-Lekeu, F. (1973) Tutoiement et vouvoiement chez les lycéens français. *The French Review* XLVI (4), 773–782.
Coffen, B. (2002) *Histoire culturelle des pronoms d'adresse*. Paris: Honoré Champion.
Dewaele, J.-M. (2002) Variation, chaos et système en interlangue française. *Acquisition et interaction en langue étrangère* 17, 143–167.
Dewaele, J.-M. (2004a) The acquisition of sociolinguistic competence in French as a foreign language: An overview. *Journal of French Language Studies* 14 (3), 301–319.
Dewaele, J.-M. (2004b) *Vous* or *tu*? Native and non-native speakers of French on a sociolinguistic tightrope. *IRAL* 42 (4), 383–402.
Dewaele, J.-M. and Planchenault, G. (2006) 'Dites-moi tu'?! La perception de la difficulté du système des pronoms d'adresse en français. In M. Faraco (ed.) *La classe de langue: théories, méthodes et pratiques* (pp. 147–166). Aix-Marseille: Publications de l'Université de Provence.
Gardner-Chloros, P. (1991) Ni tu ni vous: principes et paradoxes dans l'emploi des pronoms d'allocution en français contemporain. *Journal of French Language Studies* 1 (2), 139–155.
Guesle-Coquelet, C. (2009) *Les Termes d'adresse en français*. Paris: L'Harmattan.
Huart, H. (2012) L'immigration récente en Aquitaine est teintée d'accent britannique. *INSEE Aquitaine*, Aquitaine e-publications, octobre 2012, n°17, accessed 12 July 2014. http://www.insee.fr/fr/themes/document.asp?reg_id=4&ref_id=19109
Kinginger, C. and Farrell, K. (2004) Assessing development of meta-pragmatic awareness in study abroad. *Frontiers: The Interdisciplinary Journal of Study Abroad* 10, 19–42.
Lambert, W.E. and Tucker, G.R. (1976) *Tu, vous, usted: A social-psychological study of address patterns*. Rowley: Newbury House.
Liddicoat, A.J. (2006) Learning the culture of interpersonal relationships: Students' understandings of personal address forms in French. *Intercultural Pragmatics* 3 (1), 55–80.
Lyster, R. (1994) The effect of functional-analytic teaching on aspects of French immersion students' sociolinguistic competence. *Applied Linguistics* 15 (3), 263–287.
Lyster, R. and Rebuffot, J. (2002) Acquisition des pronoms d'allocution en classe de français immersif. *Acquisition et interaction en langue étrangère* 17, 51–72.
Maley, C. (1972) Historically speaking, *Tu* or *Vous*? *The French Review* XLV (5), 999–1006.
Morford, J. (1997) Social indexicality in French pronominal address. *Journal of Linguistic Anthropology* 7 (1), 3–37.
Noiriel, G. (2002) *Atlas de l'immigration en France: exclusion, intégration*. Paris: Autrement.
Peeters, B. (2004) Tu ou vous. *Zeitschrift für Französische Sprache und Literatur* 114, 17–32.
Planchenault, G. (2009) Celui qui est *tu* n'est pas toujours le plus fort: choix des pronoms d'adresse dans les écrits d'étudiants de FLE et de lycéens français. In B. Peeters and K. Ramière (eds) *Tu ou vous: l'embarras du choix* (pp. 223–237). Limoges: Lambert-Lucas.

Rehner, K. and Mougeon, R. (2003) The learning of sociolinguistic variation by advanced FSL learners: The case of *nous* versus *on* in immersion French. *Studies in Second Language Acquisition* 25 (1), 127–156.
Schoch, M. (1978) Problème sociolinguistique des pronoms d'allocution: 'tu' et 'vous'. Enquête à Lausanne. *La Linguistique* 14 (1), 55–73.
Smallwood, D. (2007) The integration of British migrants in Aquitaine. In C. Geoffrey and R. Sibley (eds) *Going Abroad: Travel, Tourism and Migration* (pp. 119–131). Cambridge: Cambridge Scholars' Publishing.
van Compernolle, R.A. (2010) Towards a sociolinguistically responsive pedagogy: Teaching second-person address forms in French. *The Canadian Modern Language Review* 66 (3), 445–463.
van Compernolle, R.A., Williams, L. and McCourt, C. (2011) A corpus-driven study of second-person pronoun variation in L2 French synchronous computer-mediated communication. *Intercultural Pragmatics* 8 (1), 67–91.
Warren, J. (2009) *Tu* et *vous* en français contemporain à Paris et à Toulouse. In B. Peeters and K. Ramière (eds) *Tu ou vous: l'embarras du choix* (pp. 67–80). Limoges: Lambert-Lucas.

Appendix A

Fiche Individuelle

NOM (facultatif)	SEXE	PROFESSION
PRENOM (facultatif)	NATIONALITE	
AVEZ-VOUS DES ENFANTS?	VOTRE TRANCHE D'AGE	
SI OUI, DE QUEL(S) AGE(S)?	moins de 20 ans	
moins de 10 ans?	20–29 ans	
11–15 ans	30–34 ans	
16–20 ans	35–39 ans	
21–25 ans	40–49 ans	
26–30 ans	50–59 ans	
30 ans et plus	60 ans et plus	
	LANGUE(S) MATERNELLE(S)	

1. En quelle année avez-vous décidé de vous installer en France?

2. Votre présence en France découle-t-elle
   de la volonté de vivre à l'étranger
       sur le plan géographique   oui / non
       sur le plan culturel   oui / non
       sur le plan linguistique   oui / non

   du choix délibéré en amont de vivre en France
       pour des raisons géographiques   oui / non
       pour des raisons culturelles (ex. rythme de vie)   oui / non
       pour des raisons linguistiques   oui / non
       pour des raisons professionnelles   oui / non

   du choix délibéré – après être arrivé en France – de vivre dans ce pays
       pour des raisons géographiques   oui / non
       pour des raisons culturelles (ex. rythme de vie)   oui / non
       pour des raisons linguistiques   oui / non
       pour des raisons professionnelles   oui / non

   Remarques éventuelles:

3. Etes-vous arrivé en France en ayant déjà appris le français?   oui / non
   Si oui, comment l'avez-vous appris?
       Ecole primaire   Centre de langues
       Collège   Entreprise

Lycée	Cours particuliers
Université	Autre

4. Avez-vous continué à suivre des cours pour améliorer votre français après votre arrivée en France? oui / non
   Si oui, dans quel cadre:

Mairie	Université
Association	Cours particuliers
Centre de langue	Autre

   Si vous n'avez pas poursuivi votre apprentissage, pourquoi?

5. Aujourd'hui, selon vous, quel est votre niveau en français?
   débutant (A1) pré-intermédiaire (A2) intermédiaire (B1) avancé (B2) perfectionnement (C)

6. Travaillez-vous? Si oui, travaillez-vous principalement en français, en anglais, les deux (ou autre langue)?

7. A quelle fréquence (en pourcentage) évaluez-vous votre utilisation du français au travail? *Remarques éventuelles*:

8. Si vous avez un conjoint, sa langue maternelle est-elle le français?
   oui / non
   Si non, quelle est sa langue maternelle?
   Quelle(s) langue(s) parlez-vous ensemble? le français / l'anglais / les deux / autre(s) langue(s)
   A quelle fréquence (en pourcentage) jugez-vous votre utilisation du français avec votre conjoint?

9. Si vous avez des enfants, quelle(s) langue(s) parlez-vous avec eux?
   le français / l'anglais / les deux / autre(s) langue(s)
   A quelle fréquence (en pourcentage) jugez-vous votre utilisation du français avec vos enfants?

10. Avez-vous des amis français? Quelle(s) langue(s) parlez-vous avec eux?
    le français / l'anglais / les deux
    A quelle fréquence (en pourcentage) jugez-vous votre utilisation du français avec vos amis français?

11. Positionnez-vous sur cet axe (en plaçant un **X** en dessous de la ligne) pour répondre à la question suivante: Vous sentez-vous intégré dans votre milieu social en France?

    ```
              1        2        3        4        5
    Négatif ←――――――――――――――――――――――――――――――――→ Positif
    ```

Remarques éventuelles:

12. Positionnez-vous sur cet axe (en plaçant un **X** en dessous de la ligne) pour répondre à la question suivante: Vous sentez-vous intégré dans votre milieu professionnel en France?

    Négatif ←─────1─────2─────3─────4─────5─────→ Positif

Remarques éventuelles:

13. Selon vous, existe-t-il aujourd'hui des freins à votre intégration en France? oui / non
    Si oui, ces freins sont-ils :
       d'ordre linguistique
       d'ordre social
       d'ordre culturel
       autre
    Remarques éventuelles:

Appendix B

Questionnaire sur votre usage de « TU » ET DE « VOUS »

Entourez les réponses qui vous conviennent
  T=tu, V=vous. *Si par exemple, vous entourez la réponse T-V à la question 1, cela signifie que vous tutoyez votre mari (votre femme) mais qu'il (elle) vous vouvoie. Si vous entourez la réponse V-V, cela signifie que vous vous vouvoyez réciproquement. La première lettre désigne toujours votre usage et la seconde celui de votre interlocuteur.*
  Il vous est ensuite parfois demandé de préciser la façon dont vous appelez la personne, puis la façon dont elle-même vous appelle: cela peut être Monsieur, Madame ou Mademoiselle seuls, Monsieur, Madame ou Mademoiselle suivis du prénom, Monsieur, Madame ou Mademoiselle suivis du nom de famille, le prénom seul, ou le nom de famille seul, ou (rien).

Famille et proches

En français, comment vous adressez-vous et comment s'adresse(nt) à vous
1 – Votre mari / femme / compagnon / compagne?   T-T   V-V   T-V   V-T

2 – Le père de votre mari / femme / compagnon / compagne?
                                                 T-T   V-V   T-V   V-T
Comment l'appelez-vous et comment vous appelle-t-il?

3 – La mère de votre mari / femme / compagnon / compagne?
                                                                      T-T   V-V   T-V   V-T
Comment l'appelez-vous et comment vous appelle-t-elle?

4 – Vos enfants, si vous en avez?   T-T   V-V   T-V   V-T
Remarques:

5a – Lorsque vous rencontrez une personne pour la première fois, comment vous adressez-vous à elle?
- je tutoie spontanément
- je vouvoie spontanément
- cela dépend
Remarques :

5b – Si vous avez répondu « cela dépend », de quel(s) critère(s) selon vous cela dépend-il?
(plusieurs réponses sont possibles, classez-les par ordre d'importance)
- de l'âge de la personne
- du sexe de la personne
- du statut / de la profession de la personne
- de l'apparence de la personne
- de la situation (dans un magasin, dans un bureau, à la plage, dans une soirée, dans un club de sport,…)
- autres raisons :
Remarques :

6 – Un(e) ami(e) que vous tutoyez vous présente un(e) de ses ami(e)s qu'il ou elle tutoie. Comment vous adressez-vous à cette personne?
- je tutoie spontanément   + prénom   + nom   + (rien)
- je vouvoie spontanément   + prénom   + nom   + (rien)
                                        + M./Mme/Mlle
- cela dépend
- j'attends de voir comment il / elle s'adresse à moi
Remarques :

7 – Si vous avez des enfants, comment vous adressez-vous à leurs ami(e)s, et comment leurs ami(e)s s'adressent-ils/elles à vous? *(plusieurs réponses sont possibles)*   T-T   V-V   T-V   V-T

Diriez-vous que cela dépend?   oui / non
Comment les appelez-vous et comment vous appellent-ils?
Diriez-vous que l'âge de ces ami(e)s de vos enfants entre en ligne de compte?
                                                                                                      oui / non

Remarques :

8 – De façon très générale, tutoyez-vous plus facilement quelqu'un qui est de même sexe que vous?   oui / non
Remarques :

9 – Supposez que vous rencontriez un Français que vous n'avez pas vu depuis au moins un an. A cette époque-là, vous vous tutoyiez. Comment vous adressez-vous aujourd'hui à cette personne?   T ou V
De quoi votre choix va-t-il dépendre?
Remarques :

Travail

10 – Imaginez un supérieur et un subalterne qui se tutoient. Comment d'après vous s'adressent-ils l'un à l'autre dans une réunion officielle, publique, solennelle? (vous pouvez distinguer les trois si vous le souhaitez)
(la première lettre désigne le supérieur)   T-T   V-V   T-V   V-T
<u>supérieur</u>: M./Mme seul, M./Mme + prénom, M./Mme + nom, prénom seul, nom de famille seul, *ou* (rien)
<u>subalterne</u> M./Mme seul, M./Mme + prénom, M./Mme + nom, prénom seul, nom de famille seul, *ou* (rien)
Remarques :

**Si vous ne travaillez pas ou vous ne travaillez jamais en français, ne répondez pas aux questions 11–21
11 – Que dites-vous à un supérieur hiérarchique (ou à un professeur, doyen, recteur, directeur, patron, chef de bureau…) et que vous dit-il?
                                          T-T   V-V   T-V   V-T
Est-ce que cela peut changer avec le temps?   oui / non
<u>vous</u>: M./Mme seul, M./Mme + prénom, M./Mme + nom, prénom seul, nom de famille seul, *ou* (rien).
<u>votre sup.</u>: M./Mme seul, M./Mme + prénom, M./Mme + nom, prénom seul, nom de famille seul, *ou* (rien)
Remarques :

12 – Que dites-vous à un subalterne, et que vous dit-il?
                                            T-T   V-V   T-V   V-T
<u>vous</u>: M./Mme seul, M./Mme + prénom, M./Mme + nom, prénom seul, nom de famille seul, *ou* (rien).
<u>votre sub.</u>: M./Mme seul, M./Mme + prénom, M./Mme + nom, prénom seul, nom de famille seul, *ou* (rien)
Remarques :

13 – Comment vous adressez-vous, et comment s'adresse à vous
un(e) élève   T-T   V-V   T-V   V-T
un(e) étudiant(e)   T-T   V-V   T-V   V-T
un(e) stagiaire,   T-T   V-V   T-V   V-T
vous: M./Mme seul, M./Mme + prénom, M./Mme + nom, prénom seul,
   nom de famille seul, *ou* (rien).
élève/étudiant/stagiaire: M./Mme seul, *ou* M./Mme + prénom, *ou* M./Mme
   + nom, *ou* prénom seul, *ou* nom de famille seul, *ou* (rien)
Remarques :

14 – Là où vous travaillez (faculté, entreprise, bureau...), y a-t-il une tendance générale à se tutoyer entre collègues de même statut hiérarchique?
oui / non
Remarques :

15 – Là où vous travaillez (faculté, entreprise, bureau...), y a-t-il une tendance générale à se tutoyer quel que soit le statut hiérarchique de chacun?
oui / non
Remarques :

16 – Si ce n'est pas le cas, quel est le motif qui fait que vous vous tutoyez entre quelques-uns?
- idées communes, sympathie mutuelle   - même école ou même promotion
- relation extra-professionnelle   - autres raisons :
- amitié, même âge...
Remarques :

17 – Pensez-vous
que le passage du *vous* mutuel au *tu* mutuel modifie automatiquement les rapports?   oui / non
que le *tu* permet plus de familiarité?   oui / non
que le *tu* autorise un certain relâchement dans l'attitude et le langage?
oui / non
Remarques :

18 – Si vous vous vouvoyez entre supérieur et subalterne, pensez-vous que le fait de vous tutoyer
changerait les relations de travail?   oui / non
rendrait moins sensible le rapport hiérarchique?   oui / non
laisserait une plus grande liberté de comportement?   oui / non
Remarques :

19 – Si votre patron, ou quelqu'un qui vous est hiérarchiquement supérieur, vous proposait le tutoiement réciproque, pourriez-vous refuser?

oui / non

Remarques :

20 – Si vous appartenez à un syndicat, comment vous adressez-vous et comment s'adressent à vous
les dirigeants?   T-T   V-V   T-V   V-T
les autres membres?   T-T   V-V   T-V   V-T
Comment vous appelez-vous les uns les autres?
Remarques :

21 – Définissez en quelques mots les règles d'adresse qui sont en usage dans votre entreprise :

Dans la vie quotidienne

22 – Si vous appartenez à un club de sport, comment vous adressez-vous et comment s'adressent à vous
les professeurs ou moniteurs   T-T   V-V   T-V   V-T
les autres membres   T-T   V-V   T-V   V-T
comment vous appelez-vous les uns les autres?
Remarques :

23 – Tutoyez-vous *tous* vos amis français?   oui / non
Si non, est-ce pour des raisons
– de différence d'âge?   oui / non
– de différence dans le statut social?   oui / non
– par respect mutuel?   oui / non
– parce que vous estimez n'être pas assez proches?   oui / non
– parce que vous ne vous voyez pas assez souvent?   oui / non
– parce que certains de vos amis vous vouvoient   oui / non
– autres raisons?
Remarques :

24 – Y a-t-il des cas où vous hésitez entre *tu* et *vous*? Lesquels? Y a-t-il des cas où vous évitez de faire la distinction? Pouvez-vous donner des exemples de tels cas et de la façon dont vous contournez le problème?

25 – Quelle expression utilisez-vous pour faire comprendre à quelqu'un que vous aimeriez passer du vouvoiement mutuel au tutoiement mutuel? Laquelle ou lesquelles?

26 – Vous arrive-t-il (ou vous est-il arrivé) de tutoyer une personne à certains moments et de la vouvoyer à d'autres moments? En quelle(s) circonstance(s)?

27 – Vous est-il déjà arrivé d'avoir tutoyé une personne lors d'une première rencontre et de vous sentir tenu de la vouvoyer à la rencontre suivante?

28 – Que signifient pour vous, personnellement,   le tutoiement?
                                                                      le vouvoiement?
Remarques :

29 – Pensez-vous qu'il soit souhaitable d'abandonner la distinction *tu / vous* comme cela a été le cas en anglais? Pourquoi / pourquoi non?

30 – Y a-t-il eu une évolution, depuis que vous êtes en France, dans le choix que vous faites entre *tu* et *vous*? Laquelle?

31 – Parlez-vous une autre langue en plus du français, qui fait aussi la distinction entre *tu* et *vous*? Si oui, quelle langue? Quand vous parlez cette langue, appliquez-vous les mêmes critères de distinction qu'en français? Si non, en quoi sont-ils différents?
Remarques générales

4 L2 English Vocabulary in a Long-residency Swedish Group Compared to a Group of English Native Speakers

Britt Erman and Margareta Lewis

Introduction and Aim

Finding words can be hard even for someone who has lived and worked in the L2 community for a considerable time. L2 vocabulary is, in fact, one very central aspect of late attainment studied in the research program 'High-level proficiency in L2 use', of which the research reported here is a part.[1] Studies of L2 vocabulary have so far in the program focused on advanced vocabulary, i.e. low-frequency single words (e.g. Bardel *et al.*, 2012) and formulaic language ('multiword structures') (Erman *et al.*, 2014; Forsberg & Fant, 2010). The study of Bardel *et al.* (2012) involves spoken L2 French and L2 Italian and a study by Forsberg Lundell and Lindqvist (2014) focuses on correlations between test results involving receptive and productive L2 French. Erman *et al.* (2014) studied the use of multiword structures (henceforth MWS) in the speech of three Swedish L2 groups involving three target languages, viz. English, French and Spanish. The two studies presented in this chapter involve L2 English in the speech of a Swedish group resident in the UK. They are an attempt to combine two aspects of English L2 vocabulary, i.e. the L2 users' knowledge of MWSs and their knowledge of single words. On all the measurements to be presented a matched group of native English speakers has been used as benchmark.

The notion of the advanced L2 speaker is rather broad, frequently including 'all learners who have moved beyond an intermediate level of acquisition' (Forsberg Lundell & Lindqvist, 2013: 29). In view of this, the non-native speaker group in focus in this chapter, having lived and worked professionally several years in the L2 country (the UK), would indeed be characterised as very advanced.

The main aim of both studies is to disclose potential similarities and differences in the spoken production of the London Swedes (henceforth LS) and native speakers (henceforth NS groups) in the number of multiword structures and the number of high- and low-frequency words. Learning a foreign language obviously takes time and requires a great deal of experience and input. The Swedes living in London are integrated in the target language community, which, presumably, favours the acquisition of their L2 (Forsberg & Fant, 2010; Groom, 2009). A second aim was to find out to what extent the L2 performance could be related to different situations; to this end the participants performed several tasks. Finally, we aimed at examining the degree of variation in the speech of the LS and NS groups and across the tasks, which required the study of types and tokens in both studies (see Lindqvist, 2010: 415 for the importance of also including types in the analysis).

Earlier Research

Multiword structures

Although formulaic, conventionalised language has gained considerable attention during the last few years in SLA research (e.g. Schmitt, 2004), it has remained relatively unexplored in the spoken production of very advanced, long-residency L2 speakers. The majority of studies of collocations within SLA have found that non-native speakers tend to use fewer collocations compared to native speakers in writing (Bolly, 2009; Erman, 2009; Granger, 1998; Howarth, 1998). Some have shown that non-native speakers use the same quantity of collocations as native speakers but use significantly more high-frequency collocations (Durrant & Schmitt, 2009). Significant correlations between quantity of MWSs and general proficiency were found in written production (Lewis, 2009).

As mentioned, there is an imbalance between studies of formulaic language in written and spoken material, which is presumably due to the complicated procedure of collecting speech data. The few studies of spoken production that exist have mainly addressed the role of formulaic sequences as fluency devices, which were found to be used more frequently by L2 learners as a production strategy (Raupach, 1984). Studies linking multiword structures in spoken production to proficiency include Boers *et al.* (2006), Stengers *et al.* (2011) and Forsberg Lundell *et al.* (2014), who conclude that the learners' general proficiency level seems to coincide with their degree of mastery of MWSs.

The importance of interaction with native speakers for progress in acquiring formulaic sequences was shown in a study by Adolphs and Durow (2004). They investigated the 10 most frequent three-word formulaic sequences in the spoken production of two female Chinese students on two occasions four months apart and noted that the participant that was more integrated in the British society had larger gains in formulaic sequences.

Cognates

Words and phrases that are similar across languages are commonly referred to as 'cognates' (e.g. Lotto & de Groot, 1998; Kroll et al., 2002) or 'translation equivalents' (e.g. Wollter & Gyllstad, 2011). In the present study the term 'cognate' has been adopted to refer to MWSs that are similar between Swedish and English (see Study 1, section Cognates, below).

Ringbom (2007) through his emphasis on the role of positive transfer has noted the advantage of cross-linguistic similarity in learning a foreign language. Indeed, the role of similarity between L1 and L2 and its importance in L2 acquisition are issues that have been addressed in several earlier studies. For example, studies of vocabulary acquisition showed that high-frequency words and cognate words were easier to learn than low-frequency words and non-cognate words (Lotto & de Groot, 1998). Another study showed that cognate words were significantly quicker to translate from English into L2 French (Kroll et al., 2002). Wollter and Gyllstad (2011) compared reaction times between English native speakers and Swedish L2 speakers for (i) collocations with translation equivalents in Swedish (L1) and English (L2), (ii) non-translation equivalents (L2 specific collocations) and (iii) unrelated items. Both the NSs and NNSs displayed significantly different reaction times between the collocations and the unrelated combinations, the former being accessed more readily. However, the NNSs had significantly shorter reaction times for translation equivalents, not found in the NS data. In a study comparing the written production of French advanced learners of L2 English with an NS group it was found that adverb and adjective collocations were used to a lesser extent by the NNSs (Granger, 1998), whereas certain intensifiers directly transferable from their L1, such as *totally* and *completely*, were used more frequently by the NNS group compared to the native speakers.

Single word study

While there are a number of studies of receptive vocabulary knowledge based on vocabulary tests and reading comprehension tests, studies of productive vocabulary knowledge are scarce and typically based on written production (e.g. Albrechtsen et al., 2008; Lemmouh, 2010). Apart from the studies referred to in the Introduction of this chapter there are few studies on vocabulary in spoken production for native and non-native speakers alike (but see Ovtcharov et al. (2006) for L2 French, and Lindqvist et al. (2011) for L2 French and L2 Italian). This study seeks to fill this gap by analysing the vocabulary in the spoken production of the same two groups as in the study of MWSs (see Multiword structures and cognates, above), performing three tasks, a role play, an online retelling task (i.e. the same two tasks as in the previous study) and in addition an interview.

Establishing methods that relate vocabulary knowledge to different proficiency levels in L2 production has in the last few years been a major concern (e.g. Daller *et al.*, 2007; Lindqvist, 2010; Lindqvist *et al.*, 2011; Lindqvist *et al.*, 2013; Milton, 2007; Tidball & Treffers-Daller, 2007). There is evidence to prove that frequency plays an important role in L2 acquisition, implying that high-frequency words are shared by more L2 users than low-frequency words (Tidball & Treffers-Daller, 2007). A basic assumption underlying several of these studies is that the higher the percentage of words beyond the 2000 most frequent words is in an L2 user's production, the more advanced is this person's vocabulary knowledge (see also Laufer, 1995; Laufer & Nation, 1995). This is commonly referred to as lexical richness (or lexical sophistication) in the literature. The results from studies of lexical richness have shown that quantitative results of frequency bands are able to distinguish, not only L2 users at different proficiency levels, but also native from non-native speakers, which is of interest to the present study (e.g. Lindqvist *et al.*, 2011). Laufer's 'Active vocabulary threshold hypothesis' (1991) involving that 'our productive lexicon will grow only until it reaches the average level of the group in which we are required to function' (1991: 446) may explain limitations in L2 vocabulary.

Some advanced non-native speakers of L2 French have been shown to reach native-like levels in their use of low-frequency lemma tokens. But if some of these were removed from the list containing many low-frequency words (i.e. the 'Off-list'; see Study 2, section Method), such as thematic words occurring in teaching materials and words that are similar in L1 and L2, no non-native speaker of either L2 French or L2 Italian reached native-like levels (Bardel *et al.*, 2012). Furthermore, there were indications that lemma types were considerably fewer in the non-native data in Lindqvist (2010).

Participants and Material

Participants

The number of the participants contracted by the research group within the program totals 20, 10 Swedes living in London (LS) and 10 native speakers (NS) shown in Table 4.1.

The selection of the London Swedes met the following three criteria: they should (1) have completed upper secondary studies in Sweden, entailing at least nine years of English as a foreign language in school,

Table 4.1 Participants

Informants	Time with English	Average age
10 Native speakers	Life	32
10 London Swedes	9 years at school and an average of 7.3 years' residency in London	32

(2) have had at least five years' residency in the target language country and (3) at the time of testing be resident in the target language country, using the L2 as a principal means of communication. Most of the participants also had experience of academic studies and some of the Swedes had received some formal instruction of English in England. People growing up in Sweden have had a great deal of exposure to English from early childhood through input from films (with subtitles), TV, music, computers and the internet, in fact most aspects of young people's lives. Nevertheless, English has the status of a foreign language in Sweden.

The migrants of the present study

All the participants of this study are resident in London. London is one of three 'world cities' (alongside with New York and Tokyo) providing headquarters for finance, being 'focal points for social and technological innovation' as well as driving globalisation at large (Graddol, 2012: 133). For decades English cultural products, such as films, music and fashion have had considerable attraction for young people worldwide. Furthermore, English is the first foreign language taught in Swedish schools, starting no later than grade three; some schools teach English from grade one. All of this taken together may have played a role for the migrants of the present study when deciding to move to London. Nevertheless, several of them did not come to London to settle down as testified by one of them:

(1) I didn't plan to stay this long but things have happened that way and ...
I quite like it and now, you know, I got lots of friends here and have built up relationships with people

There is one aspect that had an essential cultural impact on them and to some had been an important part of their everyday life and that is life at the pub; this is the place where people meet to socialise. A feeling of cultural affinity may have been a contributing reason. As is clear from the quote in (2), Sweden and Swedes fall short by comparison:

(2) so...they're [British people are] very polite and very friendly. Compared anyway to Swedish people, it's very easy to chitchat and talk with them

Although they have lived and worked several years in the UK, they do not seem to have settled to the extent that they are prepared to stay there for good, as this quote shows:

(3) I like London, but I wouldn't like to live ... I wouldn't want to live in London ...in the future

What seems to appeal the most is the global outlook of the capital, London, as summarised by this non-native participant in (4):

(4) It truly is a global place and very, very cosmopolitan. You find every corner of the world is....is represented and anyway at least in the environment I actually live....people have a global view on things

These migrants differ from the notion of cultural migrant applied in this volume in that they do not explicitly claim cultural motives for migrating to the UK. However, as became clear in the interviews and as has been shown in some of the above quotations they have come to internalise cultural motives post-hoc as it were, gradually appreciating the *global* and cosmopolitan atmosphere of its capital.

As mentioned, the two studies to be reported in this chapter are part of the aforementioned larger project aiming at accumulating knowledge of the very last steps in L2 acquisition. The focus of both studies described below is the 'migrants', i.e. the group of Swedes living and working in London; a group of native English speakers is used as a control. Both studies deal with vocabulary; the first study (Study 1) focuses on the participants' command of 'multiword structures' (formulaic language), and the second study (Study 2) focuses on their knowledge of single words.

Tasks

L2 performance can be related to different situations, hence the multitask design of the study. The participants perform the following tasks: two different types of dialogic (interactive) tasks, a role play and an interview, and one monologic task, an online retelling of a film clip. The study of multiword structures is based on two of the tasks, i.e. the role play and the retelling task, while the single word study involves all three tasks. The three tasks were recorded and transcribed and total close to 90,000 words distributed over tasks and groups in Table 4.2.

The tasks do not only put different demands on the participants but also involve different goals, domains and scenarios. The role play involves two speakers and is similar to one of the tasks used by Taguchi (2007). In this task, the participant is given a written scenario, according to which he/she is requested to call his/her boss and ask for two days

Table 4.2 Total number of words over three tasks and the native speakers (NS), and the London Swedes (LS)

Tasks

Participants	Interview	Role play	Retelling task
LS	25184	3354	16236
NS	23061	3761	17693

off, since his/her sister is getting married and the wedding day has been changed so that it will clash with a very important business meeting. The participant is given five minutes to read and contemplate the scenario and then make the call. The mean duration of the task is five minutes, but given its open-ended format there is individual variation. The performance of this task is facilitated by its dialogic and everyday character.

The retelling task is what might be called a classic SLA task. The participant is asked to simultaneously narrate a video clip consisting of the first 14½ minutes from the film *Modern Times* by and starring Charlie Chaplin. In this task the participants were not allowed any planning time and were only told to imagine that they were describing what they saw on the screen to someone who could not see it, which means that it was important to create a story that was as coherent as possible.

The third task is a semi-structured interview. Some of the questions asked by the interviewer included biographical data, such as their experience with English before moving to the UK, their current work and family situation. Some of the questions focused on cultural differences between Sweden and the UK.

The role play and the retelling task put high demands on the participants, the role play in the sense that it is pragmatically challenging and the on-line narration because it is cognitively complex, encoding new visual information into linguistic form and involving some infrequent lexis as well as production on-line under time pressure. Although the role play is also on-line the fact that this format allows the participants to get support from the other interlocutor is presumably to the L2 user's advantage.

Research Questions and Hypotheses

In view of the results from previous research, it could be hypothesised that there will be differences between the LS and NS groups. The main hypothesis of both the MWS study and the single word study was that the LS group as a result of daily exposure to English at work as well as at home would perform in a similar way to the native speakers in the role play, whereas the results from the retelling task performed under considerable time pressure would deviate from the native speakers (NS).

The MWS study also involves a substudy, notably establishing the degree to which the LS and NS groups use 'cognates' (see Study 1, section Cognates). In view of results from earlier research showing that non-native speakers have more immediate access to L2 words and phrases that have equivalents in their L1 (see Earlier research, section Cognates) it was hypothesised that the LS group would have more cognates in the retelling task given its time constraints than in the role play, and hence would diverge from the NS group in this task. In the role play, by contrast, they have support from a native speaker and the task is less constrained. As mentioned, the single word study, which is a separate study, involves the same two tasks as the previous study, i.e. the role play and the retelling task, and in addition, a third task, an interview. Like the role play the interview was judged to be facilitated by its dialogic, everyday character, and thus the LS group was hypothesised to perform in a similar way to the native speakers in both tasks in this study.

Similarities and differences between the LS and NS groups will be established through the following four research questions, two per study:

(1) How many types and tokens of phrasal MWSs/100words are there across the two groups in the role play and the retelling task?
(2) How do the two groups differ with regard to the proportion of phrasal cognate MWSs in the two tasks?
(3) How many types and tokens/100 words of high-frequency words are there in the interview, role play and retelling task in the two groups?
(4) How many types and tokens/100 words of low-frequency words are there across these three tasks in the two groups?

Study 1: The Multiword Study

Introduction

We will start this section by providing a definition of an MWS. Following Erman and Warren (2000: 31) a multiword structure is defined as:

> *a conventionalized combination of at least two graphic words favoured by native speakers in preference to (an) alternative combination(s) which could have been equivalent had there been no conventionalization.*

It is a well-known fact that the identification of MWSs is difficult. There are many reasons for this, two of which will be brought up here. One reason is that an MWS to some members of a language community need not be an MWS to all members, since MWSs will be dispersed and entrenched to different degrees in a language community. Another reason is that MWSs, being such an integral part of language, are easy to overlook and can therefore go undetected. In other words, the identification of 'all and only' the MWSs in a text is indeed difficult.

In order to minimise the risk of subjectivity in the identification of MWSs, and in line with our definition of an MWS above, the identification of MWSs in the present study involves 'restricted exchangeability' of members (Erman & Warren, 2000: 32). This means that either one member cannot be replaced by a synonymous word without loss of idiomatic meaning, as in *I can't see a thing*, which cannot be **I can't see an object*, or there are strong restrictions on the choice of potential collocate/s, as in the collocation *pull a lever*. In Mel'čuk's framework, *lever* would be a 'keyword', whose referent is 'designed to', involve the activity denoted by its 'lexical correlate' (which is *pull*), and together with it form a collocation (1998: 38ff). In other words, '*pull* the lever' would be the expected way to use the noun 'lever' in the situation and overall context of the scene described in the retelling task (*Modern Times*).

Method and categories

The MWSs were manually extracted and intersubjectively evaluated. The lexical category was subdivided into phrasal (see below) and clausal MWSs (examples of clausal MWSs include *how are you doing, here we go, (it's) time for a break*). Only the results from the study of phrasal MWSs will be included in this study. The reason for focusing phrasal MWSs is that this category, in particular collocations, has been found to differ in non-native written as well as spoken production.

Examples of phrasal MWSs include *do a jigsaw puzzle, fall behind, swat a fly, light a cigarette, conveyor belt, have a bad day, all of a sudden*. As is clear from these examples some multiword structures in particular collocations, require complementation and grammatical adaption at the moment of use.

Cognates

Acknowledging that English and Swedish are Germanic languages, 'cognate' in the present study has been given quite a narrow definition. For an MWS to be categorised as a cognate there has to be semantic, structural and formal equivalence between the English and a Swedish MWS; this definition is close to Wollter and Gyllstad's definition of a 'translation equivalent' (2011: 435). For example, the English MWS *for all involved* has a semantic, structural and formal equivalent in the Swedish MWS 'för alla inblandade'. However, the fact that the tasks performed in the present study represent different situations it was necessary to add one more criterion for an MWS to be categorised as a cognate: It should also be functionally equivalent, which means that it should be used in similar contexts. In both English and Swedish the above MWS would meet also this last criterion, which makes them functionally equivalent, hence qualifying as cognate. In fact, an MWS may be equivalent in one context and not in another. For example, the English polysemous MWS *come up* has a formal, structural and semantic correspondence in Swedish 'komma upp', but would only qualify as functionally cognate in the context 'his name came up' (but not in e.g. 'the man came up to me', where Swedish has a different particle). It should be apparent from these examples that cognate MWSs are fully acceptable English MWSs. Indeed, the results show that both groups use cognates but to different degrees.

The multiword study: Results

The results for the number of MWSs phrases per 100 words in both tasks corroborate the results in Erman *et al.* (2014), involving the same Swedish and English groups. However, the MWSs in the present study were measured in slightly different ways, since cognates have been included, whereas in Erman *et al.*'s study they were excluded. How did this affect the results? In fact, including cognates in the results obviously did not make a difference for the LS group in the retelling task, since they still used significantly fewer MWS phrases compared to the NS group (Table 4.3). The chi-square test (goodness-of-fit) has been used in both studies (http://www.quantpsy.org/chisq/chisq.htm), in order to compare the NS and NNS groups. The NS group functions as benchmark, and the threshold for significance is set at $p<.05$.

Furthermore, the LS group used significantly more phrasal cognates compared to the NS group in the retelling task. In fact, all p-values in this task are highly significant ($p<.000$), i.e. for types and tokens/100 words and for the proportion of phrasal cognates types and tokens. In the role play,

Table 4.3 Types and tokens/100 words of phrasal MWSs (incl.phrasal cognates) in the role play and the retelling task over the native speakers (NS), and the London Swedes (LS); No. of phrasal cognates (phr cognates) within brackets

Phrasal MWSs	NS types	NS tokens	LS types	LS tokens
Role play	161	173	161	187
/100 wds	4.3	4.6	4.8	5.6
No.Phr Cognates	(38)	(41)	(43)	(57)
Retelling task	1188	1607	823	1051
/100 wds	6.7	9.1	5.0 ***	6.5 ***
No. Phr Cognates	(316)	(397)	(313)***	(397)***

by contrast, the LS group used phrasal MWSs, both types and tokens, in a native-like way, i.e. there was no significant difference between the two groups. Furthermore, the LSs employed a proportion of phrasal cognates that was comparable to the native speakers in this task. Interestingly, the NS group had the same proportion of phrasal cognates in both tasks, between 23% and 24%, whereas the LS group used significantly more phrasal cognates in the retelling task compared to the role play ($p<0.02$). To illustrate this, the distribution of phrasal cognates over the two tasks and groups in terms of percentage figures is shown in Figure 4.1.

In sum, the LSs are native-like in the role play on all measurements, whereas they use a significantly smaller number of phrases (types and tokens) in the retelling task compared to the native speakers. Furthermore, the LS group uses a significantly larger number of phrasal cognates in the retelling task compared to the NS group (i.e. LS 38% vs NS 24%). How should we interpret the different outcomes of the LSs in these two tasks? It could be argued that the retelling task is more cognitively challenging, since it is monologic with no support from another or other interlocutor(s), and it is online, demanding quick access to phrases. As the examples above showed (see Study 1, section Method and categories), the MWSs are not necessarily difficult or infrequent. We suggest that the principal reason is that the task is performed under considerable time pressure, with little time for pausing and reflection on language. The fact that there were no significant differences between the two groups in the role play suggests that this task was less demanding. Indeed, it was less demanding on several counts: (1) it is a dialogic task, allowing support from the interlocutor; (2) it presumably reflects an activity (making a request) that should be fairly familiar to somebody living in the country; (3) it does not involve the same time constraints as

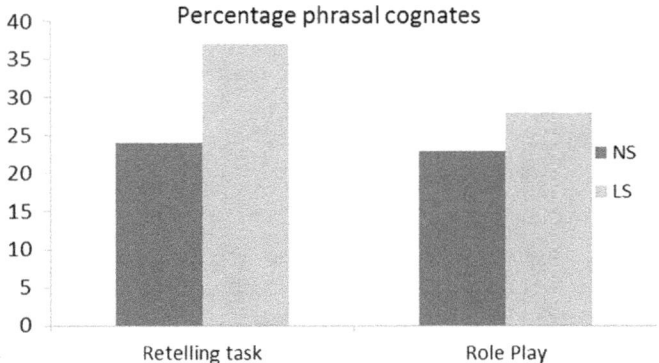

Figure 4.1 % of phrasal cognates in the role play and the retelling task over the LS and NS groups

the retelling task. Furthermore, the effects of the English instructions for the participants to read through and contemplate (approx. five minutes) should also be taken into account. The only instructions for completing the retelling task were that the participant should describe and narrate the scenes and events shown in the film clip as coherently as possible to an imagined hearer while the film was running.

The fact that the LS group used significantly more cognate phrases in the retelling task, could be a reflection of the time constraints inherent in the task, the Swedes having more immediate access to English phrases that had equivalents in Swedish. What speaks in favour of this interpretation is the fact that the native speakers used about the same proportion of phrasal cognates in both tasks (less than 25%). The results from the proportion of phrasal cognates among the phrasal MWSs being larger in the LS group in the retelling task give support for Wollter and Gyllstad's result (2011). The reaction times were significantly shorter for the Swedish L2 English speakers in their use of translation equivalent L1 Swedish collocations compared to their use of non-translation equivalents, results that were not found in the NS data.

Study 2: The Single Word Study

Introduction

This study compared words from different frequency ranges in the oral production of the same two groups as in the study of multiword structures. As mentioned the study involved three tasks representing three different situations. In addition to the two tasks presented in Study 1 (a role play and a retelling task) this study included a semi-structured interview. Unlike several earlier studies the present study includes not only results from frequencies of tokens but also frequencies of types, seeing diversity as an important aspect of the knowledge of words (cf. Daller & Xue, 2007; Vermeer, 2000). Analysing the knowledge of words in the spoken production of the same groups producing different texts is seen as an important aspect of the study.

Method

The facility used is the Lexical Frequency Profile (LFP), which is accessible in LexTutor via the program Vocabprofile (Cobb[2]), a limitation being that the frequency bands are based on written production. In Vocabprofile all the words of the data set of the study are registered in terms of type and token frequency, and listed alphabetically, which makes the data easily accessible allowing various kinds of analyses. The words in the lists have not been lemmatised, which means that type frequencies are indicated in terms of 'word forms'; for example, *museum, museums* and *call, calls, called, calling* are all registered as six separate types, while representing two lemmas. The LFP program maps the word forms onto their lemmatised forms (i.e. 'call' and 'museum' for the six word forms above) in four categories (or lists): the first most frequent 1000 words, the second most frequent 1000 words, and the Academic Word List (AWL; Coxhead, 2000). The fourth category is a separate list, called the Off-list, comprising any word (or item, e.g. word fragment) outside the 2000 most frequent words and the words in the AWL list in the data. The counting unit in Vocabprofile is 'word family', i.e. a base word, and its inflected and semantically closely related derived forms. It should be mentioned that although some types, especially in the high-frequency 1–1000 list, are inflections of one and the same lemma, as in the examples above, the majority belong to different lemmas. For example, in the interview the majority of word forms (i.e. types in LexTutor) in the 1–1000 frequency list belong to different lemmas.

In the present study the 1–1000 and 1000–2000 lists have been merged. The Off-list, as the name suggests, contains any word or item that is outside of the 2000 most frequent words and the AWL. In order to avoid a situation where words, because they are outside the frequency bands of the first 2000 words and the AWL, would unduly be considered advanced or low frequency, the Off-list was scrutinised and certain items were removed (cf. Lindqvist, 2010; Lindqvist *et al.*, 2013). All the words in the LexTutor Off-list that were deemed as not being part of a language's vocabulary, such as voiced pausing and word fragments, were removed. Furthermore, apart from **names** (of people, regions, places, continents and countries) the following types of items in the Off-lists have been removed: **languages** and **nationalities**, many of which are similar in Swedish and English, therefore more readily accessible; cf. Horst and Collins, 2006; Lindqvist *et al.* 2013; Milton 2007, **feedback** words (*yea, yeah, ok, huh, mm*), **foreign words** (*cher*), **contractions** (*wanna, gonna, gotta, coz*), **swear words** (*fucking*), **slang words** (*kids, guys, crap, ass*), **voiced pausing** (*eh, uh/uhm/um(m)*) and, finally, **fragments** of words (*Thur, archi,* etc.).

The AWL list has been merged with the modified version of the Off-list as outlined above, and both are subsumed in the beyond 2000 frequency range (henceforth the 2000+ range; cf. Laufer, 1995). Two main frequency ranges were thus examined: the first 2000 words (1–2000 frequency range), and those outside the first 2000 words (the 2000+ frequency range).

Apart from the overall aim of both studies, notably detecting similarities and differences between the LS group and the NS group, this study compares the LS and NS groups as regards types and tokens per 100 words in these two frequency ranges across the three tasks. We repeat that, although our focus is on advanced vocabulary, i.e. the rate of low-frequency words, we examine the participants' degree of variation in both frequency ranges. Below are the results from these two frequency ranges.

The single word study: Results

As mentioned, the results are divided into two main groups, the 1–2000 words frequency range and the 2000+ frequency range. We start by accounting for types and tokens per hundred words pertaining to the 2000 most frequent words, i.e. the high-frequency range (Table 4.4), followed by a corresponding account of the results from the 2000+ frequency range, i.e. the low-frequency range (Table 4.5). All statistical results below are related to the NS group functioning as benchmark. The threshold for significance is set at $p<.05$.

Results from the 1–2000 frequency range

It is worth noting, again, that high-frequency words, i.e. words within the 1–2000 frequency range, cover a major part of the texts (approx. 90%) as can be seen in number of tokens per 100 words in all three tasks in Table 4.4.

While the LS group is native-like on tokens per hundred words in the interview, they differ significantly from the NS group in the number of types. The results for the interview diverge from those for the role play and the retelling task. In fact, the LS group is native-like on all measurements within the 1–2000 frequency range in these two tasks. Our hypothesis that the Swedes would reach native-like levels in the role play was confirmed. Furthermore, the results give support for the inclusion of types in the analysis.

Table 4.4 1–2000 range; Number of Types and Tokens; Number of Types/100 wds, and Number of Tokens/100 wds in Interview, Role play and Retelling task

Tasks	No. Type Token	Types/100 wds	p	Tokens/100 wds	p
Interview					
NS	1416 20470	6.1		88.76	
LS	1366 22712	5.4	.001	90.2	0.23
Role play					
NS	391 3155	10.9		88.2	
LS	382 3015	11.1	0.84	87.6	0.84
Retelling task					
NS	1080 15699	6.1		88.8	
LS	1030 14899	6.3	0.50	91.1	0.11

Table 4.5 2000+ range; Number of Types and Tokens; Number of Types/100 wds, and Number of Tokens/100 wds in Interview, Role play and Retelling task

Tasks	No. Type Token	Types/100 wds	p	Tokens/100 wds	p
Interview					
NS	627 1077	2.7		4.7	
LS	537 1041	2.1	.000	4.1	.005
Role play					
NS	56 109	1.57		3.0	
LS	59 123	1.7	0.62	3.6	0.23
Retelling task					
NS	440 1074	2.5		6.1	
LS	282 614	1.7	.000	3.7	.000

Results from the 2000+ range

As mentioned, in the present study the 2000+ frequency range, i.e. words beyond the 2000 most frequent words (Table 4.4) is composed of a pruned version of the words in the Off-list (see Study 2, section Method) combined with the words in the AWL list (Table 4.5).

The LS group is native-like on all measures in the role play for this frequency range as well as for the 1–2000 range. With regard to the interview, the results for this task are closer to those of the retelling task for this frequency range. The LS group uses significantly fewer types and tokens per hundred words in both the interview and the retelling task compared to the native group. In fact, on three of the six measurements in the 2000+ range the *p*-values are either zero (for types *and* tokens/100 words in the retelling task, which parallels the results for the multiword study in this task.), or close to zero (for types/100 words in the interview). One possible explanation for the outcomes of the retelling task is that the NS group uses more specific vocabulary prompted by the task compared to the LS group. For example the NS group uses *swat the wasp* and *nuts and bolts,* where the LS group uses, respectively, *kill the insect* and *metal things* (both examples are from the retelling task, i.e. *Modern Times*). The tendency for native speakers to use more specific vocabulary has also been found in earlier studies (e.g. Lindqvist, 2012). A tentative explanation for the results relating to the interview is that the interviewee can talk freely about anything that comes to mind in answering the questions asked by the interviewer, which apparently was to the native speakers' advantage.

In sum, the tasks where the LS group deviated the most from the NS group in both frequency ranges are the interview and the retelling task. Measurements of types as well as tokens verified this. In the final analysis, it seems reasonable to suggest that a contributing factor for the differences between the LS and NS groups is the amount and variation of exposure and input, and this has consequences for the whole range of productive word knowledge.

Discussion and Conclusion

Results and hypotheses

The first research question concerned differences between the LS and NS groups regarding types and tokens/100 words in the multiword study. The results show that the LS group, in accordance with our hypothesis, was similar to the NS group on both types and tokens of MWSs in the role play, while they differed significantly from the NS group on both types and tokens of MWSs in the retelling task.

The MWS study also involved a comparison of the proportion of cognate MWSs in these two tasks across the two groups, which was our second research question. Based on results from earlier studies we expected the LS group to exhibit a larger proportion of cognate MWSs in the retelling task given its time-constraint, while they would have a similar proportion of phrasal cognates in the role play in view of its everyday character. In accordance with our hypothesis the proportion of phrasal cognates was significantly higher in the retelling task compared to the NS group. Interestingly, the NS group used the same proportion of phrasal cognates in both tasks.

Our third and fourth research questions pertain to the single word study and concerned comparisons between the LS and NS groups with regard to types and tokens/100 words in the 1–2000 frequency range (i.e. high-frequency words) and the 2000+ frequency range (i.e. low-frequency words), respectively. Our hypothesis regarding the results from this study was only partly confirmed. In accordance with our hypothesis the results for the LS group were similar to the NS group regarding both types and tokens per 100 words in both frequency ranges in the role play. However, our hypothesis that the LS group would be native-like also in the interview given its interactive character was not corroborated. In this task the LS group differed significantly from the NS group on types per 100 words in both frequency ranges. Furthermore, the results showed that it was in the interview and the retelling task that the LS group differed the most from the NS group in the range of low-frequency words (i.e. the 2000+ range) for both types and tokens.

The results of the two studies indicate that the native speakers have more immediate access not only to specialised vocabulary but also to low-frequency words more generally as well as MWSs. Nevertheless, these results point to the importance of exposure and clearly show that living and working in the L2 country has a positive effect, which was most evident in the role play where there were no differences between the groups in either the single word or multiword study.

Comparison with earlier research

The results from the present study are in line with Boers *et al.* (2006), Stengers *et al.* (2011) and Forsberg Lundell *et al.* (2014), who all conclude that learners' general proficiency level seems to coincide with their degree of mastery of MWSs. The results from the study of proportion of phrasal cognates indicate that the LS group has more immediate access to MWSs that are similar in L1 and L2, which is in line with results from earlier studies (e.g. Kroll *et al.*, 2002; Wollter & Gyllstad, 2011). Furthermore, the results of the present study confirm results from several earlier studies of written production (Bolly, 2009; Erman, 2009; Lewis, 2009), who have found that MWSs are not only a stumbling block for advanced L2 learners, but also a sign of proficiency.

The importance of interaction with native speakers for progress in acquiring formulaic sequences has partly been borne out by the results in this study (cf. Adolphs & Durow, 2004). Thus there were no significant differences between the LS and NS groups in the role play, involving a common activity in everyday life, viz. making a request. Indeed, the fact that the LS group is integrated in the target language community may explain the positive results from both the single word and multiword study where they performed in a similar way to the NS group in this task.

As illustrated by the NS results from the single word study it is in the interview where the interviewee can talk about anything that comes to mind in response to the questions asked by the interviewer, that the native speakers distinguish themselves regarding types per 100 words in both frequency ranges. This is also what Lindqvist observed in her investigation of non-native speakers of different proficiency levels and native speakers, although analysis of types was not part of the general framework of Lindqvist's study (2010).

Notes

(1) Thanks are due to generous funding by *The Bank of Sweden Tercentenary Foundation*, Sweden.
(2) Available at www.lextutor.ca

References

Adolphs, S. and Durow, V. (2004) Socio-cultural integration and the development of formulaic sequences. In N. Schmitt (ed.) *Formulaic Sequences* (pp. 107–126). Language Learning & Language Teaching Series. Amsterdam: John Benjamins.
Albrechtsen, D., Haastrup, K. and Henriksen, B. (2008) *Vocabulary and Writing in a First and Second Language*. Basingstoke: Palgrave Macmillan.

Bardel, C., Gudmundson, A. and Lindqvist C. (2012) Aspects of lexical sophistication in advanced learners' oral production: Vocabulary acquisition and use in L2 French and Italian. In N. Abrahamsson and K. Hyltenstam (eds) *High-Level L2 Acquisition, Learning and Use*. Thematic issue of *Studies in Second Language Acquisition* 34 (2), 269–290.

Boers, F., Eyckmans, J., Kappel, J., Stengers, H. and Demecheleer, M. (2006) Formulaic sequences and perceived oral proficiency: Putting a lexical approach to the test. *Language Teaching Research* 10 (3), 245–261.

Bolly, C. (2009) The acquisition of phraseological units by advanced learners of French as an L2: High-frequency verbs and learner corpora. In E. Labeau and F. Myles (eds) *Revisiting Advanced Learner Varieties: The Case of French*. Oxford: Peter Lang.

Cobb, H. and Horst, M. (2004) Is there room for an academic word list in French? In P. Bogaards and B. Laufer (eds) *Vocabulary in a Second Language: Selection, Acquisition, and Testing* (pp. 15–38). Amsterdam: John Benjamins.

Coxhead, A. (2000) A new academic word list. *TESOL Quarterly* 34 (2), 213–238.

Daller, H., van Hout, R. and Treffers-Daller, J. (2003) Lexical richness in spontaneous speech of bilinguals. *Applied Linguistics* 24 (2), 197–222.

Daller, H., Milton, J. and Treffers-Daller, J. (eds) (2007) *Modelling and Assessing Vocabulary Knowledge*. Cambridge: Cambridge University Press.

Daller, H. and Xue, H. (2007) Lexical richness and oral proficiency of Chinese EFL students. In H. Daller, J. Milton, and J. Treffers-Daller (eds) *Modelling and Assessing Vocabulary Knowledge* (pp. 150–165). Cambridge: Cambridge University Press.

Durrant, P. and Schmitt, N. (2009) To what extent do native and non-native writers make use of collocations. *IRAL* 47 (2), 155–177.

Erman, B. and Warren, B. (2000) The idiom principle and the open choice principle. *Text* 20 (1), 29–62.

Erman, B. (2009) Formulaic language from a learner perspective: What the learner needs to know. In R. Corrigan, E.A. Moravcsik, H. Ouali and K.M. Wheatley (eds) *Formulaic Language* (pp. 27–50). Amsterdam/Philadelphia: John Benjamins.

Erman, B. Denke, A., Fant, L. and Forsberg Lundell, F. (2014) Nativelike expression in the speech of long-residency L2 users: A study of Multiword structures in L2 English, French and Spanish. *International Journal of Applied Linguistics*. doi: 10.111/ijal.12061.

Forsberg, F. (2008) *Le Langage Préfabriqué: Formes, fonctions et frequences en français parlé L2 et L1*. Bern: Peter Lang.

Forsberg, F. and Fant, L. (2010) Idiomatically speaking: The effects of task variation and target language on the use of formulaic sequences in high-level use of French and Spanish. In D. Wood (ed) *Perspectives on Formulaic Language* (pp. 47–70). London/New York: Continuum.

Forsberg Lundell, F. and Lindqvist, C. (2012) Vocabulary development in advanced L2 French: Do formulaic sequences and lexical richness develop at the same rate? *Language, Interaction, Acquisition (LIA)* 3 (1), 73–92.

Forsberg Lundell, F., Bartning, I., Engel, H., Gudmundson, A., Hancock, V. and Lindqvist, C. (2014) Beyond advanced stages in high-level spoken L2 French. *Journal of French Language Studies* 24 (2), 255–280.

Forsberg Lundell, F. and Lindqvist, C. (2014) Lexical aspects of very advanced L2 French. *The Canadian Modern Language Review* 70 (1), 28–49.

Graddol, D. (2012) The impact of macro socioeconomic trends on the future of the English language. Doctoral thesis, English Department, Stockholm University, Sweden.

Granger, S. (1998) Prefabricated patterns in advanced EFL writing: Collocations and formulae. In A.P. Cowie (ed) *Phraseology, Theory, Analysis and Applications* (pp. 145–160). Oxford: Oxford University Press.

Groom, N. (2009) Effects of second language immersion on second language collocational development. In A. Barfield and H. Gyllstad (eds) *Researching Collocations in Another Language: Multiple Interpretations* (pp. 21–33). Basingstoke: Palgrave Macmillan.

Horst, M. and Collins, L. (2006) From faible to strong: how does their vocabulary grow? *The Canadian Modern Language Review* 63 (1), 83–106.

Howarth, P. (1998) Phraseology and second language proficiency. *Applied Linguistics* 19 (1), 24–44.

Kroll, J.F., Michael, E., Tokowicz, N. and Dufour, R. (2002) The development of lexical fluency in a second language. *Second Language Research* 18 (2), 137–171.

Laufer, B. (1991) The development of L2 lexis in the expression of the advanced learner. *Modern Language Learner* 75 (4), 440–448.

Laufer, B. (1995) Beyond 2000: A measure of productive lexicon in a second language. In L. Eubank, L. Selinker and M. Sharwood Smith (eds) *The Current State of Interlanguage: Studies in Honor of William E. Rutherford* (pp. 265–272). Amsterdam: John Benjamins.

Laufer, B. and Nation, P. (1995) Vocabulary size and use: Lexical richness in L2 written production. *Applied Linguistics* 16 (3), 307–322.

Lemmouh, Z. (2010) The relationship among vocabulary knowledge, academic achievement and the lexical richness in writing in Swedish University students of English. PhD thesis, English Department, Stockholm University.

Lewis, M. (2009) *The Idiom Principle in L2 English: Assessing Elusive Formulaic Sequences as Indicators of Idiomaticity, Fluency, and Proficiency*. Saarbrücken: VDM Verlag.

Lindqvist, C. (2010) La richesse lexicale dans la production orale de l'apprenant avancé de français. *La revue Canadienne des Langues Vivantes/The Canadian Modern Language Review* 66 (3), 393–420.

Lindqvist, C. (2012) Advanced learners' word choices in French L3. In J. Cabrelli Amaro, J. Flynn and J. Rothman (eds) *Third Language Acquisition in Adulthood* (pp. 255–280). Amsterdam: John Benjamins.

Lindqvist, C., Bardel, C. and Gudmundson, A. (2011) Lexical richness in the advanced learner's oral production of French and Italian L2. *International Review of Applied Linguistics (IRAL)* 49 (3), 221–240.

Lindqvist, C., Gudmundson, A. and Bardel, C. (2013) A new approach to measuring lexical sophistication in L2 oral production. *Eurosla Monographs Series* 2, 109–126.

Lotto, L. and De Groot, A.M.B. (1998) Effects of learning method and word type on acquiring vocabulary in a new language. *Language Learning* 48 (1), 31–69.

Mel'čuk, I. (1998) Collocations and lexical functions. In A.P. Cowie (ed.) *Phraseology. Theory, Analysis, and Applications* (pp. 23–53). Oxford: Clarendon Press.

Milton, J. (2007) Lexical profiles, learning styles and the construct validity of lexical size tests. In H. Daller, J. Milton, and J. Treffers-Dallers (eds) *Modelling and Assessing Vocabulary Knowledge* (pp. 133–149). Cambridge: Cambridge University Press.

Ovtcharov, V., Cobb, T. and Halter, R. (2006) La richesse lexicale des productions orales: mesure fiable du niveau de compétence langagière. *The Canadian Modern Language Review* 63 (1), 107–125.

Raupach, M. (1984) Formulae in second language speech production. In H.W. Dechert, D. Möhle and M. Raupach (eds) *Second Language Production* (pp. 114–137). Tübingen: Gunter Narr Verlag.

Ringbom, H. (2007) *Cross-Linguistic Similarity in Foreign Language Learning*. Clevedon: Multilingual Matters.

Schmitt, N. (ed.) (2004) *Formulaic Sequences* (pp. 107–126). Language Learning & Language Teaching Series. Amsterdam: John Benjamins.

Stengers, H., Boers, F. and Housen, A. (2011) Formulaic sequences and L2 oral proficiency. *International Review of Applied Linguistics in Language Teaching* 49 (4), 321–343.

Taguchi, N. (2007) Task difficulty in oral speech act production. *Applied Linguistics* 28 (1), 13–135.
Tidball, F. and Treffers-Daller, J. (2007) Exploring measures of vocabulary richness in semi-spontaneous French speech. In H. Daller, J. Milton and J. Treffers-Daller (eds) *Modelling and Assessing Vocabulary Knowledge* (pp. 133–149). Cambridge: Cambridge University Press.
Vermeer, A. (2000) Coming to grips with lexical richness in spontaneous speech data. *Language Testing* 17 (1) 65–83.
Wollter, B. and Gyllstad, H. (2011) Collocational links in the L2 mental lexicon and the influence of L1 intralexical knowledge. *Applied Linguistics* 32 (4), 430–449.

Part 2

Culture as a Decisive Factor in L2 Attainment

5 Migratory Experience and Second Language Acquisition Among Polish and Chinese Migrants in Dublin, Ireland[1]

Chloé Diskin and Vera Regan

Introduction

In an increasingly globalised and urbanised world, migration has become a way of life for significant numbers of people. Within sociolinguistics, the study of migration, especially to and from the world's megacities, has formed the backdrop to a broadening field of enquiry. Moreover, migration has created vast and complex sites of language contact, and has thus become a pertinent topic within the field of Second Language Acquisition (SLA).

Viewing migration purely from a demographic perspective can give a broad vision of the movement and settlement of peoples over time. However, migration studies have become more complex and the conventional vision of the 'immigrant' has evolved from an individual who makes a more or less permanent move from one setting to another, to an active agent who moves more fluidly across boundaries. These movements are based on decisions which can be of an economic, personal or cultural nature. Individuals may be in search of better employment or education, may be following friends or a spouse, or may wish to experience another culture and improve their language skills. In fact several or all of these motivations may be at play in the decision of the individual. For many, it is a combination or continuum of these motivations and varying degrees of embeddedness within social fields which ultimately shapes this experience (Levitt & Jaworsky, 2007: 130).

Migration research has thus shifted from assimilationist and integrationist perspectives to studies of transnationalism. Within the context of the developed world, transnational migrants are highly mobile individuals with tenuous ties to traditional nation states – they may be re-defined as 'trans-destinational' (King-O'Riain, 2008: 219). They move through cultural spaces fluidly, and make calculated decisions on their next destination based on the economic and human capital there is to be gained.

The sociolinguistic landscape has changed in recent years to encompass notions of superdiversity (Vertovec, 2007) and globalisation (Blommaert, 2010). These notions can also be applied to sociolinguistic SLA, in the sense that for many, the essentialist dichotomy of non-native speaker (NNS) versus native speaker (NS) has shifted. It is not the degree to which the NNS is proficient or deficient as compared to the (idealised) NS, but rather how any speaker can participate in multilingual language practices (see Jørgensen, 2008; Li, 2011) and can move fluidly between various 'lects', such as ethnolects or sociolects.

This study examines the acquisition of discourse-pragmatic features by migrants in Ireland. It aims to fill a gap within sociolinguistic SLA by focusing on the acquisition of non-standard forms by NNS. It has been shown that the degree to which a NNS feels integrated within a speech community correlates positively with the frequency of their use of discourse-pragmatic markers (DPMs) in the target language (Sankoff *et al.*, 1997). This chapter will follow on from these studies by analysing discourse-pragmatic variables and while it will not look at integration per se, it will take migration, and specifically migratory experience, as a context for SLA.

The data to be analysed comes from a corpus of over 50 hours of sociolinguistic interviews recorded in Dublin, Ireland in 2012[2]. The participants are recently arrived Polish and Chinese migrants and native Dubliners. By understanding migration as a multi-faceted phenomenon, this analysis will expand on sociolinguistic categories such as gender, age, length of residence (LOR) etc. and will use migratory experience as a lens for acquisition. Specifically, it will slice the migratory experience of the participants into four different groups: academic migrants, chain migrants, cultural migrants and economic migrants. The groups are defined according to particular criteria based on the content of the interviews. The analysis will address the following research questions: Does migratory experience affect SLA? Does this correlate with other factors such as language proficiency, gender, LOR, nationality or level of education? Do migrants in Ireland mirror patterns of NS of Irish English in their choice and frequency of use of DPMs?

Ireland and Immigration

This study was conducted against the backdrop of in-migration to Ireland, which peaked during the economic boom or 'Celtic Tiger' years, particularly 2002–2006, but continues to develop, even in the current period of economic recession. Between 2002 and 2012, the number of non-Irish nationals residing in Ireland increased from 224,261 to 544,357, a growth of 143% (Central Statistics Office, 2012a: 7). Ireland was previously (even famously) a country of high outward-migration; however the demographics have shifted and it is set to remain a country of in-migration.

Polish migration to Ireland

The demographic shift in Ireland is due in part to the fact that when 10 new states joined the European Union (EU) in 2004, Ireland was one of three countries, along with Sweden and the UK, to allow immediate, unrestricted labour market access to Polish citizens. This has contributed to the growing population of Poles in Ireland and Polish nationals now represent the largest non-Irish group (in terms of nationality) in Ireland, with a population of 122,585 or 2.7% of the Irish population (Central Statistics Office, 2012b: 33). Ireland is the third most popular destination for post-accession Polish migrants, chosen by 10% of the whole number of those who have left Poland since May 2004[3] (Grabowska-Lusińska, 2008 cited in Debaene, 2013: 19).

Polish migration to Ireland in the early Celtic Tiger years was for the most part motivated by economic factors. Unemployment was as high as 15% in some regions in Poland during this period, and wages were four times higher in Ireland than in Poland (Kropiwiec cited in King-O'Riain, 2008: 215). In more recent years, however, this migratory flow has been characterised by increased levels of chain migration, family reunification and a high birth rate. A 'critical mass' of Polish social networks developed in Ireland during the Celtic Tiger years, which enabled Polish migrants to continue to migrate to Ireland, even when the job market was not as attractive (King-O'Riain, 2008: 215). The Polish population in Ireland grew by almost 94% in the period 2006–2012, going from 63,276 to 122,585 (Central Statistics Office, 2012a).

Polish migration to Ireland has also been described as a 'misnomer' and that 'mobility' may be a more accurate term for this phenomenon (Szumowski, 2007 personal communication cited in Debaene, 2013: 19). Indeed, as EU citizens, there is no reason that Poles would stay in Ireland if they were to find better opportunities in another EU state. In the words of one Polish migrant, some people are 'keeping their options open.' (Debaene, 2013: 21). Ease of mobility as well as advances in technology have changed the process of migration and offers increased agency to individuals. This particular study has thus chosen the term 'migratory experience' rather than (e)migration.

Chinese migration to Ireland

Migration from mainland China to Ireland is also a recent phenomenon. Mainland China, much like Poland, is in the wake of early capitalism and has only in recent decades opened its borders. It has since seen a surge of outward migration, particularly from the burgeoning middle classes. The vast majority of Chinese migrants entering Ireland are permitted on a student visa scheme. For some, this scheme permits them to pursue cultural and linguistic capital, by acquiring assets such as improved English language skills, qualifications from well-regarded English-speaking universities and work experience abroad. The experience is seen as an investment for the future (King-O'Riain, 2008: 217). For others, the student visa offers a step in to the labour market and the academic programme for which they have enrolled is not a priority. Certain English language schools have been reportedly sponsoring these visas for students who do not attend classes, in exchange for a fee (Pan, 2011: 275). Other students may remain undocumented in the state.

In terms of population, Wang and Chiyoko King-O'Riain (2006) estimated that there were between 60,000 and 100,000 Chinese nationals in Ireland in 2006, whereas the Census of 2011 gave the much more conservative figure of 10,896 (Central Statistics Office, 2012a). It is thus not easy to define the scope of Chinese migration to Ireland. It certainly appears to be a tenuous, transient phenomenon which has decreased since the Celtic Tiger. Indeed, many of the participants in this particular study did not intend to remain long-term in Ireland. Nonetheless, Chinese migrants have made a permanent cultural imprint on the city of Dublin, particularly with the visible growth of unofficial Chinatown areas on Capel Street and Parnell Street.

Overview of Recent Discourse-Pragmatic Research

The linguistic analysis of this study comprises of a quantitative analysis of the frequency of use of DPMs and quotatives among NS and NNS. The variables chosen are the discourse-pragmatic markers (DPMs) 'like', 'you know' and 'I mean' and the quotatives 'like', 'say', 'go' and the zero quotative.

Discourse-pragmatic variables were chosen as an object of analysis since they are relatively understudied among NNS and they provide an interesting insight into language acquisition on an interpersonal and communicative level. The DPMs 'like', 'you know' and 'I mean' in particular have been identified as salient features of everyday, informal Irish English (see section *The DPMs 'like', 'you know' and 'I mean' in Irish English*). The NNS in this study are exposed to Irish English on a daily basis and may find themselves 'picking up' these DPMs as a feature of their spoken interaction. This study is ultimately an analysis of how NNS accommodate to Irish English NS patterns.

Theoretical approaches to discourse-pragmatic markers

There has been a wealth of research in the area of DPMs, a branch of the wider study of pragmatics, especially in the English language. There has been disagreement over the grammatical category, meaning, function and positioning of a DPM. This is not surprising considering the amount of words that can be considered to belong to this category. Brinton (1996: 32) counts the following 'pragmatic markers': 'Ah', 'actually', 'after all', 'almost', 'and', 'and {stuff, things} like that', 'anyway', 'basically', 'because', 'but', 'go say', 'if', 'I mean/think',' just',' like', 'mind you', 'moreover', 'now', 'oh', 'o.k'., 'or,' 'really', 'right/all right/that's right', 'so', 'say', 'sort of/kind of', 'then', 'therefore', 'uh huh', 'well', 'yes/no', 'you know/y'know', 'you see'.

DPMs have been termed 'pragmatic markers', 'discourse markers', 'pragmatic particles', 'interactional signals' and 'smallwords' (Andersen, 2001: 38), as well as 'comment clause', 'connective', 'continuer', 'discourse connective', 'discourse-deictic item' (Brinton, 1996: 29) and 'pragmatic expression' (Erman, 1986). This chapter will employ the more multifunctional term 'discourse-pragmatic marker' (DPM), acknowledging both the discourse and pragmatic scope of these items and aligning itself with recent work by Tagliamonte (2012).

DPMs are characterised by many defining features, including orality, high frequency, stylistic stigma, phonological reduction, semantic shallowness and optionality (Brinton, 1996: 33). In terms of the functionality of DPMs, it is generally understood that DPMs do not carry much lexical import on their own but instead function as integrated parts of an utterance. In fact, they are far more flexible, creative and semantically rich than their surface lexical meanings. They do not have a fixed meaning, but 'meaning potential' (Aijmer, 2013: 12).

Schiffrin (1987: 267) proposes that DPMs act as textual co-ordinates within an utterance while Andersen (2001: 31) argues that they help to make the utterance as relevant as possible through the least amount of processing time- a guarantee of optimal relevance (Aijmer, 2013: 11). The former is known as an integrative theory, which 'involves multiple contextual components which contribute to the overall sense of "the coherence" of discourse' (Aijmer, 2013: 10). The latter is known as relevance theory, which has 'the potential to provide a theory of utterance interpretation which is consistent with generative grammar' (Blakemore, 2002: 7). This chapter aligns itself with the integrative approach and views the context as selecting the meaning of the DPM, rather than the relevance approach, where the DPM 'looks for a context which is compatible with communicative principles' (Aijmer, 2013: 12).

Of particular importance among DPMs is their position within the clause, utterance or turn sequence. Erman (1986: 132) wrote that pragmatic expressions in an utterance-medial position were 'intrusive' elements and she classed those between clauses as 'connective' elements. She writes that establishing the syntactic environment is crucial in ascertaining the meaning of a DPM. Lennon (1990), made a similar distinction between 'juncture pauses', which occur at major syntactic boundaries, and 'hesitation pauses', which occur within syntactic units. According to Lennon, listeners are more tolerant of the former than of the latter, and pauses within syntactic units are likely to be perceived as longer than those of equivalent length at syntactic boundaries. This study supports this framework and presents data on the differing syntactic environments of 'like' in particular, which will be shown to occupy various semantic and pragmatic properties depending on its position.

Functions and social evaluations of discourse-pragmatic markers

Table 5.1 lists the functions of DPMs as identified and coded in this study, in order of their frequency in the data. The functions were identified by adapting previous work on functions of DPMs, particularly Müller (2005). Before the analysis began, a pilot coding project with a portion of the data confirmed the most prevalent functions of DPMs in this study. Some of Müller's functions were retained, such as reference to shared knowledge, others were discarded, such as quotative 'you know' (of which there were no tokens in this data) and more were added, such as the mitigating function, which is more specific to the Irish context.

'Like' has been found to occupy a variety of functions, including giving examples, expanding, acting as a filler or hesitation device, an approximative adverb or a quotative. In most varieties of English, it is negatively evaluated as being a feature of young, female, dysfluent speech, perhaps due to its origins in 'Valley Girl' speech. Its function as a filler and as a quotative seems to be over-represented in the media. Many may actively avoid it (Moore, 2011); however as a quotative it has undergone grammaticalisation (Tagliamonte, 2012) and global diffusion (Tagliamonte & Hudson, 1999). It is understood to be a salient, robust and frequent feature of the quotative system of most varieties of English. Nonetheless, 'like' may be avoided by language users and learners aspiring towards 'standard' English, due to views such as those held by Underhill: '["like"] is entirely ungrammatical in standard English and makes sentences seem disjointed to many listeners' (1988: 234). This is relevant to this study concerning NNS and thus 'learners' of English.

'You know' can refer to shared knowledge, invite responses in the form of a tag question or introduce information. It can act as a social monitor or occupy a hedging function. 'I mean' on the other hand organises discourse (Erman, 2001: 1340–1341). Fox Tree and Schrock (2002: 744) write that 'you know' is addressee-oriented, whereas 'I mean' keeps the focus on the speaker's thoughts. In terms of social evaluation, 'you know' and 'I mean' are regarded more neutrally than 'like'. Stubbe and Holmes (1995) found that 'you know' was more frequent among young male working class speakers in New Zealand; however Macaulay (2002) did not find social class to have an effect on its distribution in Scotland.

The research listed above would indicate that there may be a relationship between DPMs and text or interaction type. For example, people partaking in a large group conversation, where there is constant turn-taking and

Table 5.1 Functions of DPMs in this study

Function	Description	Example	Total number used (overall total=2462)	Percentage used for this function
Illustrating/ Expanding/ Explaining	Used to expand on what the speaker is saying and is followed by an explanation or extension.	*Maybe you don't know about this. Like a stamp four, you know?* (Liqiu)	1462	59.38%
Filler/false start/ hesitation	Used when the speaker hesitates, or as a filler while they search for or plan the appropriate expression.	*But sometimes I'm like kind of ah…. It's very difficult to-to you know um…* (Agnieszka)	277	11.25%
Exemplifying	Precedes the provision of an example.	*Every vegetables, lots of different, like potatoes, tomatoes, cucumbers….* (Mei Hua)	260	10.56%
Invite response/tag question	It invites a response from the interlocutor. Frequently occurs with rising intonation in clause-final position or between units.	*The government that probably wouldn't be seen as ah politically correct in any ways, you know?* (Agnieszka)	168	6.82%
Reference to shared knowledge	The speaker makes allusion to what they consider to be common or general knowledge about the world, or to knowledge that is shared between the interlocutors.	*D'you know like the way you'd have a like sewer kinda thing…* (Pearl)	96	3.9%
Approximative adverb	Used to express an approximate number or quantity.	*Yeah so it was like two, maybe two and a half months.* (Agnieszka)	82	3.33%

(Continued)

Table 5.1 (Continued)

Function	Description	Example	Total number used (overall total=2462)	Percentage used for this function
Mitigator/hedge	Serves to reduce or soften the force of an utterance; avoid a face-threatening act or coming across as an 'expert'.	Yeah but yeah hopefully the Italian, I'll just – but at least it'll keep me working at it like. (David)	49	1.99%
Self-correction/ replacement/repair	Serves to frame the correction of an error, misinformation or a false start.	I decided after too many staff room chats where I couldn't fit – like follow anything, that I'm gonna start going to all these films… and watching the news. (Niamh)	42	1.71%
Open floor	Speaker signals that they wish to take the floor. Can be an interruption or overlap. Often followed by a (personal) opinion or assertion.	You know, I know the difference, but I don't – can't tell… (Marcin)	13	0.53%
Completion of an information unit	Signals the end of an information unit and may open up a turn for the other interlocutor. Often accompanied by falling intonation.	I think now when we have a good manager maybe will be better you know. (Eliza)	11	0.45%
Forewarner for adjustments/ disagreements	Frames or introduces a disagreement with what has previously been said. Indicates certainty. May be an interruption.	I mean I – when Michal should be one person and I have two other lads here in the South […]. (Andrzej)	2	0.08%

floor-holding, may differ largely from those partaking in a one-on-one conversation. This is relevant for this study, where the interaction type was the sociolinguistic interview, where the participant engages in long stretches of uninterrupted speech. Perhaps the participants would have been more inclined to use speaker-oriented DPMs, such as 'I mean', rather than listener-oriented ones, such as 'you know'.

The DPMs 'like', 'you know' and 'I mean' in Irish English

The DPMs 'like', 'you know' and 'I mean' have been the object of marginal yet increasing interest in the pragmatics of Irish English. In particular, recent research has focused on the position of 'like' within the clause, which has been shown to have particular idiosyncrasies.

Kallen (2006) conducted a corpus-based study of the DPM 'like' in Irish English (ICE-Ireland, 1997) as compared to British English (ICE-Great Britain, 1998) and found that 'like' is much more common in Irish English, both as an 'internal discourse marker' and as a tag. Kallen describes these differences as 'dramatic' (2006: 18). He claims that although in other varieties of English, 'like' in clause-final position (henceforth CF 'like') is 'recessive' and 'dialectal'; in Irish English it is 'robust' (2006: 14).

Schweinberger (2012: 196) conducted an analysis of ICE-Ireland (1997) and found that the DPM 'like' was confined to younger cohorts but was not subject to gender differentiation. He also examined the positional distribution of 'like' and found that 'clause-final LIKE with backward scope is the most frequently used variant in the Irish data' (Schweinberger, 2012: 197). CF 'like' has also been identified as a feature of Northern (British) English, particularly Tyneside English, but its use is declining over time (Bartlett, 2013).

Siemund et al. (2009) found a preference in ICE-Ireland (1997) for 'like' in clause-marginal position – a collapsed category encompassing both clause-initial and CF 'like'. Interestingly, they also found this pattern in Indian English. When compared to four other varieties of English, they found statistically significant results to show that Irish English has the highest frequencies of DPM 'like' overall. In terms of position, the contrary was found by Amador-Moreno (2010), who reported that clause-medial 'like' was the preferred position of 'like' for middle and upper class speakers living in the southern suburbs of Dublin. 'Like' in Irish English thus indexes a number of meanings, such as Irishness (particularly CF 'like') and affluence (particularly clause-medial 'like'), as well as what it indexes more generally in English, such as young female talk and dysfluency.

In 2005, Kallen conducted a small-scale study comparing the use of the DPMs 'you know' versus 'I mean' in Irish and British English using ICE-corpora. He found that within Irish English spoken interactions, the proportion of 'you know' (3.27 instances per 1000 words) relative to 'I mean' (1.26 instances per 1000 words) was much higher. Quite the opposite was found for British English, where 'I mean' (4.43 instances per 1000 words) was preferred to 'you know' (3.6 instances per 1000 words). Kallen's hypothesis for this is that 'you know' is the 'silent partner' of 'I mean': 'I mean' reinforces the illocutionary intent of speaker, whereas 'you know' acts as a downgrader (Kallen, 2005: 63). He argues that Irish English speakers favour 'methods of expression that are more indirect than might commonly be expected in the English-speaking world' (Kallen, 2005: 66). It seems as though 'you know', along with CF 'like', indicates Irishness more strongly than the other DPMs and positions in this study.

DPMs and non-native speakers

DPMs in conversation occupy both a structural and phatic function; however they are often not taught explicitly by language instructors (Hellermann & Vergun, 2007). They require sociolinguistic competence and their absence or misuse can have implications for successful communication in the L2. Svartvik wrote:

> If a foreign language learner says 'five sheeps' or 'he goed', he can be corrected by practically every native speaker. If, on the other hand, he omits a 'well', the likely reaction will be that he is dogmatic, impolite, boring, awkward to talk to etc., but a native speaker cannot pinpoint an 'error' (Svartvik, 1980: 171).

Echoing this view, Aijmer (2002: 3) claims that incorrect use or underuse of discourse markers by NNS may lead to misunderstandings and Hansen wrote that this can be 'less significant but certainly far less easy to resolve than the incorrect use of a content word' (1998: 199). Indeed, it seems as though language instruction and testing are focused on the acquisition of phonology, content words and grammar, whereas aspects of language such as DPMs do not appear to be as explicitly taught, especially those considered to belong to the informal domain, such as 'like' and 'you know'. This can have implications for SLA, as migrants may be avoiding what they consider to be non-standard features of speech, at the risk of losing some of the nuances of conversation.

Previous studies of DPMs and NNS have shown that in general the frequency patterns of NNS do not mirror those of NS. Fuller (2003) found that her German, French and Spanish L1 participants (highly proficient academic staff in American universities) used DPMs less than their NS counterparts, especially for 'you know', 'like' and 'I mean'. Only their frequency of use for 'oh' and 'well' mimicked that of the NS. Müller (2005) found that her German L1 participants (university students on exchange in the US) used 'you know' and 'like' far less than her NS participants.

On the other hand, the NNS used 'well' and 'so' much more than the NS. She attributed this to an over-representation of 'well' in German EFL textbooks, a perception amongst NNS that 'well' and 'so' sound 'native' and the function of 'well' as an avoidance strategy in NNS speech. Hasselgreen (2004) found that Norwegians with a high proficiency in English used DPMs at a rate closer to that of NS (although NS still used them the most). Neary-Sundquist (2014) also found that as proficiency increased among NNS, so too did their frequency and variety of DPMs. 'You know' was found to be used 10 times more frequently among high proficiency speakers as compared to low proficiency speakers (Neary-Sundquist, 2014: 650). This suggests that the DPM 'you know' is acquired relatively late among learners of English.

Romero Trillo (2002) found that NNS were capable of acquiring what he termed 'operative markers' ('look' and 'listen') which contribute to the flow of conversation. However, when it came to 'involvement markers' ('you know', 'I mean', 'well') they did not attain a NS level. Hellermann and Vergun (2007) found that among adult beginner learners of English, proficiency and exposure to NS increased their use of the DPMs 'like', 'you know' and 'well'. In particular they found that more acculturated NNS were more likely to use a higher frequency of DPMs (Hellermann & Vergun, 2007: 168).

Few studies have examined the use of DPMs among NNS of Irish English in particular. Nestor et al. (2012) provides an exception to this paucity of research. Their study with Polish migrants in Ireland found that the DPM 'like' was frequently used and was significantly favoured in clause-marginal positions, reflecting what Siemund et al. (2009) discovered in ICE-Ireland. Almost 80% of the tokens of 'like' in their corpus, which consisted of eight participants and approximately eight hours of speech, were in clause-marginal position. Although they expected NNS living in rural County Mayo to make more use of CF 'like' than those living in the urban area of Dublin, this was not found to be an effect.

Quotatives

A 'quotative' in this study is understood as a marker that indicates and precedes either a direct or a hypothetical quote. It is also known as a 'quotative complementizer' or an introducer of constructed dialogue (Ferrara & Bell, 1995: 265). A direct quote is reported speech; it is a person quoting what another person said, usually in a series of interchanges to which the protagonist responded (Tagliamonte, 2012: 248). Hypothetical or indirect speech reports a feeling or attitude of an individual or group of people, e.g. 'I was like, "Oh my God!"'.

There has been a surge of research into quotatives and variation, especially since the rapid and salient grammaticalisation of 'like' as a quotative has gained ground in many varieties of English. It can vary according to age, sex and even ethnicity (D'Arcy, 2010: 62). Quotative 'like' now competes with more traditional quotative verbs such as 'say', 'go', 'think', 'tell', or quotative zero.[4] The use of quotative 'like' in particular is an interesting area of study as its use is stratified in terms of age and sex, i.e. the trend tends to be led by young females, and continued on by young males and subsequently older speakers (Tagliamonte, 2009: 89).

Studies of quotatives among NNS are relatively rare; however a recent study by Meyerhoff and Schleef (2013) showed that young Polish migrants in Edinburgh used the same quotatives as their native Edinburgh peers ('like', 'say', 'go', and zero), but that they only used quotative 'like' half the amount of times. Instead, they made use of the zero quotative twice as much. Meyerhoff and Schleef write that 'native speaker (NS) variation is rarely replicated exactly' (2013: 2).

As regards quotatives and Irish English, the popular Ross O'Carroll-Kelly novels have been described from a sociolinguistic perspective by Amador-Moreno (2010). In these novels, the speech of the protagonist is laden with DPM 'like' and quotative 'like' and this is generally accepted within media discourses as being stereotypical of South Dublin English. However, his speech is more than likely exaggerated for comic effect. It thus does not provide a reliable measure of quotative use in Irish English.

In addition, there are a number of studies that identify quotative 'like' in Irish English (e.g. Kallen, 2006; Luckmann, 2009; Nestor, 2013; Nestor *et al*., 2012; Schweinberger, 2012; Siemund *et al.* 2009), but do not compare it to the use of other quotatives. Therefore this study does not have a point of reference for what is considered 'frequent' or 'typical' for quotatives of Irish English. The same was said by Meyerhoff and Schleef (2013: 5–6) who wrote '[...] we do not know what the norms are for Edinburgh English. It is not clear, a priori, whether this variable will be more or less successfully acquired by the NNSs in our corpus'.

The Sample

A total of 48 participants were interviewed throughout 2012 for this study. Their nationality and gender are summarised in Table 5.2. There was

Table 5.2 Participants

Nationality	Male	Female	Total
Chinese	8	12	20
Polish	10	11	21
Irish	3	4	7

a fairly even balance between the Polish and Chinese participants, as well between the males and females. The Irish group was smaller, since its main function was to act as a control group.

Participants were recruited via the friend-of-a-friend approach, snowballing, by approaching migrant organisations such as the Chinese Gospel Church in Ireland and by placing advertisements in migrant media sources such as the newspaper *Polski Express*. All the participants were resident in Dublin city at the time of interview and the Irish contingent were all native Dubliners from both the north and south of the city. The participants were aged from 19 to 49; however the sample was on average relatively young with most participants in their late twenties or early thirties. The mean age of the participants was 29.7 years ($SD=6$).

In terms of proficiency, the NNS participants were asked to self-assess[5] their level of English according to a questionnaire based on the Common European Framework of Reference for Language (Council of Europe, 2001). This involved selecting statements that best corresponded to their proficiency in English in five areas: listening, reading, spoken interaction, spoken production and writing. Below is an example of one of these statements, which corresponds to a B2 level in spoken interaction:

> I can interact with a degree of fluency and spontaneity that makes regular interaction with native speakers quite possible. I can take an active part in discussion in familiar contexts, accounting for and sustaining my views (Council of Europe, 2001).

The participants' scores in the five areas were averaged so that each speaker was assigned a general score. These scores are provided in Table 5.3. The average assessment was close to a B2. All the participants had had some level of English instruction, normally within the formal school system, prior to arrival[6]. The lack of A1 users in this study has to do with fact that participants were told in advance that they would be having a conversation in English for one hour. Thus only those NNS capable of this chose to participate in the study.

Table 5.3 Proficiency in English of the NNS

Proficiency (adapted from CEFR)	N
A1 (Basic user)	0
A2 (Basic user)	2
B1 (Independent user)	13
B2 (Independent user)	11
C1 (Proficient user)	14
C2 (Proficient user)[7]	1

The participants' level of education was also recorded and was included as an independent variable in this study. Level of education was defined as the highest level of education the participant had completed. All of the participants had completed a minimum of 2nd level education. The responses were divided into 2nd level (completed secondary school), 3rd level (earned an undergraduate or Bachelor's degree) and 4th level (earned a postgraduate degree).

The participants' occupations were for the most part in the lower middle class bracket, particularly in the retail industry. 30% of the sample was students (undergraduate and postgraduate). Social class was difficult to assess in this study. Many participants experienced status inconsistency and social class displacement upon arrival in Ireland and found themselves working in occupations that were not commensurate with their qualifications[8]. Thus their current professions were not necessarily an accurate measure of their social class. This trend, coupled with the significant proportion of students in this study, resulted in the omission of social class as a variable.

Migratory experience was also included as an independent variable in this study. Each NNS participant was assigned to one of four categories. Despite the possible essentialism of grouping participants into such broad categories, in quantitative sociolinguistics it can be very useful for finding emerging patterns within data and for drawing conclusions about large datasets. See Table 5.4 for a summary.

The decision on the type of migrant was made by the first author based on the content of the interview data. Since the question 'what was your reason for coming to Ireland' (or similar) was a question in all of the interviews, ascertaining the type of migrant was relatively straightforward. However, on occasions the categories did overlap. For example, some Chinese nationals who came to Ireland to study also cited

Table 5.4 Grouping according to migratory experience

Type of Migrant	Justification	N
Academic	Came to Ireland solely or primarily to enrol in full-time higher-level education.	13
Chain	Came to Ireland solely or primarily to accompany or join a relative or friend.	10
Cultural	Came to Ireland as they had an interest in learning about another culture and language, wanted a new experience, wanted to see more of the world, wanted to take a 'gap year'. Identify with transnationalism, consider themselves 'trans-destinational' (King-O'Riain 2008: 219)	6
Economic	Came to Ireland primarily to seek employment, a better salary, a higher standard of living.	12

finding a part-time job alongside their studies as an important aspect of their lives in Ireland. There were also some grey areas within the chain migration group as certain participants followed other academic or economic goals once they had made the initial move to Ireland to join their contact there. This was visible among a cohort of the Polish women in this study, whose initial sole motivation to migrate was to join their husbands in Ireland, but who later on developed more reasons to stay. A grouping of this kind will always present difficulties when the classification is not merely categorical or clearly quantifiable. This classification aimed to be as consistent as possible by focusing on the migrants' initial and principal reasons for migrating.

Methodology

The sociolinguistic interview

All the participants met with the first author at various stages throughout 2012. The interviews were either held in public places, such as cafes, or in the participants' own homes (following invitation on the part of the participants). The interviews lasted between one and three hours and were recorded using a discreet digital voice recorder (smaller than a mobile phone) which could be placed on a table or ledge near the participant without causing disruption. As well as having the conversation, the participants were requested to fill out the CEFR questionnaire (see section *The sample*).

The participants were interviewed using the method of the sociolinguistic interview, which elicits long stretches of unmonitored speech and vernacular style (Labov, 1972). This was appropriate for the analysis of features of informal, spoken speech. The interview was loosely structured and resembled a chat. The interviewer did most of the listening and let the participants relax into the conversation. There was a list of question modules; however this was only used as a guide and was not visible to the participants. Nonetheless, there were certain topics that were covered with all participants, such as employment, education, social networks and reason for migrating. This resulted in the necessary demographic data being collected, while at the same time the participant was not made to feel as though they were being interrogated.

Transcription and coding

Following the interviews, the recordings were anonymised and transcribed and coded using ELAN[9], resulting in a time-aligned corpus. Although the interviews were transcribed in their entirety, for the purpose of this analysis, a 20-minute segment from the middle portion of each interview was extracted and coded. It was felt that a segment from the middle of the interview would contain the 'richest' data, i.e. where the interviewer had established topics of interest and the participant had been given the opportunity to take the floor. The segmentation resulted in an analysis of 100,853 words with an average of 2101 words per speaker being coded. Within ELAN, the DPMs and quotatives under investigation were tagged using controlled vocabularies. A total of 2821 tokens were used in this analysis. The frequencies were then normalised and calculated per 1000 words, to avoid discrepancies in the length of each individual segment. Each token was tagged for type of DPM or quotative, position (initial, medial, final or between units[10]) and function.

Starting hypotheses

The DPMs 'like', 'you know' and 'I mean' are understood as both structural and phatic components of interaction within this study. They are also considered to be features of everyday, informal, vernacular speech within Irish English. It is understood that NNS are exposed to them once they have even minimal contact with NS and that these DPMs consist of a valid variable context within SLA. In terms of the overall frequency of DPMs, it is hypothesised that NNS' use of DPMs will be lower than that of NS. Within the NNS, DPMs will be more frequent among cultural migrants (due to their integrative motivations), participants who are more proficient in English and participants with a longer LOR in Ireland[11].

In terms of the DPM 'like', it is hypothesised that due to its relatively marked status as non-standard, it will be less frequent among the NNS overall, and again will be more frequent among cultural and longer residence migrants. It is also predicted that NNS with a high proficiency in English will be more likely to use the DPM 'like' since the L1s of the NNS in this study (Polish, Mandarin and Cantonese) do not have an equivalent for 'like'. Thus the prediction is that it is more difficult to acquire for low proficiency speakers. It is also hypothesised that the position of the DPM 'like' will display differences. Those participants wishing to sound more Irish may use the uniquely Irish CF 'like'. It is hypothesised that it is the cultural migrants who will aspire more to sounding Irish than the other migrants. Overall, it is predicted that CF 'like' will be more prevalent among the Irish, due to its 'in-group' status.

It is expected that the DPM 'you know' will display less differences than with 'like' due to its socially unmarked status and its equivalents in all L1s of the NNS. It is predicted that the between-group differences for 'you know' will be minimal. Following Kallen (2005), it is predicted that 'you know' will be more frequent in the speech of the Irish in this study, but that there will be less difference among the NNS.

In terms of the functions of the DPMs in this study, it is predicted that 'like' will be used most often as a filler, since in at least the folk linguistic domain, it seems to be one of its most salient functions. It is predicted that 'you know' will be used most often for inviting responses (as a tag question) and referring to shared knowledge.

Within the quotative system, it is hypothesised that the socially marked quotative 'like' will behave much like the DPM 'like': it will be more frequent among cultural, more proficient and longer residence migrants. In addition, as with the DPM 'like', it has no L1 equivalent and is thus predicted to feature more in the speech of more proficient migrants. A similar trend is expected for quotative 'go'. Quotative 'say' and 'zero' will be expected to be more frequent in the speech of the NNS, since they will be making less use of 'like' and 'go' than their Irish counterparts. Quotative other is expected to display low rates across all groups, with slightly higher frequencies among the NNS.

Results

Choice and frequency of DPMs

In terms of the choice of DPMs among the participants in this study, Figure 5.1 shows that 'like' and 'you know' were used to very similar degrees – between 9 and 11 times per thousand words (Figure 5.1).

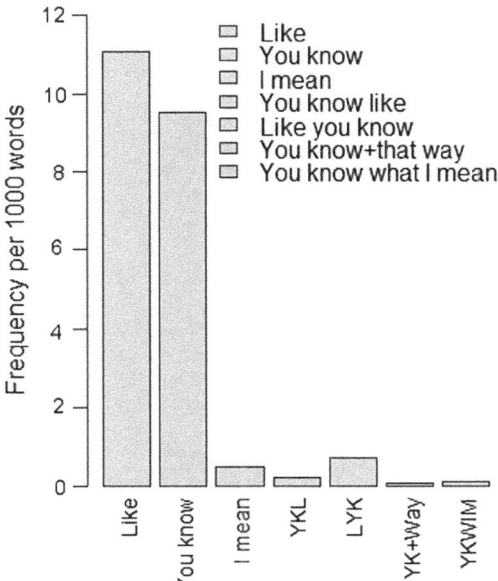

Figure 5.1 Frequency of DPMs

Despite these similar rates, a Pearson correlation test found no correlation between frequency of use of 'like' and 'you know' across all participants, $r(46) = -0.16$, $p = 0.25$. In other words, those participants who made frequent use of 'like' did not necessarily make frequent use of 'you know' and vice versa. 'I mean' was not as frequent as a DPM and was uttered just under once per 1000 words. There were also a small number of collocations: 'you know like', 'like you know', 'you know (that) way' and 'you know what I mean' (Figure 5.1). However, due to their low rates they were not used in further analyses. Instead, they were later collapsed into the 'like', 'you know' or 'I mean' categories (Figure 5.2).

Following this data visualisation, an analysis of variance (ANOVA) test was conducted to test the effect of the independent variables (nationality, gender, type of migrant, proficiency, LOR and level of education) on the dependent variable (frequency of DPMs per 1000 words). The results are summarised in Table 5.5. Initially, none of the independent variables were found to have an effect, as shows in the 'significance level' column.

However, by simply eyeballing the means, it seemed as though the cultural migrants and those participants with four years LOR (in bold) had higher means of DPM use than the other groups. The ANOVA test was then repeated, but without the Irish cohort. Within the type of migrant and LOR categories, they had simply been coded as 'Irish', since those variables were

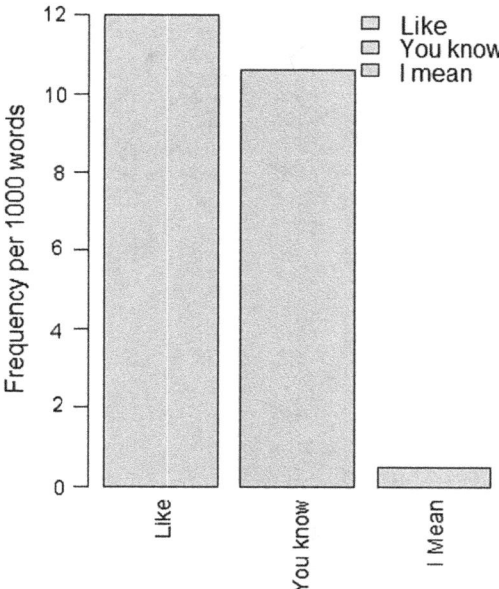

Figure 5.2 Frequency of DPMs (collapsed)

Table 5.5 Analysis of Variance (ANOVA) of the Frequency of DPMs

Independent variable	Dependent variable: mean number of DPMs (grand mean=20.26)	F statistic (rounded)	Significance level (p)	Irish removed
Nationality	Chinese=15.7 Irish=21.5 Polish=23.9	F=1.38	p=0.262	F=2.986, p=0.0921
Gender	Female=21.1 Male=19.3	F=0.15	p=0.7	F=0.844, P=0.364
Type of migrant	Academic=14 Chain=23.9 **Cultural=32.8** Economic=17.3 Irish=21.5	F=1.79	p=C.15	**F=2.664, p=0.0625**
Proficiency in English	A2=17.2 B1=18.1 B2=18 C1=23.9 Irish=21.5	F=0.31	p=C.87	F=0.43, p=0.733
Length of Residence	1 year=7 2 years=10 3 years=20.6 **4 years=27.1** 5 years=17.4 6 years+=25.1 Irish=21.5	F=1.22	p=0.316	**F=5.865, p<0.0203***
Level of education	2nd level=27 3rd level=20.7 4th level=16.1 Irish=21.5	F=0.96	p=C.42	F=1.557, p=0.224

specific to the migrant experience. Following this, significance was found for LOR and near significance for type of migrant (see 'Irish removed' column). Thus the differences in means did reflect actual differences in the data.

Another common statistical test within quantitative sociolinguistics was then applied to the LOR and type of migrant variable: linear regression. This test gives more information on what exactly is the predictor of the differences in means, and not simply which broad grouping has an effect. The results of two regression analyses are summarised in Table 5.6. The first is a regression analysis including the Irish, and the second without. The results confirm that those participants with a four year and six year– LOR (as initially observed by examining the means) differ significantly from the participants in the other LOR groups. This is an interesting finding, and suggests that the longer one resides in Ireland, the more likely

Table 5.6 Regression output for DPMs and length of residence

	Estimate	Standard Error	t value	Pr(>|t|)	Irish removed
(Intercept)	7.000	7.837	0.893	0.3771	0.3508
LOR: 2 years	3.025	11.083	0.273	0.7863	0.7743
LOR: 3 years	13.600	13.574	1.002	0.3224	0.2961
LOR: 4 years	20.125	11.083	1.816	**0.0769**	**0.0629**
LOR: 5 years	10.411	9.419	1.105	0.2756	0.2498
LOR: 6 years+	18.129	8.710	2.081	**0.0438***	**0.0344***
Irish	14.543	9.824	1.480	0.1466	n/a

Residual standard error: 15.67 on 40 degrees of freedom.
Multiple R-squared: 0.1547, Adjusted R=squared: 0.02793.
F-statistic: 1.22 on 6 and 40 DF, p-value: 0.3163

one is to use DPMs that are typical of Irish English. The hypothesis was further tested by a Pearson correlation test. A weak but positive correlation was found for LOR at $r(38)=0.37$, $p<0.02$.

Figure 5.3 depicts the distribution of DPMs by type of migrant and LOR. It shows the high degree of interspeaker variation, particularly among the six+ LOR cohort. It also shows that the majority of the academic migrants (indicated by the diamond) had LORs of one to three years, whereas the six year+ category had a broad range of types of migrant. Thus there were discrepancies in distribution; however overall there were very few empty cells.

Table 5.7 summarises a regression analysis which confirms the findings in Table 5.5 that cultural migrants, especially once the Irish are removed from the analysis, are significant predictors of frequency of DPMs.

The DPM 'Like'

The first analysis in this study showed that LOR and type of migrant were significant predictors of frequency of use of overall DPMs ('like', 'you know' and 'I mean' together). The second analysis looked at the DPM 'like' in isolation. As before, ANOVA tests were carried out. Table 5.8 summarises the results. The results show that the strongest effects on 'like' usage were nationality and, to a lesser extent, level of education. However, when the Irish were excluded from the analysis, no significance was found. This suggests that being Irish is the only significant effect on 'like' usage, and that among the migrants, there are no significant predictors, i.e. all the migrant groups use 'like' to more or less equal degrees.

A regression analysis further confirmed this trend: the Irish came out significant within each analysis of the independent variables. However, when the Irish were then excluded from the regression analysis, significance was found within LOR, at the three, four and six year mark. The results are summarised in Table 5.9.

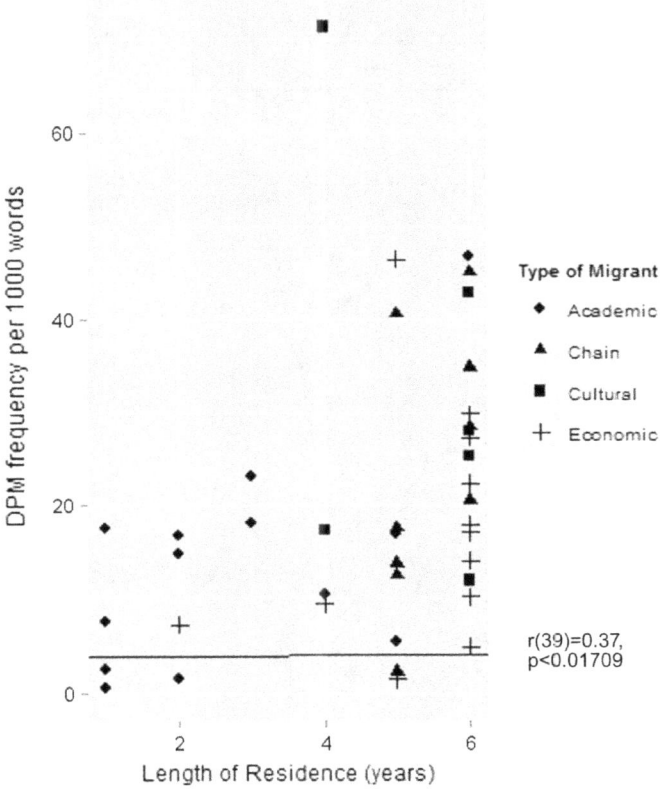

Figure 5.3 Length of residence, type of migrant and DPMs

Table 5.7 Regression output for DPMs and type of migrant

	Estimate	Standard Error	t value	Pr(>|t|)	Irish removed
(Intercept)	13.977	4.266	3.277	0.00211**	0.00134**
Type of Migrant: Chain	9.956	6.669	1.493	0.14294	0.12170
Type of Migrant: Cultural	18.806	7.591	2.478	**0.01734***	**0.01247***
Type of Migrant: Economic	3.348	6.157	0.544	0.58946	0.56729
Irish	7.566	7.210	1.049	0.30003	n/a

Residual standard error: 15.38 on 42 degrees of freedom.
Multiple R-squared: 0.1454, Adjusted R-squared: 0.06403.
F-statistic: 1.787 on 4 and 42 DF, p-value: 0.1495

Table 5.8 Analysis of Variance (ANOVA) of the frequency of DPM 'like'

Independent variable	Dependent variable: mean number of DPM 'like' (grand mean=9.04)	F statistic	Significance level (p)	Irish removed
Nationality	Chinese=8.17 **Irish=17.7** Polish=6.92	F=3.505	**p<0.0387***	p=0.569
Gender	Female=9.22 Male=8.82	F=0.018	p=0.895	p=0.271
Type of migrant	Academic=7.24 Chain=8.94 Cultural=10.4 Economic=5.32 **Irish=17.7**	F=2.017	p=0.109	p=0.455
Proficiency in English	A2=5.5 B1=5.31 B2=8.12 C1=9.38 **Irish=17.7**	F=2.011	p=0.11	p=0.463
Length of Residence	1 year=0.4 2 years=8.47 3 years=11.4 4 years=10.2 5 years=4.7 6 years+=9.36 **Irish=17.7**	F=1.869	p=0.11	p=0.124
Level of education	2nd level=4.88 3rd level=8.09 4th level=8.42 **Irish=17.7**	F=2.561	**p=0.0673**	p=0.429

As before, a Pearson correlation test was conducted to test whether LOR and frequency of use of DPM 'like' are positively correlated. The result showed a weak correlation at r(38)=0.22, p=0.1544. This is visible in Figure 5.4. Thus it cannot be said that as LOR increases, so too does frequency of 'like' usage. However, it can be said that 'like' is predominantly a feature of NNS with a minimum LOR of three years. This suggests that NNS may require a minimum period of exposure to DPM 'like' before incorporating it into their speech.

Position of the DPM 'like'

When it comes to the DPM 'like', position matters. This is particularly true of speakers of Irish English, as explained in section *The DPMs 'like',*

Table 5.9 Regression output for DPM 'like' and length of residence (migrants only)

	Estimate	Standard Error	t value	Pr(>|t|)
(Intercept)	0.400	3.244	0.123	0.9026
LOR: 2 years	8.075	4.588	1.760	0.0874
LOR: 3 years	11.050	5.619	1.966	**0.0575**
LOR: 4 years	9.775	4.588	2.130	**0.0404***
LOR: 5 years	4.300	3.899	1.103	0.2779
LOR: 6 years	8.965	3.606	2.486	**0.0180***

Residual standard error: 6.489 on 34 degrees of freedom.
Multiple R-squared: 0.2162, Adjusted R=squared: 0.101
F-statistic: 1.876 on 5 and 34 DF, p-value: 0.1245

'you know' and 'I mean' in Irish English. Figure 5.5 shows the general trend of the position of 'like' as selected by all the participants in this study. The figures are expressed as percentages of the total occurrences of DPM 'like', i.e. clause initial 'like' was selected just over 30% of the times 'like' was

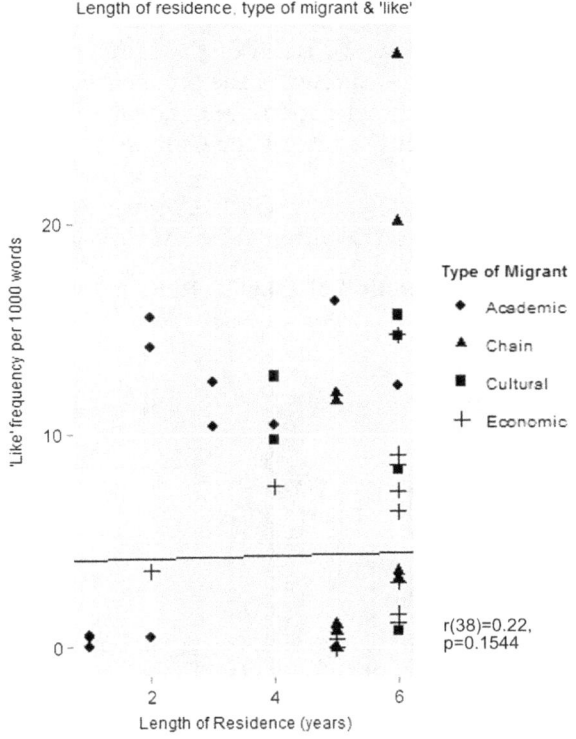

Figure 5.4 Length of residence, type of migrant and 'like'

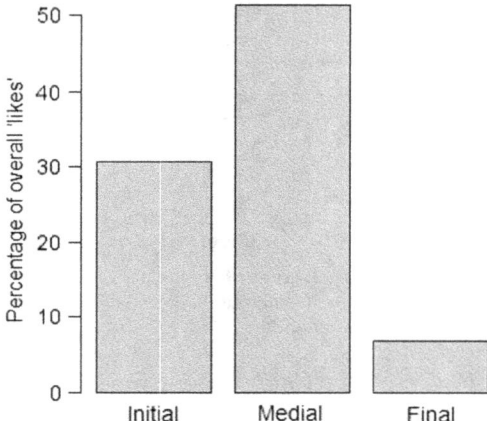

Figure 5.5 Position of 'like' (all groups)

used, clause-medial 'like' over 50% and CF 'like' under 10% of the time. Figure 5.6 shows this breakdown in terms of nationality. It shows that all three nationalities follow the trend of the sample as a whole. What is most notable about this breakown is the preference the Irish appear to have for CF 'like' over the other nationalities: about 15% compared to the mean of 10%, or five times the rate of the Chinese and twice the rate of the Polish.

A visualisation of the differences in CF 'like', which displayed the highest degree of variability across the different nationality groups, is provided

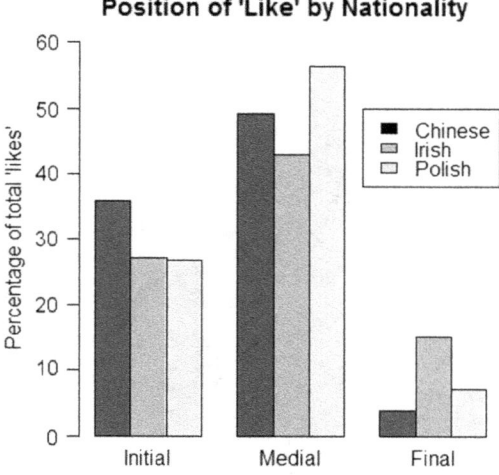

Figure 5.6 Position of 'like' by nationality

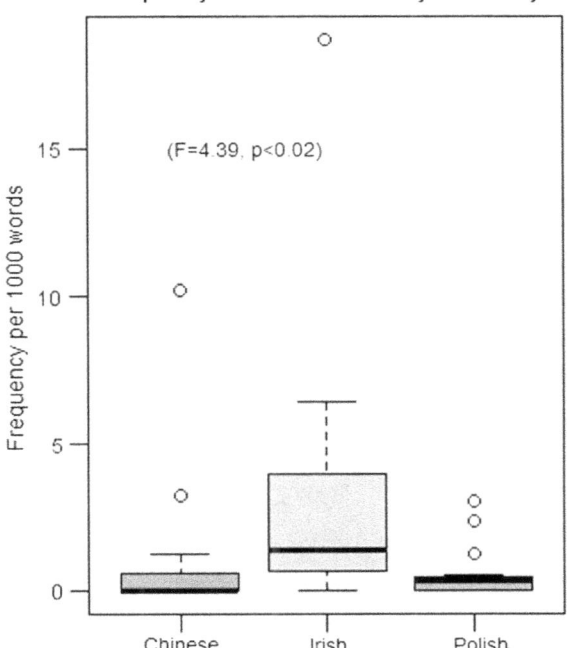

Figure 5.7 Frequency clause – Final 'like' by nationality

in the boxplot in Figure 5.7. It includes the output from an ANOVA test, showing that the differences between the different nationality groups were found to be significant at $p<0.02$.

Table 5.10 provides output from a mixed effects linear regression, with the speaker as a random effect. This shows that type of migrant was found to be significant. The chain and economic migrants, as well as the Irish, were found to be significant predictors of usage of CF 'like'.

The only difference found for clause-medial 'like' was that cultural migrants were found to be near significant predictors ($p=0.09$). For clause-initial 'like', again, no differences were found except for cultural migrants to disfavour its use ($p=0.06$). These results show that cultural migrants continue to exhibit patterns that differ from the rest of the migrant groups.

The DPM 'you know'

The boxplots in Figure 5.8 show the distribution of 'you know' (per 1000 words) spread across the range of independent variables. The long tails and outlier points show the high levels of interspeaker variation. However, within 'nationality' there is a clear difference between Polish and the other

Part 2: Culture as a Decisive Factor in L2 Attainment

Table 5.10 Regression output for clause-final 'like' and type of migrant

	Estimate	Standard Error	z value	Pr(>|t|)
(Intercept)	−4.5084	0.6963	−6.475	9.47e−11***
Type of Migrant: Chain	1.5805	0.7987	1.979	0.047837*
Type of Migrant: Cultural	1.1186	0.8782	1.274	0.202748
Type of Migrant: Economic	2.4841	0.7822	3.176	0.001494**
Irish	2.9204	0.8103	3.604	0.000313***

Log Likelihood −354.6
Correlation of fixed effects[12] (Type of Migrant: Economic*Intercept): r=−0.85

two nationalities. In general, the means for Irish use of 'you know' also appear to be much lower than that of the migrants. ANOVA tests were implemented to test these observations. The results are summarised in Table 5.11. Nationality was found to have a significant effect on 'you know',

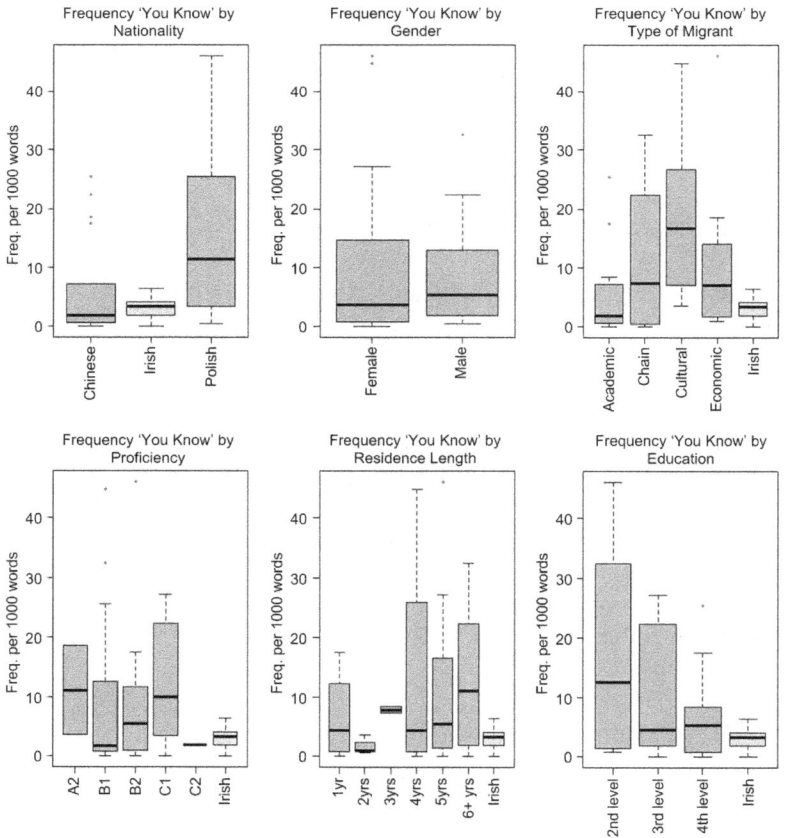

Figure 5.8 DPM 'you know'

Table 5.11 Analysis of Variance (ANOVA) of the frequency of DPM 'you know'

Independent variable	Dependent variable: mean number of DPM 'you know' (grand mean=9.5)	F statistic	Significance level (p)	Irish removed
Nationality	Chinese=6.12 Irish=3.1 **Polish=14.9**	F=4.837	***p<0.0125****	***p<0.0199****
Gender	Female=10.2 Male=8.57	F=0.241	p=0.626	p=0.575
Type of migrant	Academic=5.82 Chain=11.6 **Cultural=19.3** Economic=10.6 Irish=3.1	F=2.255	***p=0.0788***	p=0.164
Proficiency in English	A2=11.1 B1=10.1 B2=9.43 C1=12.5 C2=1.9 Irish=3.1	F=0.695	p=0.63	p=0.922
Length of Residence	1 year=6.6 2 years=1.55 3 years=7.85 4 years=13.4 5 years=12.4 6 years+=12.2 Irish=3.1	F=1.069	p=0.396	p=0.65
Level of education	2nd level=18.7 3rd level=10.3 4th level=6.79 Irish=3.1	F=3.424	***p<0252****	p=0.0517

both with and without the omission of the Irish, suggesting that it is, as the means suggest, the Polish that have the strongest effect. A regression analysis confirmed this (see Table 5.12).

A regression analysis (Table 5.13) also shows the cultural migrants to be significant predictors of frequency of use of 'you know'. A regression analysis was then performed to test whether there was an interaction between type of migrant and nationality, i.e. to test whether it is Polish cultural migrants in particular that are leading this trend. However, this was not found to be significant.

Education was also further investigated through a regression analysis (Table 5.14). Those educated to 4th level were found to have a significant

164 Part 2: Culture as a Decisive Factor in L2 Attainment

Table 5.12 Regression output for DPM 'you know' and nationality

	Estimate	Standard Error	t value	Pr(>|t|)
(Intercept)	6.125	2.404	2.548	0.0143*
Nationality: Irish	−3.025	4.722	−0.641	0.5250
Nationality: Polish	8.737	3.359	2.601	**0.0125***

Residual standard error: 10.75 on 45 degrees of freedom.
Multiple R-squared: 0.1769, Adjusted R=squared: 0.1404
F-statistic: 4.837 on 2 and 45 DF, p-value: 0.01251

negative effect on frequency of use of DPM 'you know'. A Pearson correlation analysis found a weak yet negative correlation at r(39)=−0.37, p=0.01809. This shows that, to a certain degree, as level of education increases among migrants, use of 'you know' decreases.

Functions

All DPMs in the analysis were coded according to function. This section will focus on the functions of 'like' and 'you know' only. Out of the nine possible functions for these two DPMs, six were particularly frequent: illustrate, filler, exemplify, invite response, reference to shared knowledge and mitigator (see Table 5.1 for more detail). Figure 5.9 shows the most significant correlations across the DPMs and functions in this study. 'Like' was highly positively correlated with the illustrate, exemplify, mitigator functions and to a lesser extent with the filler function. 'You know' was highly positively correlated with the reference to shared knowledge and invite response function.

Quotatives

Figure 5.10 shows the distribution of quotatives within the data. The figures displayed are expressed as a percentage of the total number of quotatives used, e.g. the Irish used 'like' 27% of the time they were using a quotative. The barplot shows a preference among the Irish participants

Table 5.13 Regression output for DPM 'you know' and type of migrant (Irish omitted)

	Estimate	Standard Error	t value	Pr(>|t|)
(Intercept)	5.823	3.287	1.771	0.0847
Type of Migrant: Chain	5.807	4.985	1.165	0.2516
Type of Migrant: Cultural	13.460	5.850	2.301	**0.0271***
Type of Migrant: Economic	4.752	4.745	1.002	0.3231

Residual standard error: 11.85 on 37 degrees of freedom.
Multiple R-squared: 0.1275, Adjusted R=squared: 0.05677
F-statistic: 1.803 on 3 and 37 DF, p-value: 0.1636

Table 5.14 Regression output for DPM 'you know' and level of education (Irish omitted)

	Estimate	Standard Error	t value	Pr(>|t|)
(Intercept)	18.744	3.861	4.855	2.08e−05***
Education: 3rd level	−8.480	4.948	−1.714	0.0947
Education: 4th level	−11.956	4.728	−2.528	0.0157*

Residual standard error: 11.58 on 38 degrees of freedom.
Multiple R-squared: 0.1444, Adjusted R=squared: 0.09932
F-statistic: 3.206 on 2 and 38 DF, p-value: 0.05171

for quotative 'like'. There is a preference for quotative 'say' among both the Polish and Chinese participants. All the participants make notable use of quotative zero. Quotative 'go' was used almost exclusively by the Irish participants. The proportion of quotative 'other'[13], especially among the Polish participants, was unexpectedly large.

Regression analyses were employed to test these observations. Mixed effects models were used. The advantage of using mixed effects models are that they can take into account by-speaker and by-item correlations and estimate both between-group effects, such as nationality, and within-group effects, such as the individual speaker (Tagliamonte, 2012: 138). Quotative 'go' was excluded from this analysis as there were only four tokens of it in the total dataset. In all of the mixed models described below, the speaker was included as a random effect, to decrease the possibility of the perceived group differences to be down to variation between speakers.

Quotative 'like'

No significant difference was found among rates of quotative 'like' among NS as compared to NNS. Nationality was also not found to be a significant predictor. However, when nationality was considered in interaction with gender, it was found that Polish males were the least likely to use quotative 'like'. The results are summarised in Table 5.15. No other predictors (including type of migrant) were found to have an effect.

Quotative Zero

For quotative zero, gender was found to be a near significant predictor, with males being more likely to use it than females ($p=0.0645$). Gender was not found to be significant in interaction with any other possible predictors for quotative zero. Type of migrant was found to be a significant predictor, with economic migrants the most likely to use quotative zero (Table 5.16). Level of education was also found to have an effect on use of quotative zero, with university-educated migrants (3rd and 4th level) less likely to use it ($p<0.02$ in both instances).

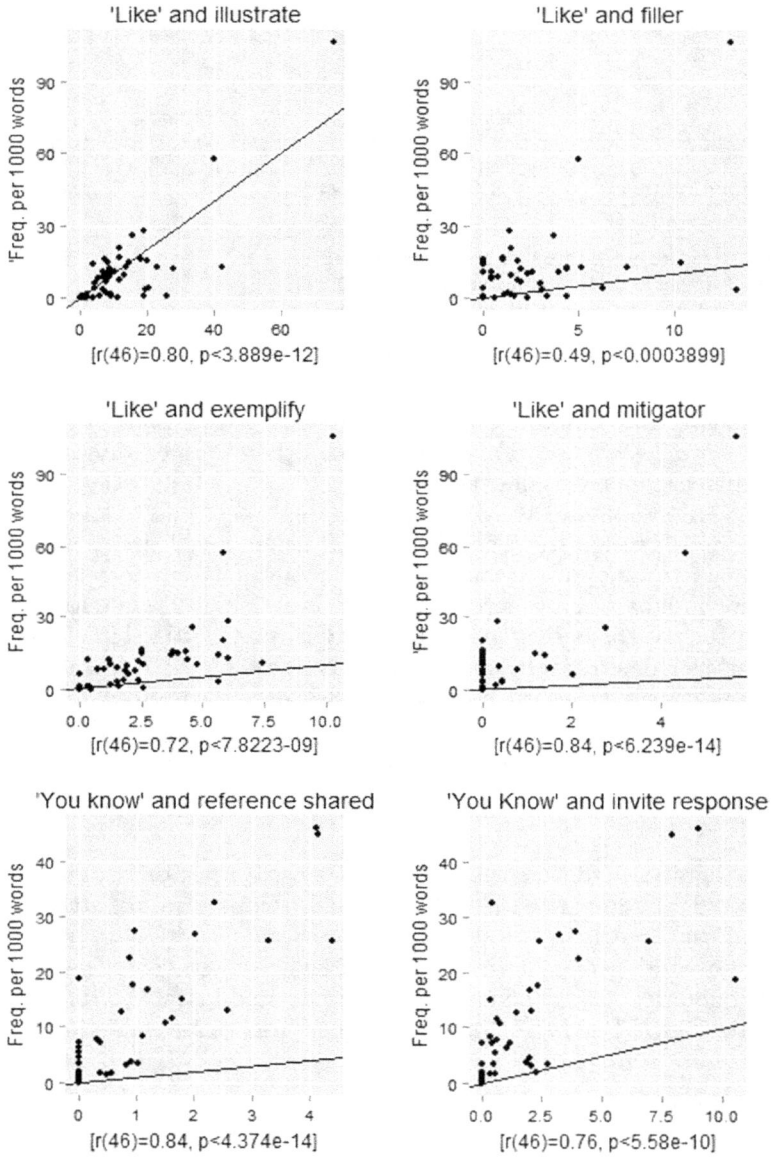

Figure 5.9 Function correlations

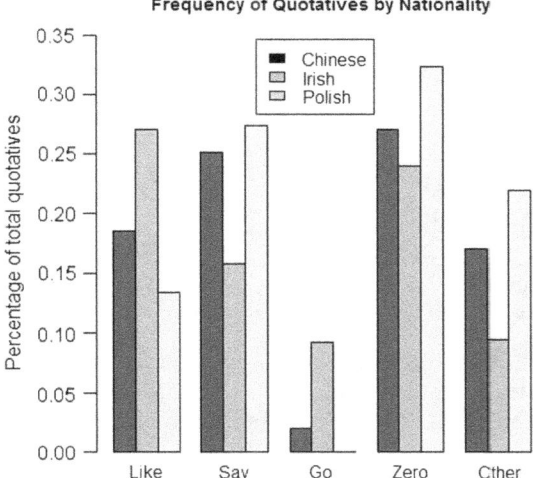

Figure 5.10 Frequency of quotatives by nationality

Quotative 'say'

For quotative 'say', nationality was found to be a near significant predictor, with the Irish being the least likely to use it ($p=0.0677$). Males were also found to be highly significant predictors of quotative 'say' (Table 5.17). No interactions or other predictors were found to be significant.

Quotative other

For quotative other, the least likely to use this quotative were the Irish and migrants with a LOR of six years or longer (Table 5.18). However, no

Table 5.15 Mixed effects model (interaction) for quotative 'like', nationality and gender

	Estimate	Standard Error	z value	Pr(>|t|)
(Intercept)	−1.0839	0.6120	−1.771	0.0765
Nationality: Irish	0.1605	1.1013	0.146	0.8841
Nationality: Polish	−1.8407	0.8759	−2.101	**0.0356***
Gender: Male	−2.6048	1.2282	−2.121	**0.0339***
Nationality Irish*Gender Male	2.8300	1.9610	1.443	0.1490
Nationality Polish*Gender Male	3.6497	1.5182	2.404	**0.0162***

Log Likelihood -144.9
Correlation of fixed effects (Nationality Polish: Gender Male*Gender Male): r=−0.828

Table 5.16 Mixed effects model for quotative zero and type of migrant

	Estimate	Standard Error	z value	Pr(>|t|)
(Intercept)	−2.2284	0.6196	−3.597	0.000322***
Type of Migrant: Chain	1.0121	0.7459	1.357	0.174816
Type of Migrant: Cultural	1.1571	0.7658	1.511	0.130826
Type of Migrant: Economic	1.9553	0.7014	2.788	**0.005305****
Irish	1.2129	0.8059	1.505	0.132350

Log Likelihood −205.2
Correlation of fixed effects (Type of Migrant: Economic*Type of Migrant: Chain): r=0.742

correlation was found for LOR and use of quotative other [r(39)=−0.02, $p=0.8831$]. Males were also found to be a significant predictor of non-usage of quotative other ($p<0.010363$). Economic migrants were also significant non-users of quotative other (Table 5.19).

Discussion

In terms of the overall rate of DPMs, it had been hypothesised that the NNS would use DPMs less than the NS. However, this was not found to be the case. This shows that DPMs are indeed a part of the communicative and pragmatic system for NNS and that there do not seem to be any particular constraints on their acquisition. Indeed, proficiency in English was not found to have an effect on frequency of DPM use. This goes against previous findings of a link between proficiency and frequency of DPMs among NNS (Hasselgreen, 2004; Neary-Sundquist, 2014).

Nonetheless, the expected hypothesis that those participants with a longer LOR would use more DPMs was found to be true. Also, in terms of migratory motivations, the cultural migrants used DPMs more than the other types of migrant. This suggests that DPM use is not a question of proficiency or linguistic competence, but it is a question of accommodation. Those with more integrative motivations towards Irish culture or simply those who have been in Ireland longer, have incorporated DPMs into their interactions more than others. This reflects the findings of Hellermann

Table 5.17 Mixed effects model for quotative 'say' and gender

	Estimate	Standard Error	z value	Pr(>|t|)
(Intercept)	−1.351247	0.001632	−828.1	<2e−16***
Gender: Male	0.252695	0.001631	154.9	**<2e−16*****

Log Likelihood −189.9
Correlation of fixed effects: r=0.00

Table 5.18 Mixed effects model for quotative other and length of residence

	Estimate	Standard Error	z value	Pr(>|t|)
(Intercept)	−0.006926	1.002934	−0.007	0.9945
LOR: 2 years	−0.597051	1.362950	−0.438	0.6613
LOR: 3 years	0.028662	1.406461	0.020	0.9837
LOR: 4 years	−0.479890	1.133892	−0.423	0.6721
LOR: 5 years	−1.125314	1.080876	−1.041	0.2978
LOR: 6 years+	−2.337663	1.072628	−2.179	**0.0293***
Irish	−3.061931	1.300793	−2.354	**0.0186***

Log Likelihood −165.9
Correlation of fixed effects (Nationality: Irish*Residence: 6 years+): r=−0.732

and Vergun (2007), who found a positive correlation between increased acculturation, longer LOR and use of DPMs.

When the analysis was broken down by individual DPM, it was shown that all participants preferred 'you know' to 'I mean'. This mirrors what was found in Kallen (2005) for speakers of Irish English as compared to British English. It is an interesting trend to observe among the NNS, who are orienting more towards Irish English rather than British English, even if their perceived notion of 'standard' may be more akin to British English features (as tends to be the trend in instructed English language settings outside of the English-speaking world).

Another take on 'you know' and 'I mean' could be text type. Fox Tree and Schrock (2002: 744) write that 'you know' encourages listeners to focus more on their own thoughts, and that 'I mean' encourages listeners to focus more on speakers' thoughts. Perhaps within the sociolinguistic interview, where the participant engages in long stretches of uninterrupted speech, participants are more concerned with their own thoughts than if they were partaking in a conversation with a lot of turn-taking and floor-holding. However, quite the opposite of Fox Tree and Schrock's observation was found in this study, with speakers opting for 'you know' even when

Table 5.19 Mixed effects model for quotative other and Type of Migrant

	Estimate	Standard Error	z value	Pr(>|t|)
(Intercept)	−0.6247	0.5270	−1.185	0.2358
Type of Migrant: Chain	−0.7677	0.6976	−1.101	0.2711
Type of Migrant: Cultural	−1.0213	0.7503	−1.361	0.1734
Type of Migrant: Economic	−1.3870	0.6688	−2.074	**0.0381***
Irish	−2.5715	1.0211	−2.518	**0.0118***

Log Likelihood −170.5
Correlation of fixed effects (Type of Migrant: Economic*Intercept): r=−0.735

they were concentrating on their own thoughts. Since all the interviews in this study were conducted under the same conditions, however, it is difficult to make any firm claims about variability within text type in relation to this study.

DPM 'like' showed a more nuanced distribution. The Irish used 'like' more as a DPM than the migrants. It was hypothesised that this would be the case due to its relatively marked status as non-standard and its associations with 'Valley Girl' speech and dysfluency. Whereas DPM (and quotative) 'like' have become grammaticalised in most varieties of English, for NNS, it may still be a salient and undesired variable which is being avoided. It was falsely predicted that proficiency in English would have an effect. The fact that DPM 'like' does not have equivalents in Polish, Mandarin or Cantonese may be a factor, however more proficient L2 users still do not use it more frequently. Instead, those participants with a longer LOR (and thus more exposure to the target language) used DPM 'like' more; specifically, those at the four year and six year+ mark.

It had been predicted that the Irish would be more likely to use CF 'like', since it is an almost uniquely Irish variable to which the participants would not have been exposed to prior to their arrival in Ireland. This was found to be the case. Being Irish was the single most significant predictor of CF 'like' use. The chain and economic migrants were also found to be significant predictors of usage of CF 'like'. This was unexpected. It suggests that chain and economic migrants may desire to accommodate more to Irish patterns than those migrants with cultural motivations. Indeed, the cultural migrants exhibited a preference for clause-medial 'like', which reflects a growing feature of South Dublin English (Amador-Moreno, 2010), but also a more general trend towards a 'global' preference for 'like' in this position.

One explanation for these trends is that CF 'like' is considered to be strongly indexical of 'Irishness' and that the NNS in this study did not aspire to 'sound Irish', but rather to sound unmarked, 'normal' and 'standard' (see Excerpt 1). It could be that the participants associated CF 'like' with sounding non-standard or incorrect and that for NNS, correctness in English is the aim, and not sounding native. Indeed, many migrants do not wish to lose the established sense of national identity from their country of origin and feel they may be disconnected from other migrants if they try to 'act' Irish (see Excerpt 2).

Excerpt 1

I try not to do the Irish accent too much. I don't want to have an accent. I just want to have a normal English accent. Instead of being like, classified or being stereotyped, like 'Oh you have an Irish accent' (Jemma; 20-year-old Chinese female; eight years living in Ireland; chain migrant)

Excerpt 2
You know, I am Polish... You hear my lovely Polish accent in everything that I'm saying. That's natural. I'm proud of it, okay. I will not lose it. I know people that try to lose the Polish accent. And that's not funny for me, because that sounds like acting. That you're trying to be somebody else that you're not really. I love my accent – as long as people can understand it, alright? (Aleksander; 33-year-old Polish male; six years living in Ireland; economic migrant)

It was expected that 'you know' would not display many inter-group differences, due to its socially neutral status and its equivalents in the L1s of the NNS. Surprisingly, however, the Polish contingent used 'you know' more than both the Chinese and the Irish. The most likely explanation is L1 transfer, and that *wiesz* ('you know') is used more frequently in Polish than in English and that it is easily transferred by NNS due to its salience and relatively liberal syntactic constraints. However, no previous quantitative studies on this topic were found to confirm this hypothesis.

'You know' was also employed more frequently by cultural migrants (both Polish and Chinese), and was employed the least by migrants educated to 4th level. There is no clear pattern here, however it could be surmised that 'you know' is used more by cultural migrants because of its interpersonal function, since cultural migrants are more interested in learning about the cultures of others. Perhaps those with a higher education had more fixed notions of 'standardness' in English and considered 'you know' to be too informal in the context of the sociolinguistic interview, where they were in conversation with the first author, who was also educated to 4th level.

In terms of the functions of DPMs in this study, it was found that, contrary to popular opinion, DPM 'like' is not primarily used as a filler. Instead, its most frequent function was as an illustrator and exemplifier. Thus DPM 'like' occupies crucial structural and communicative functions in interaction and is not simply something that is employed by a speaker who is 'buying time', trying to think of what to say next. As expected, 'you know' was positively correlated with referring to shared knowledge and inviting responses.

The quotative system also exhibited signs of inter-group variation. Interestingly, the quotative system was the only variable context in this study that displayed gender differences. Starting with quotative 'like', it had been hypothesised that it would behave much like the DPM 'like': it would be more frequent among cultural, more proficient and longer residence migrants. However, the only effect that was found was that Polish males had a negative effect on its usage. This suggests that quotative 'like' is not necessarily difficult to acquire by NNS. Quotative 'like', along with DPM 'like' has a perceived association with young females within the folk linguistic realm, and perhaps as a result, this feature was least desired by Polish males.

It was noteworthy that proficiency did not have an effect on quotative 'like' in this study, whereas Meyerhoff and Schleef (2013) found that their less proficient Polish participants in Edinburgh did not make use of quotative 'like' more than once in their entire corpus. Meyerhoff and Schleef attributed the lack of 'uptake' of quotative 'like' to its 'complex syntax-discourse interface' and agreed with Sorace (2003) that variable aspects of the grammar that require interface knowledge are particularly difficult to acquire to native-like standards (cited in Meyerhoff & Schleef, 2013: 15).

Gender differences were also encountered with quotative 'say' and zero, with males being the most likely to use them. Moreover, economic migrants were the most significant users of quotative zero whereas highly educated migrants were the least likely to use it. 'Say' is arguably the most conservative and unmarked form of quotative. Quotative zero is also unmarked. Usage of quotative 'say' is generally perceived as adhering to the 'standard' and is more formal than the other quotatives. It is also arguably the most frequent quotative featuring in English language textbooks and curricula at large. Indeed, the Irish were the least likely to use quotative 'say', perhaps because they also had 'like' and 'go' at their disposal, having been exposed to English in many more domains than the NNS. It could be argued that it is the Polish, lower-educated, economic migrant males (Polish males being the significant non-users of quotative 'like') that are driving the trend behind quotative 'say' and zero.

Quotative 'other' in this study was coded as such as it had been expected that its frequency counts would be very low, due to the other four quotatives covering the majority of quotatives within the system. In fact, quotative other occupied a central place within the quotative system of the NNS in this study, particularly among the Polish migrants. In terms of significance, again, there were more negative predictors than positive ones. Males, economic migrants, Irish and LOR of 6 years+ were the least likely to use quotative 'other'. Males and economic migrants were already found to be significant users of 'say' and zero; this thus explains their lower usage of 'other' (and 'like'). The Irish and LOR 6 years+ already aligned on DPM 'like', thus it is not surprising to see them behaving similarly in this domain also. It can be surmised that it is thus the Polish females that are the leading the quotative 'other' trend, although this did not explicitly emerge from the analysis.

Taking the domain of migratory experience in isolation, economic and cultural migrants displayed the greatest degrees of variation. This suggests that it is these two motivations in particular that can influence SLA in the context of migration. It had been expected that the cultural migrants, who are interested in migration from the perspective of learning about other cultures, would mirror the trends of the Irish more. However, it seems as though their cosmopolitan and 'trans-destinational' (King-O'Riain, 2008: 219) outlook means that they do not always align themselves with regionally or nationally bound features. A tentative hypothesis might be that the cultural migrants, who move fluidly across national boundaries and identify with a heterogeneous, transnational identity, are more 'standard' in their language use. They are content to index a number of different meanings, depending on the context in which they find themselves. This stance is observed in Excerpt 3:

Excerpt 3
I think in Europe, especially this time, we kind of like um, you know your personal identity or your nationality is not- it's kind of like more flexible and kind of like... It wouldn't be something that I would just... like being a Pole, a Polish woman, wouldn't be the very first thing that I would say about myself. There'd be other um... descriptions that would come first [...] Europe I think, people being so you know like, working here and there, travelling here and there, working for a few months here and then moving somewhere else....I don't think it's that important, and, you know, especially for our generation I guess (Agnieszka; 30-year-old Polish female; six years living in Ireland; cultural migrant)

Conclusion and Future Directions

This chapter has shown the importance of taking the migratory experience into account when conducting an analysis of SLA among NNS migrants. The division of the participants by type of migrant showed that there appeared to be examples of stance taking and identity work on the part of the economic and cultural migrants. The division by nationality showed that the Poles had a preference for 'you know', providing some evidence for L1 transfer. All the NNS followed the NS in their preference for 'you know' over 'I mean', showing that accommodation, especially when it is less socially marked, is happening at all levels of proficiency and length of residence. Finally, the avoidance of the 'Irish variable', clause-final 'like', by the NNS, shows a sensitivity to varietal variation and displays evidence of distinction and identity construction, which can be as much a process of countering trends as well as replicating them.

While this study focused heavily on inter-group differences in a migratory context, an interesting future direction would be to focus on the individuals themselves. Studies in indexicality (Eckert, 2008) focus on the situated use of variables in context, and emphasise the importance of style and stylistic variation. It would be fruitful to go deeper into the interview data to reveal more language attitudes and ideologies (such as the examples given in the previous section) especially in the realm of ideologies about standardness in language. It would also be useful to look at actions such as stance-taking at particular junctures where DPMs are being used, which may shed light on the positional variation of 'like'. There is a paucity of literature on CF 'like' in particular and it would be worthwhile to focus on this variable as indexing Irishness in particular. In the words of Mair (2009: 22), '"Like" and "be like" [...] are among the fastest-spreading constructions in English today'. It comes as no surprise that these innovations are also reflected in the English of non-native speakers.

Notes

(1) The authors would like to thank two anonymous reviewers, as well as the volume editors, for valuable comments on earlier drafts of this chapter. All further errors are our own.
(2) The data was collected by Chloé Diskin.
(3) While this percentage may not seem particularly high, it must be understood in the context of the long and ongoing tradition of Polish migration to Germany, due to factors such as geographical proximity.
(4) Quotative zero is when a quote is not introduced by any particle or marker, e.g. 'And then 'How about you? You and my dad, how are you?'' (Mei Hua).
(5) Self-assessment is not always a fully reliable method of assessing proficiency; however it was felt that if the participants were to be assessed more formally, they would feel under pressure throughout the conversation to conform to correctness, which was not the aim of the sociolinguistic interview.
(6) However, this was not a variable in this study. Kobiałka (2015) included this as a variable in her study and found it to have no significance.
(7) This participant was found to be an extreme outlier for most of the analyses in this study and was subsequently excluded from the majority of results described in this chapter.
(8) Kobiałka (2015) discusses this phenomenon in more detail.
(9) ELAN is an open source annotation tool suitable for creating complex annotations of both audio and video resources.
(10) Due to its low frequency, the clause position 'between units' was subsequently discarded from the analysis provided in this chapter.
(11) In Regan (2013), LOR and proficiency were found to be significant predictors of acquisition of vernacular norms.
(12) In all of the tables containing mixed effects regression output, only the most significant correlation of fixed effects has been included.
(13) The majority of quotative 'other' was quotative 'ask' or 'tell'.

References

Aijmer, K. (2002) *English Discourse Particles. Evidence from a Corpus*. Amsterdam/Philadelphia: John Benjamins.

Aijmer, K. (2013) *Understanding Pragmatic Markers. A Variational Pragmatic Approach*. Edinburgh: Edinburgh University Press.
Amador-Moreno, C.P. (2010) *An Introduction to Irish-English*. London: Equinox.
Andersen, G. (2001) *Pragmatic Markers and Sociolinguistic Variation. A Relevance-Theoretic Approach to the Language of Adolescents*. Amsterdam/Philadelphia: John Benjamins.
Bartlett, J. (2013) 'Oh I just talk normal like': A corpus-based, longitudinal study of constituent-final like in Tyneside English. *Newcastle Working Papers in Linguistics* 19 (1), 1–21.
Blakemore, D. (2002) *Relevance and Linguistic Meaning: The Semantics and Pragmatics of Discourse Markers*. Cambridge: Cambridge University Press.
Blommaert, J. (2010) *The sociolinguistics of globalization*. Cambridge: Cambridge University Press.
Brinton, L.J. (1996) *Pragmatic Markers in English: Grammaticalization and Discourse Functions*. Berlin: Mouton de Gruyter.
Central Statistics Office (2012a) *Profile 6: Migration and Diversity*. Dublin: Stationery Office.
Central Statistics Office (2012b) *This is Ireland: Highlights from Census 2011, Part 1*. Dublin: Stationery Office.
Council of Europe (2001) Common European framework of reference for languages: Learning, teaching, assessment. Strasbourg: Language Policy Unit. www.coe.int/lang-CEFR (accessed 24 July 2014).
D'Arcy, A. (2010) Quoting ethnicity: Constructing dialogue in Aotearoa/New Zealand. *Journal of Sociolinguistics* 14 (1), 60–88.
Debaene, E. (2013) Emigration versus mobility. The case of the Polish community in France and Ireland. In D. Singleton, V. Regan and E. Debaene (eds) *Linguistic and Cultural Acquisition in a Migrant Community* (pp. 1–27). Bristol: Multilingual Matters.
Eckert, P. (2008) Variation and the indexical field. *Journal of Sociolinguistics* 12 (4), 453–476.
Erman, B. (1986) Some pragmatic expressions in English conversation. In G. Tottie and I. Bäcklund (eds) *English in Speech and Writing. A Symposium* (pp. 131–147). Acta Univ. Ups., Studia Anglistica Upsaliensia 60. Uppsala: Academiae Upsaliensi.
Erman, B. (2001) Pragmatic markers revisited with a focus on *you know* in adult and adolescent talk. *Journal of Pragmatics* 33, 1337–1359.
Ferrara, K. and Bell, B. (1995) Sociolinguistic variation and discourse function of constructed dialogue introducers: The case of Be+Like. *American Speech* 70, 265–290.
Fox Tree, J.E. and Schrock, J.C. (2002) Basic meanings of you know and I mean. *Journal of Pragmatics* 34, 727–747.
Fuller, J.M. (2003) Discourse marker use across speech contexts: A comparison of native and non-native speaker performance. *Multilingua* 22, 185–208.
Hansen, M.-B.M. (1998) *The Function of Discourse Particles. A Study with Special Reference to Spoken Standard French*. Amsterdam/Philadelphia: John Benjamins.
Hasselgreen, A. (2004) *Testing the Spoken English of Young Norwegians: A Study of Test Validity and the Role of 'smallwords' in Contributing to Pupils' Fluency*. Cambridge: Cambridge University Press.
Hellermann, J. and Vergun, A. (2007) Language which is not taught: The discourse marker use of beginning adult learners of English. *Journal of Pragmatics* 39 (1), 157–179.
ICE-Great Britain (1998) The International Corpus of English: The British Component. Survey of English Usage, University College London.
ICE-Ireland (1997) The International Corpus of English: The Ireland Component. Queen's University Belfast & Trinity College Dublin.
Jørgensen, J.N. (2008) Polylingual languaging around and among children and adolescents. *International Journal of Multilingualism* 5 (3), 161–176.

Kallen, J. (2005) Silence and mitigation in Irish English discourse. In A. Barron and K.P. Schneider (eds) *The Pragmatics of Irish English* (pp. 47–71). Berlin: Mouton de Gruyter.

Kallen, J. (2006) Arrah, Like, You Know: The dynamics of discourse-marking in ICE-Ireland. Sociolinguistics Symposium 16. University of Limerick, Limerick, Ireland.

King-O'Riain, R.C. (2008) Target earning/learning, settling or trampolining? Polish and Chinese immigrants in Ireland. *Irish Geography* 41, 211–223.

Kobiałka, E. (2015) Language variation, identity and social class. Unpublished PhD thesis. University College Dublin.

Labov, W. (1972) *Sociolinguistic Patterns*. Philadelphia: University of Pennsylvania Press.

Lennon, P. (1990) Investigating fluency in EFL: A quantitative approach. *Language Learning* 40 (3), 387–417.

Levitt, P. and Jaworsky, B.N. (2007) Transnational migration studies: Past developments and future trends. *Annual Review of Sociology* 33, 129–156.

Li, W. (2011) Moment Analysis and translanguaging space: Discursive construction of identities by multilingual Chinese youth in Britain. *Journal of Pragmatics* 43, 1222–1235.

Luckmann, K. (2009) The pragmatic marker like in clause-final position: Its functional and social distribution in Irish English. Unpublished MA thesis. University of Duisburg-Essen, Germany.

Macaulay, R. (2002) You know, it depends. *Journal of Pragmatics* 34, 749–767.

Mair, C. (2009) Corpus linguistics meets sociolinguistics: The role of corpus evidence in the study of sociolinguistic variation and change. In A. Renouf and A. Kehoe (eds) *Corpus Linguistics: Refinements and Reassessments* (pp. 7–32). Amsterdam/New York: Rodopi.

Meyerhoff, M. and Schleef, E. (2013) Hitting an Edinburgh target: Immigrant adolescents' acquisition of variation in Edinburgh English. In R. Lawson (ed.) *Sociolinguistic Perspectives on Scotland* (pp. 103–128). Basingstoke: Palgrave Macmillan.

Moore, R. (2011) 'If I Actually Talked Like That, I'd Pull a Gun on Myself': Accent, avoidance, and moral panic in Irish English. *Anthropological Quarterly* 84, 41–64.

Müller, S. (2005) *Discourse Markers in Native and Non-native English Discourse*. Amsterdam/Philadelphia: John Benjamins.

Neary-Sundquist, C. (2014) The use of pragmatic markers across proficiency levels in second language speech. *Studies in Second Language Learning and Teaching* 4 (4), 637–663.

Nestor, N. (2013) The positional distribution of discourse *like* – A case study of young Poles in Ireland. In D. Singleton, V. Regan and E. Debaene (eds) *Linguistic and Cultural Acquisition in a Migrant Community* (pp. 49–74). Bristol: Multilingual Matters.

Nestor, N., Ní Chasaide, C. and Regan, V. (2012) Discourse 'like' and social identity – A case study of Poles in Ireland. In B. Migge and M. Ní Chiosáin (eds) *New Perspectives on Irish English* (pp. 327–354). Amsterdam/Philadelphia: John Benjamins.

Pan, D. (2011) Student visas, undocumented labour, and the boundaries of legality: Chinese migration and English as a foreign language education in the Republic of Ireland. *Social Anthropology/Anthropologie Sociale* 19, 268–287.

Regan, V. (2013) The bookseller and the basketball player: Tales from the French Polonia. In: D. Singleton, V. Regan and E. Debaene (eds) *Linguistic and Cultural Acquisition in a Migrant Community* (pp. 28–48). Bristol: Multilingual Matters Ltd.

Romero Trillo, J. (2002) The pragmatic fossilization of discourse markers in non-native speakers of English. *Journal of Pragmatics* 34, 769–784.

Sankoff, G., Thibault, P., Nagy, N., Blondeau, H., Fonollosa, M.-O. and Gagnon, L. (1997) Variation in the use of discourse markers in a language contact situation. *Language Variation and Change* 9, 191–218.

Schiffrin, D. (1987) *Discourse Markers*. Cambridge: Cambridge University Press.

Schweinberger, M. (2012) The discourse marker LIKE in Irish English. In B. Migge and M. Ní Chiosáin (eds) *New Perspectives on Irish English* (pp. 179–202). Amsterdam/Philadelphia: John Benjamins.

Siemund, P., Maier, G. and Schweinberger, M. (2009) Towards a more fine-grained analysis of the areal distributions of non-standard features of English. In E. Pentilla and H. Paulasto (eds) *Language Contacts Meet English Dialects: Studies in Honour of Markku Filppula* (pp. 19–46). Newcastle upon Tyne: Cambridge Scholars Publishing.

Sorace, A. (2003) Near-nativeness. In C.J. Doughty and M.H. Long (eds) *The Handbook of Second Language Acquisition* (pp. 130–152). Oxford: Blackwell.

Stubbe, M. and Holmes, J. (1995) You know, eh and other 'exasperating expressions': An analysis of social and stylistic variation in the use of pragmatic devices in a sample of New Zealand English. *Language and Communication* 15, 63–88.

Svartvik, J. (1980) *Well* in conversation. In S. Greenbaum, G. Leech and J. Svartvik (eds) *Studies in English Linguistics for Randolph Quirk* (pp. 167–177). London: Longman.

Tagliamonte, S. (2009) *Be like*: The new quotative in English. In N. Coupland and A. Jaworski (eds) *The New Sociolinguistics Reader* (pp. 75–91). Basingstoke: Palgrave Macmillan.

Tagliamonte, S. (2012) *Variationist Sociolinguistics: Change, Observation, Interpretation*. Malden, MA: Wiley-Blackwell.

Tagliamonte, S. and Hudson, R. (1999) Be like et al. beyond America: The quotative system in British and Canadian youth. *Journal of Sociolinguistics* 3 (2), 147–172.

Underhill, R. (1988) *Like* is like, focus. *American Speech* 63 (3), 234–246.

Vertovec, S. (2007) Super-diversity and its implications. *Ethnic and Racial Studies* 30, 1024–1054.

Wang, Y. and Chiyoko King-O'Riain, R. (2006) *Chinese Students in Ireland*. Dublin: National Consultative Committee on Racism and Interculturalism (NCCRI).

6 Acculturation as the Key to the *Ultimate* Attainment? The Case of Polish-English Bilinguals in the UK[1]

Kate Hammer and Jean-Marc Dewaele

Introduction

Attainment in the second language is both a fascinating and controversial topic of research in the field of second language acquisition (SLA) (Abrahamsson & Hyltenstam, 2009; Hyltenstam, 2014). Ultimate attainment refers to the final stage of second language (L2) learning. In exceptional cases it can result in native-likeness, namely a unique ability to speak the L2 in the way native speakers do (Birdsong, 2006). Some researchers have claimed that absolute native-likeness is impossible and cases thereof are to be perceived as pathology no less than cases of L1 acquisition failure (Bley-Vroman, 1989). Bylund *et al.* (2012) addressed the question of a potential negative influence of L1 maintenance on L2 ultimate attainment. The authors investigated whether L1 use hampers L2 development and ultimately blocks the achievement of high proficiency levels in the L2. They found no link between L1 maintenance and ultimate attainment but stressed the importance of language aptitude in SLA research. Schumann's Acculturation Model for SLA highlighted the importance of socio-cultural and psychological aspects of ultimate attainment and recognised acculturation (ACC) as the main causal variable in SLA (Schumann, 1986). Debaene and Harris (2013), who studied Polish-English bilinguals in Ireland, pointed out that passing for a native speaker and speech accommodation in the context of migration are to be analysed in the light of social identity theory, migration theory, group identity and individualism. Investigations into proficiency in L2 and ultimate attainment, as presented in the following sections of this chapter, are typically undertaken in relation to age of acquisition, as well as linguistic accuracy, language use, immersion and acculturation.

The aim of the present chapter is to develop the line of research on the relationship between migration, acculturation and L2 attainment (Graham & Brown, 1996; Jiang et al., 2009; Maple, 1982; Schrauf, 2009; Schumann, 1986, 1978; Singleton et al., 2013) combining both quantitative and qualitative approaches. L2 attainment in this sense is understood as the highest level of proficiency achieved, and not as native-likeness. Potential links between variables traditionally linked to acculturation and SLA are investigated in this chapter in relation to L2 attainment. The following sections present an overview of the literature as well as the research questions, methods, results, discussion and some concluding remarks.

Literature Review

Age of onset

Age of onset (AoA) and the context of learning the L2 are two of the most investigated independent variables in SLA research (Cook & Singleton, 2014; Dewaele, 2013). Age of onset is of particular interest when studying and comparing early and late bilinguals (cf. Paradis, 2007; Pavlenko, 2014). Age of onset has been linked to the critical period hypothesis (CPH) which rests on the assumption that there is an ultimate point in the lifespan after which the initiation of L2 acquisition is unlikely to result in reaching high levels of L2 attainment (cf. Birdsong, 2005; Lenneberg, 1967; Singleton, 2003). SLA initiated at the age of 17 or more is said to fail to result in instances of native-likeness in the L2 (Abrahamsson & Hyltenstam, 2009). The age of nine years old, on the other hand, is associated with cognitive restructuring in monolinguals (Pavlenko, 2011). Previous studies on self-reported proficiency in multilinguals concluded that age of onset of the L2 has a significant effect on self-perceived competence in the L2 (Dewaele, 2009a, 2009b, 2010; Munro & Mann, 2005). L2 users who start learning their L2 earlier in life have been shown to reach higher level of self-perceived proficiency in the L2 and they tend to rate their communicative competence higher. Age of onset is understood in some areas of literature as age at migration; however, Pavlenko (2011, 2014) recommends that future studies continue to distinguish between these two variables. Age at migration is said to be linked with either L1- or L2-oriented naming patterns. Bilinguals with higher age on arrival are said to be under a greater influence of L1 in ways they name and classify objects (Pavlenko, 2011).

Abrahamsson and Hyltenstam (2009) conducted a study on 195 Spanish-Swedish bilinguals in order to find out if *most* early and *some* late learners of the L2 can be perceived as native speakers, and whether those who do pass for native speakers maintain that status when tested over a wide range of variables. They wanted to find out what age relations, if any, exist and what patterns, if any, emerge for the groups. They found that native-like attainment in the L2 is linked with age of onset and that passing for a native speaker does not occur for those learners whose onset would equal or exceed the end of puberty set as 17 years of age. Their conclusions were congruent with previous findings by Flege et al. (1995).

Similarly, Kopeckova (2013) found that 20 younger Polish L1 learners were able to distinguish and imitate English vowels more successfully than 20 older learners. She attributed this aptitude to increased perceptual abilities in cross-language phonetic similarity in young learners. The latter resulted in more accurate acquisition of L2 segments which ultimately translated into better pronunciation. Her findings matched those of Abrahamsson (2012) who studied 200 Spanish-Swedish bilinguals and found that lower AoA raises the likelihood of achieving native-like phonetic and morphosyntactic intuition in the L2. Participants in his study had spent on average 15 years in Sweden and were compared against a control group of 20 native speakers of Swedish. Abrahamsson found that native-like morphosyntactic and phonetic intuition ceased to occur after the age of 13. Pronunciation is a necessary element in achieving native-likeness, however, it is not sufficient in its own right to pass for a native speaker; in the same way that age of acquisition is seen to be a necessary yet not sufficient requirement for native-like attainment in the L2 (Hyltenstam & Abrahamsson, 2003).

Dewaele (2009b) found also that age of onset had an effect on language choice for emotional expression and mental calculation. In general, the earlier in life the L2 is acquired the higher the likelihood that the L2 user will choose the L2 to communicate emotions and the higher the age of onset, the more likely it is that L1 will remain the more emotional language (Dewaele, 2009b). However, a relatively age-independent hypothesis of the emotional context of learning predicts that the language which is learnt in an emotional context is more likely to be perceived as an emotional language, regardless of the age of acquisition (Harris et al., 2006). Shared emotional contexts have the potential to alter language preferences and ways of emotional expression in people. De Leersnyder et al. (2011) found that people who experience emotional situations together tend to approximate their emotional expression to match that of their companions which in case of L2 acquisition in circumstances of migration can result in the phenomenon of emotional acculturation. Studies on migrants in the USA (Korean L1) and Belgium (Turkish L1) showed correlations between patterns of emotional expression between the migrants and respective native speakers. Exposure and engagement in the L2 culture and emotional context of L2 use served as predictors of emotional acculturation (De Leersnyder et al., 2011: 460). In other words, age of onset is not the only factor to consider.

Context of acquisition

Investigations into the effect of the context of L2 acquisition provided evidence that mixed instructed and naturalistic language learning increases the likelihood of the L2 user feeling more proficient than users who experienced solely instructed language learning (Dewaele, 2010). Also prolonged contact with native speakers of the target language as well as staying abroad and language immersion were found to have a significant effect on both productive and receptive language skills in the L2 (cf. Ożanska-Ponikwia, 2013; Taguchi, 2008). Dewaele (2010) found also that speakers who experienced mixed or naturalistic language learning were more likely to consider the foreign language as their 'language of the heart' (Dewaele, 2010: 74). This in turn highlights the significance of experiencing language and accounting for the psychological and emotional dimensions of instructed language learning in the quest of becoming a proficient user of that language (cf. Dewaele, 2005, 2011).

Frequency of use

Frequency of L2 use is considered a crucial antecedent of L2 competence and high frequency of L2 use has a positive effect on language learning (Flege, 1999; Flege et al., 1997). Moreover, languages used sporadically are said to be at a risk of attrition due to decreased levels of activation (Green, 1986). Studies on the relationship between general frequency of L2 use and self-perceived proficiency show that frequency of use has a significant effect on the self-perceived level of competence (Dewaele, 2010). The more the L2 is used, the more proficient the L2 user feels in that language. Studies on L2 immersion showed that frequent target language use in the native environment for that language boosts the acquisition of different skills including sociolinguistic and pragmatic competence (Mougeon et al., 2010; Regan 2013). Increased interaction rates in the L2 are moreover associated with decreased adaptation problems and more overall fluency in the L2 (Ward & Kennedy, 1993). Evidence of rapid development of the L2 in immersion situations was found not only for communicative and cultural competence but also for a development of grammar (cf. Howard, 2005).

Bylund et al. (2012) studied 30 Spanish-Swedish early bilinguals who had lived in the L2 speaking country (Sweden) for an average of 23 years. The participants' frequency of L1 use was less than 30%. The authors wanted to answer the question whether L1 hampers the ultimate attainment in the L2. The study referred to the balance theory of bilingualism and its assumption that the two languages of the bilingual make up the total language ability in the mind which in turn makes them compete for the finite memory resources. The participants were tested in each of their languages on two occasions and both their language accuracy and aptitude were measured. Results showed a positive correlation between L1 and L2 performance and no inverse relationship between the two languages was found. High proficiency in the L1 proved to be neutral, while low L1 proficiency showed to be neither beneficial nor necessary for L2 attainment. Language aptitude, however, proved to be an important factor in the ultimate attainment and reaching the ultimate proficiency in the L2.

Gender, age and education level

Self-perceived proficiency in the L2 has also been linked to socio-biographical variables such as gender, age and education level. Previous studies show that females typically report higher self-perceived proficiency levels in comparison to males (Dewaele, 2010; Pavlenko et al., 2003). Studies by Dewaele (2010) revealed systematic age differences in self-perceived competence in the L2. A significant increase in self-perceived competence was noted after the age of 30, continuing into the 40s and 50s. Education level had a significant and systematic effect on self-perceived competence in the L2 with more highly educated participants feeling more competent in the L2 (Dewaele, 2010).

Acculturation

Schumann linked SLA with socio-cultural and psychological processes of acculturation (1978, 1986). Acculturation in this context is understood as '(...) those phenomena which result when groups of individuals having different cultures come into continuous first-hand contact with subsequent changes in the original culture patterns of either or both groups' (Redfield et al., 1936: 149). A more operational definition of acculturation was provided by Brown (1994) who defined acculturation as the 'process of becoming adapted to a new culture where reorientation of thinking and feeling is necessary' (p. 169). Acculturation level therefore refers to a degree to which a migrant adopts the new way of living in the host country, the extent to which s/he develops native-like habits, follows host-country customs, as well as the depth to which s/he internalises host country values. Acculturation level refers to a degree of socio-cultural and linguistic integration in the host country (Boski, 2008).

Schumann's Acculturation model for SLA is applicable in the context of migration and is based on the prediction that the L2 learner will acquire the target language to the degree to which s/he acculturates into the target language community. Acculturation is thus viewed as a link between SLA, cultural psychology and socio-cultural anthropology, and it serves as a multidisciplinary variable employed in post-structuralist approaches to L2 learning and L2 use (Pavlenko, 2002). The main strength of Schumann's model is not only the inclusion of psycho-social variables into the equation of SLA research but also its potential robustness to uncover the *whys* behind high levels of L2 attainment; for language is intrinsically mixed with the social context, acculturation can be viewed as a major causal variable in SLA (Pavlenko, 2011). Critics of the acculturation model point to its ambivalent approach towards instructed learning and do not see how prolonged contact with target language speakers can lead to higher proficiency levels (Kelley, 1982; Stauble, 1981). Dervin (2013) perceives acculturation as a notion detrimental to migration studies and an interaction between the cultural *self* and *other* which he perceives to be an unethical manifestation of pygmalionism (Dervin, 2013). Other researchers view acculturation as a language related variable which should be examined in order to facilitate foreign language acquisition and as means of increasing communicative competence (Spitzberg, 1988). Also the attraction of the *other* tends to be understood as a motivation strategy employed by foreign language learners in their quest to become multilingual subjects (Kramsch, 2009).

Schumann's (1978) theory combines both the affective (psychological) and integrative (social) aspects and recognises identification with the target language group as a prerequisite for successful SLA. Instructed context of acquisition is specifically not accounted for in the acculturation model (Ellis, 1994). Identification with the target language community is said to be achieved by overcoming the perceived social and psychological distance between the two cultures. The levels of social and psychological distance are seen as crucial indicators when assessing the acculturation level, for the greater the perceived distance, the more difficult it is for the learner to acquire the target language (Brown, 2007; Schumann, 1978; Ushioda, 1993). How distant or how close learners perceive themselves to be in relation to the target culture and how much they see themselves as part of that culture either fosters their language acquisition or hinders it (Damen, 1987; Ellis, 1994). Gass and Selinker (2008) stress that the level of social and psychological distance between the learner and the target language community dictates the amount of input that learners receive. As the target language input is received in the circumstances of regular contact between the learner and the target language speakers, the socio-cultural context of interaction is considered essential from the point of view of both SLA and socio-cultural adaptation (Masgoret & Ward, 2006; Norton Pierce, 1995). Perceived psycho-social proximity, as opposed to psycho-social distance, aids integrative processes and is likely to result in acculturation which 'initiates a chain reaction including contact in the middle and acquisition as its outcome' (Gass & Selinker, 2008: 404).

The relationship between linguistic performance and social interaction in the migration context has been suggested to be a reciprocal one (Clément *et al.*, 2001), which provides indirect support for the Schumann's model for SLA. Lybeck (2002) notes also that shift in pronunciation patterns to resemble native speakers is viewed as a strong marker of cultural identification with the target language group and may be a symptom of the development of a new cultural identity and thus neutralisation or eradication of the psycho-social distance. This confirms earlier studies of German-born American immigrants conducted by Hansen (1995) which showed that native-like phonation is attainable by immigrants who acculturate to a higher level. According to Ellis (1994) Schumann's model is based on developmental understanding of SLA and aims to explain inter-individual variation in the level of L2 attainment among SLA learners. The overall social and psychological circumstances as well as the attitude towards the target language and the target group community have an impact on the ultimate success of language learning experience (Ellis, 1994).

Graham and Brown (1996) conducted a study on a group of 48 native Spanish speakers in Mexico's Colonia Juarez who attended a two-way bilingual programme with English as L2 at school. The main research question was whether social and affective variables are linked to the participant's level of proficiency and whether they contribute to the development of L2 proficiency outside of the classroom and in a broader social context. The attainment of native-like proficiency in the L2 was found to be linked to positive attitudes towards the English-speaking community and developing close friendships with English speaking peers. Similar conclusions were drawn by Masgoret and Gardner (1999), who found that psychological and linguistic assimilation to the host community is significantly linked to increased L2 proficiency levels.

Jiang *et al.* (2009) conducted an exploratory study of 49 Chinese-English late SLA learners enrolled at US universities, in order to investigate whether acculturation to the host society is associated with higher levels of L2 proficiency and pronunciation. Results showed that increased levels of acculturation were strongly linked with increased levels of L2 speaking proficiency (Jiang *et al.*, 2009). Participants who acculturated to the host society to a higher degree were reported to achieve higher levels of L2 proficiency, when compared to participants whose acculturation levels were lower, and who displayed higher levels of psycho-social distance. These results confirmed earlier findings by Maple (1982), who studied the relationship between L2 proficiency and social distance in a group 190 adult Spanish students learning English L2 in the US. He found a significant link between the learners' proficiency in L2 and their level of social distance. Participants with lower levels of social distance achieved increased levels of L2 proficiency (Maple, 1982). Tight links found between the levels of L2 proficiency, social distance and acculturation provide support for Schumann's Acculturation model for SLA (Jiang *et al.*, 2009; Maple, 1982).

Schrauf (2009) measured language proficiency and language use among 60 older Puerto Ricans who migrated to the mainland and lived in ethnically concentrated neighbourhoods. Participants self-rated their English proficiency ranging from low intermediate through high intermediate to fluent and they declared their language preferences across different areas of life and in relation to different interlocutors. The study was based on the view that the level of exposure and engagement in the L2 via different sociolinguistic contexts is the main predictor of L2 proficiency level. Participants' acculturation level was measured according to the *Puerto Rican Bicultural Scale*. Results revealed significant differences between individuals and lower levels of proficiency were strongly linked to low acculturation levels as well as lower socioeconomic status. Schrauf concluded that the 'level of second language proficiency is a potent source of intracultural variation' (p. 157).

Multiple studies of Polish migrants in Ireland, Austria and France carried out in different contexts by Singleton *et al.* (2013) showed that higher levels of integration into the host society generally correlate with higher frequency of L2 use. The authors studied different waves of migration in three different locations. Language use was said to reflect the degree of integration in the L2 culture (cf. Regan, 2013).

Motivation

Motivation behind L2 learning is a prominent aspect of SLA research (Dörnyei & Ushioda, 2009). Dörnyei and Ushioda (2011) accentuate the importance of L2 self, language identity and identification as well as integrative motivation in processes of language learning. L2 learners are surrounded by dynamic contexts which are constantly changing due to processes of globalisation and evolving visions of the ideal L2 self. Processes of migration and acculturation can be seen as such dynamic contexts in which learners' motivations develop and processes of SLA take place. Schumann (1978) claimed that motivation, among other sociocultural factors, has a significant impact on SLA and that high levels of motivation are linked to increased success in SLA. According to Schumann motivation is an important element characterising the level of psychological distance in L2 learners. Also Giles and Smith (1979) and Gardner (2001) viewed motivation as the main determinant of L2 proficiency and concluded that L2 speakers will try to modify their speech accordingly to their intention of reducing social distance between them and the host community (Giles & Smith, 1979; Gardner, 2001).

Age at migration and length of residence

Age at migration is considered to be a powerful predictor of L2 proficiency (Jia *et al.*, 2002). The lower the age at migration is, the higher the possibility for a complete attainment of the L2. Finally, length of residence in the host country has an influence on L2 attainment (Bialystok, 1997). It is not only synonymous with receiving extended input of the L2 but it is connected with cognitive restructuring in bilinguals and effectively 're-naming the world' (Pavlenko, 2011: 199).

Method

Participants

A total of 149 Polish-English bilinguals took part in the study. A majority of the participants were female (86% versus 14% male). This is a typical gender distribution in online questionnaires on language issues (Wilson & Dewaele, 2010). All participants were L1-Polish/L2-English bilinguals with a university/college degree who migrated in early adulthood and were professionally or academically active in the host country. The decision to migrate to an English-speaking country in early adulthood was a life-choice decision made by all participants. The average age of the participants was 31 years old and ages ranged from 23 to 45 years (Mean=31.1, SD=4.7). The average age at migration was 23 years old and ranged from 18 to 41 years of age (Mean=23.6, SD=3.8). All participants were university or college graduates of which over a half (58.4%) held MA level qualification, followed by over a quarter (26.2%) of BA holders, 10.1% of PhD holders and the remaining 5.4% were College graduates. Almost a half of the respondents (45.6%), felt proficient in their English L2, 38.3% declared to have native-like proficiency, 14.1% self-rated as advanced speakers and 2% declared to have an intermediate level of proficiency in English. Only 20% of the participants knew a third language at the level comparable to their L2 or L1. All were sequential bilinguals who learnt the L2 in the process of SLA and the earliest age of onset of L2 acquisition was the age of 3, while the average age of onset was 12 years (Mean=12.3 years, SD=4.6). Over a half of the participants started learning English before the age of 13.

Instrument

Participants filled out an online questionnaire containing close-ended Likert scale questions as well as open-ended questions (Hammer, 2012). Fourteen participants were interviewed by the first author as part of the study. The closed questions in the online questionnaire measured levels of self-reported proficiency, frequency of L2 use and acculturation. Acculturation level was measured using the following close-ended question: *Acculturation is a process roughly defined as: social and psychological integration with the target language group. How integrated with your English language group do you feel?* Participants chose one out of five available answers which included the following levels: *Completely / Highly / Moderately / Slightly / Not at all* (Hammer, 2012). Other closed questions elicited information on context of L2 acquisition, gender, education level and motivation behind migration. Open-ended questions elicited information on age of onset, age at migration, current age and length of domicile in the English-speaking country. Semi-structured interviews and other open-ended questions in the questionnaire investigated the experience of linguistic transition between L1 and L2 following migration. The questions asked included the following: *(1) Think of the time when you first moved to this country. How did you find the change from Polish to English in the majority of public situations? Has anything changed since that time? (2) Do you think that your journey from using Polish in your daily life - to using English - has taught you something? (3) Your English and Polish today - do they have different roles in your life? How do you feel about each of them?* (Hammer, 2012). The questions served as a starting point and prompted respondents to share their linguistic experience following migration. Responses were later analysed qualitatively and the categories created included evidence of social and cultural integration, length of domicile, frequency of language use and emotional acculturation.

A one-sample Kolmogorov-Smirnov test revealed that the values for self-perceived proficiency level in L2 are not normally distributed (Kolmogorov-Smirnov Z value=2.9, $p<.0001$); therefore Kruskal-Wallis and Mann-Whitney tests were used as non-parametric equivalents of one-way ANOVAs and independent t-tests.

Research questions and hypotheses

Three research questions were formulated in order to investigate possible links between L2 attainment and (1) post-migration sociolinguistic aspects; (2) temporal predictors of L2 attainment; and (3) socio-biographical variables:

(1) Is self-reported proficiency level in the L2 linked to acculturation level and frequency of L2 use?
(2) To what extent do age of onset, age at migration and length of domicile in the host country predict self-reported proficiency in the L2?
(3) Is there a link between self-reported proficiency in the L2 and socio-biographical variables such as context of L2 acquisition, education level, age, gender and motivation behind migration?

Two hypotheses were formulated to address the first research question, which investigates the sociolinguistic aspects of L2 attainment, namely:

Hypothesis 1: Participants with higher levels of acculturation will attain higher proficiency levels in L2;

188 Part 2: Culture as a Decisive Factor in L2 Attainment

Hypothesis 2: Participants who use the L2 more frequently will attain higher proficiency levels in L2;

Three hypotheses were formulated to address the second research question, which investigates the temporal aspects of L2 attainment, namely:

Hypothesis 3: Participants with lower age of onset will attain higher proficiency levels in L2 following migration;

Hypothesis 4: Participants with lower age at migration will attain higher proficiency levels in L2;

Hypothesis 5: Participants with greater length of domicile will attain higher proficiency levels in L2;

Three hypotheses were formulated to address the third research question, which investigates the socio-biographical aspects of L2 attainment, namely:

Hypothesis 6: Participants with culturally-oriented motivation behind migration will attain higher proficiency levels in L2, than participants whose motivation behind migration was socio-economic;

Hypothesis 7: Participants who started learning the L2 in a mixed context will attain higher proficiency levels in L2, than participants whose context of L2 acquisition was purely instructed or naturalistic;

Hypothesis 8: Female participants, as well as participants with higher education level and higher age will attain higher proficiency levels in L2.

The results section presents the findings under two main strands, namely ACC and SLA. The two mains strands serve as the umbrella under which the sociocultural, temporal and socio-biographical aspects are investigated.

Results

The effect of acculturation level on self-perceived proficiency level in L2

A Kruskal-Wallis test revealed a significant effect of acculturation level on self-perceived proficiency level in L2 ($\chi^2=11.1$, $p \leq .004$) with a mean rank of 59.6 for moderately (and less) acculturated migrants, 75.15 for highly acculturated migrants and 89.1 for completely acculturated

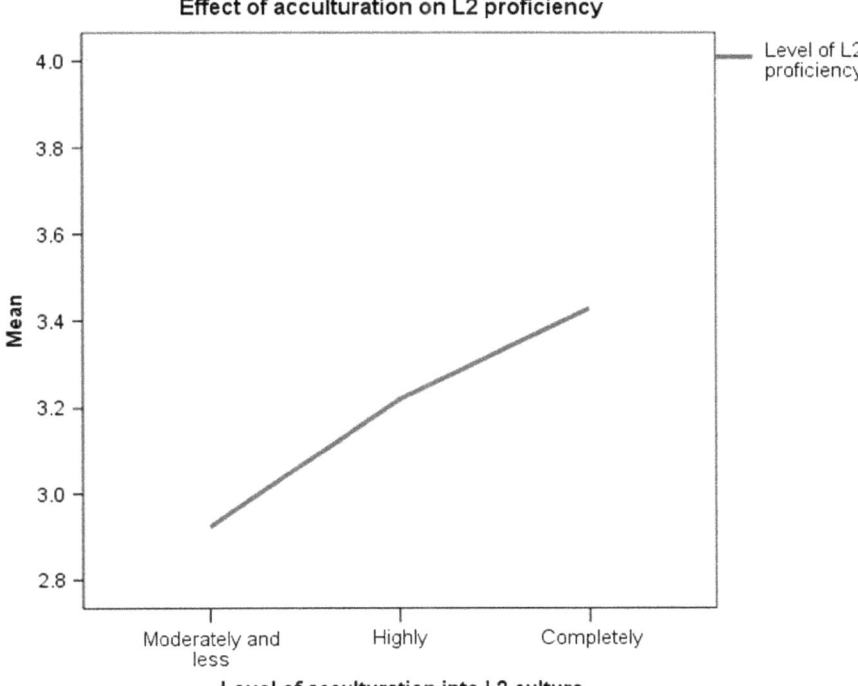

Figure 6.1 Self-perceived proficiency in L2 in relation to acculturation level (mean scores)

migrants (Figure 6.1 presents the mean scores). Participants with higher levels of acculturation reported higher scores of self-perceived proficiency in the L2. The highest levels of L2 proficiency were noted for participants who declared to be completely acculturated. This was followed by highly acculturated participants whose self-reported proficiency was proportionally high yet lower to the completely acculturated group. The lowest levels of self-reported proficiency were noted for participants who declared to be acculturated to a moderate degree or lower. Figure 6.1 represents a monotonic increase in the level of self-reported proficiency.

The effect of age at migration on self-perceived proficiency level in L2

A series of Kruskal-Wallis tests showed no significant effect of age at migration on self-perceived proficiency level in L2 ($\chi^2=2.4$, $p=.303$) with a mean rank of 69.4 for the group of 18–22 years old, 80.2 for the group of 23–26 years old and 73 for the group of 27 years old or more.

The effect of length of domicile on self-perceived proficiency level in L2

A Kruskal-Wallis test revealed that there is a significant effect of length of domicile on the self-perceived proficiency level in L2 ($\chi^2=7.1$, $p\leq.029$) with a mean rank of 66.3 for up to five years domicile, 73.8 for between 5 and 10 years of domicile and 93.4 for over 10 years of domicile (Figure 6.2). Participants who have lived in the L2 speaking country for more than 10 years declared by far the highest scores of self-rated proficiency in the L2. A significant difference was equally noted for participants with a length of domicile stretching between 5 and 10 years, who rated their self-reported proficiency level significantly higher than participants with up to 5 years of domicile.

The effect of motivation behind migration on self-perceived proficiency level in L2

A series of Kruskal-Wallis tests showed no significant effect of motivation behind migration on self-perceived proficiency level in L2

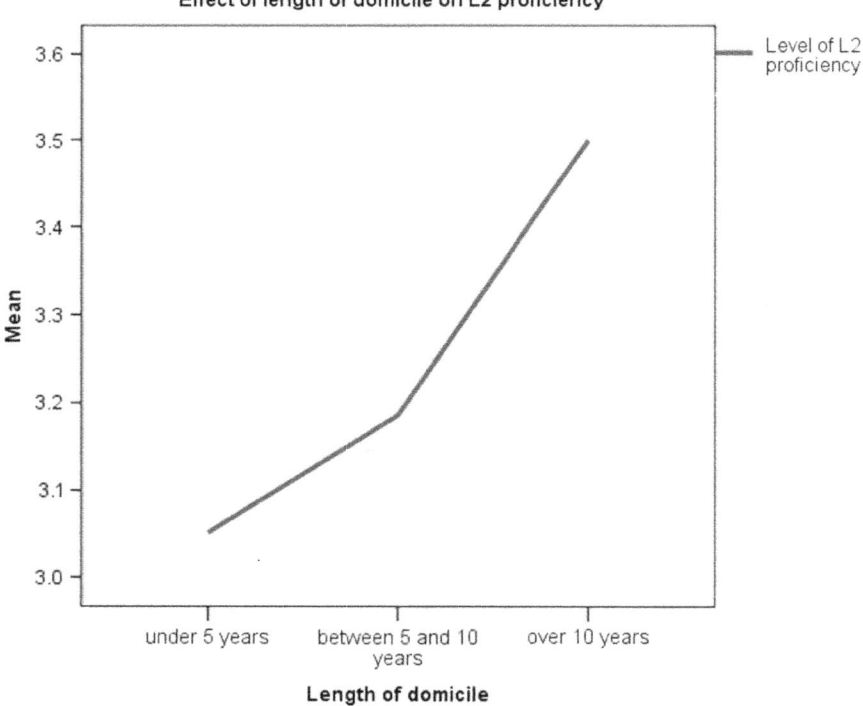

Figure 6.2 Self-perceived proficiency in L2 in relation to length of domicile (mean scores)

(χ^2=.492, p=.782) with a mean rank of 73.40 for socially/educationally oriented motivation, 74.6 for culturally oriented motivation and 80 for personally oriented motivation.

The effect of age of onset of the L2 on self-perceived proficiency level in L2

A Kruskal-Wallis test revealed that there is a significant effect of age of onset on self-perceived proficiency level in L2 (χ^2=6.3, $p \leq$.042) with a mean rank of 85.7 for ages from 0 to 9 years old, 73.1 for ages between 10 and 16 years old and 60.1 for the age of 17 years old onwards (Figure 6.3). Participants who started learning English as L2 before the age of 9 years old reported much higher levels of L2 proficiency than the other groups. Participants whose AoA ranged from the age of 10–16 years old rated their proficiency as lower, on average, when compared with younger learners, but significantly higher than learners who began their SLA after the age of 17.

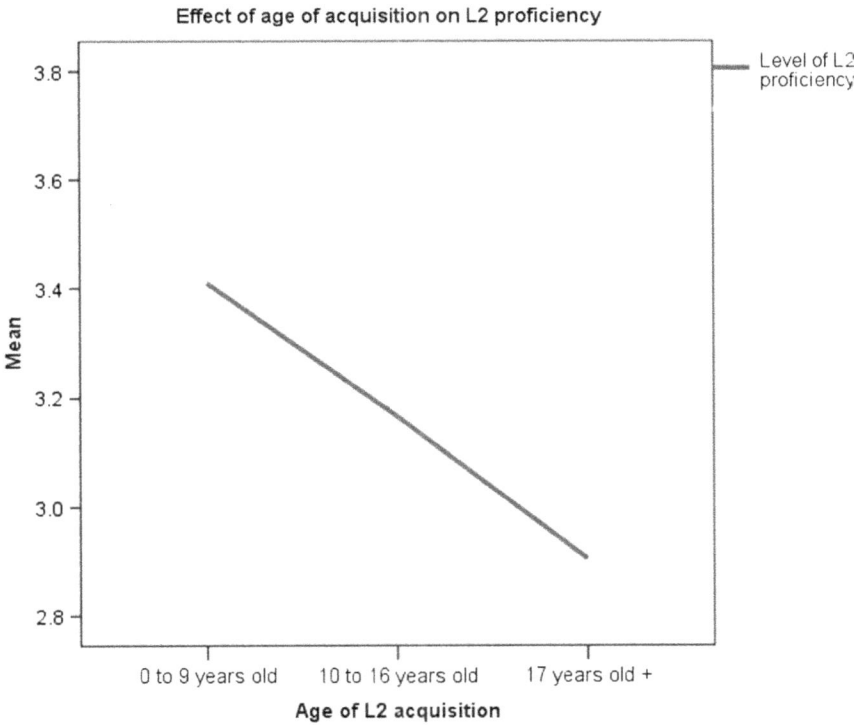

Figure 6.3 Self-perceived proficiency in L2 in relation to AoA (mean scores)

The effect of the context of L2 acquisition on self-perceived proficiency level in L2

A series of Kruskal-Wallis tests showed no significant effect of context of L2 acquisition on self-perceived proficiency level in L2 ($\chi^2=4.3$, $p=.116$) with a mean rank of 72 for instructed learning, 89.65 for mixed context of acquisition and 67.5 for naturalistic context of L2 learning.

The effect of frequency of L2 use on self-perceived proficiency level in L2

A Kruskal-Wallis test revealed that there is a significant effect of frequency of L2 use on self-perceived proficiency level in L2 ($\chi^2=10$, $p\leq.018$) with a mean rank of 52.1 for using L2 25% of the time, 68.9 for using L2 50% of the time, 82.7 for using L2 75% of the time and 94.2 for using L2 100% of the time (Figure 6.4). There was a monotonic increase in the self-reported proficiency in L2. Increased levels of frequency of L2 use are linked with increased self-reported proficiency ratings. Qualitative

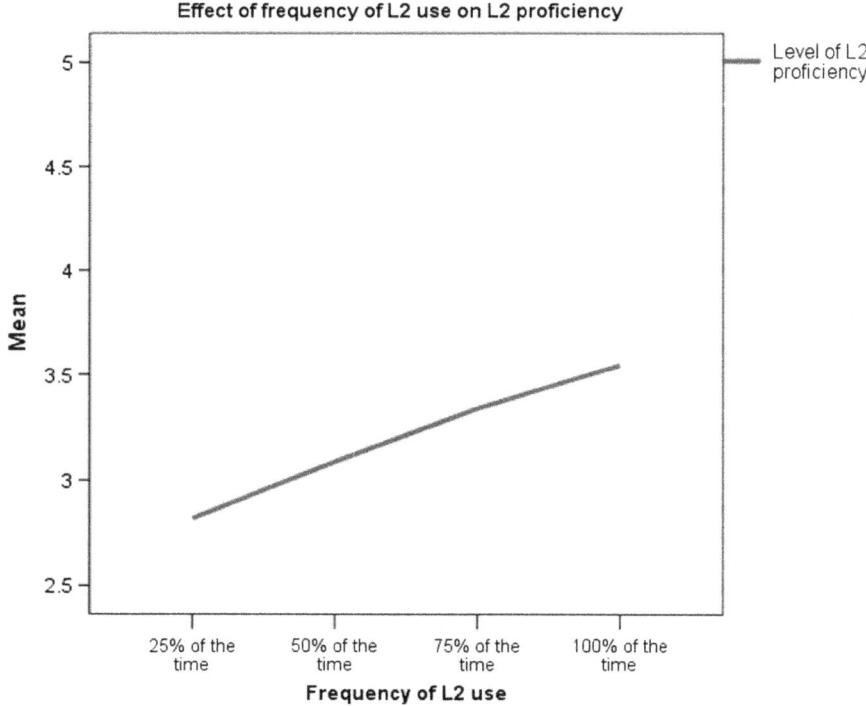

Figure 6.4 Self-perceived proficiency in L2 in relation to frequency of L2 use (mean scores)

analysis revealed that the more English participants use in daily life, the more proficient they feel in their English.

The effect of gender, age and education level on self-perceived proficiency level in L2

(a) A Mann-Whitney test showed no significant effect of gender on self-perceived proficiency level in L2 ($U=1342$, $p=.991$).
(b) A Spearman Rank analysis showed a significant link between age and self-perceived level of proficiency (Rho=.176, $p\leq.032$). In other words, older migrants felt more proficient in English than their younger counterparts.
(c) A Kruskal-Wallis test showed no significant effect of education level on self-perceived proficiency level in L2 ($\chi^2=2.25$, $p=.324$) with a mean rank of 71.2 for BA/College graduates, 74.6 for MA holders and 88.9 for PhD holders.

The feedback from the open questions and from the interviews allowed us to get a better and richer understanding of the complex interaction of variables. This emic perspective offers us the opportunity to hear the voices of the participants, and understand their perspectives and interpretations of behaviour (Dewaele, 2009b). We chose data extracts that were most illustrative and most interesting:

MI29 reported the importance of socio-cultural integration and cultural competence in improving her English skills and understanding full meaning of English words:

[When I first moved to this country] I did not feel the meaning of all English words I knew. It came with time, this social and cultural understanding. I felt sometimes stupid that I was not getting them... But going out and socialising with majority of native speakers helped a lot.

MI33 reported the experience of transition in the ability to fully express herself in English attained through acquiring cultural understanding:

Yes, it was quite difficult at the beginning. I remember saying to myself: I cannot wait to be able to fully express myself. I can say that a lot has changed since that time. I know now that understanding of any language means to understand the culture.

MI70 reported gaining full understanding of English words only after migration which increased the understanding of culture and intensified emotionality of some English words:

A lot has changed since I moved to England. I can relate more to words I had learnt while living in Poland. I can put them in the right context more easily; find the right collocations more quickly. I have also learnt the connections between words and cultural background. Some have become more emotionally charged.

MI94 reported the importance of the cultural and societal context in acquiring communicative competence and gaining confidence when speaking English:

At school we are taught certain words but they often lack context, we are unable to judge their level of (in)formality, and some very common words are absent altogether (...). As a result, initially, it is easier to understand the Queen than your neighbour. With time you learn the context and emotionally empty words become more and more familiar, until you are able to use them with confidence.

MI38 reported change in perception of his language proficiency both for L1 and L2 after migration:

When I first moved to England I felt completely lost, as back at home I was certain that my English was good. Well, it wasn't. Funny, as I visit Poland now, I carefully listen to conversations and I feel lost!

MI6 reported that length of domicile had a positive effect on her confidence when using L2:

I was more ashamed speaking in public before than nowadays. I found myself to be more confident [in my ability to speak in English] by living longer in an English speaking country.

MI8 reported that eight years of domicile in England and education in English helped to improve her proficiency level:

When I came to England 8 years ago I could not have a proper conversation. I understood 50% of what people were saying, but could not answer. During that period I went to a language school and did an MA which improved my English a lot. Now I can say that I speak English.

MI10 reported how domicile in the UK had a significant effect on his English proficiency:

When I first arrived in the UK my English was good, however since then it improved significantly. In addition, another thing which can be mentioned is that I was struggling to understand the different accents that people use. I believe that now I got used to them.

MI41 noted how 10 years domicile and acculturation affected her English proficiency:

I have been learning English since I was 6, but learning a language and knowing a language are two different things. My high school was bilingual and I considered myself to have a good understanding of the English language, good vocabulary and grammar. When I came to England 10 years ago I was in for a shock – I could not speak the language as well as I thought and I felt incredibly self-conscious of my accent and I would often doubt if I understood everything correctly, even though I had. (...) Learning a language is not only about understanding the meaning of each separate word, it's also about understanding humour, hidden meaning, understanding how what is being said links with events of the past, culture, TV shows or current affairs. After I came to the UK I made a conscious decision to integrate myself fully into the community and have achieved that.

MI28 reported that length of domicile and assimilation into L2 culture had a positive effect on English language proficiency:

At the beginning it felt completely different to what I had been taught at school and university. Pronunciation seemed different as well; even if I was very good at English I felt intimidated and was afraid to speak because I thought people would not understand me (...). Now it is completely different. It's been 5 years since I first arrived and I think I got assimilated.

Discussion

The quantitative and qualitative findings showed a systematic increase of self-reported L2 proficiency linked to acculturation level, length of domicile, age of onset, frequency of L2 use and age. Highly and completely acculturated Polish-English bilinguals rated their L2 proficiency significantly higher than moderately or less acculturated bilinguals. Level of acculturation proved therefore to be tightly linked to self-reported proficiency levels in migrants. The results also revealed that participants who use the L2 more frequently report significantly higher L2 proficiency levels than participants who report less frequent use of English. Older participants felt more proficient in their L2 than younger participants. This is congruent with the monotonic increase in L2 proficiency ratings in participants with considerable length of domicile in the UK, particularly those who have lived there for five years and over ten years respectively. Higher age and considerable length of domicile are thus linked to increased self-reported proficiency levels in migrants. An inverse age-related connection, however, was found for age of onset. Participants who started learning English L2 earlier in life, especially up to the age of nine and then up to the age of 16 respectively, rated their L2 proficiency levels systematically higher than participants whose AoA was situated after the age of 17. Age at migration, on the contrary, did not yield significant results, which points at AoA, rather than at age at migration, to be the most significant age-related variable in the context of L2 attainment.

These findings support previous research of age-related effects on SLA (Abrahamsson & Hyltenstam, 2009; Dewaele, 2009b, 2010; Hyltenstam, 2014). Participants who started learning the L2 up to the age of nine, which is the age associated with cognitive restructuring in monolinguals (Pavlenko, 2011), reported higher self-perceived proficiency scores than older participants. Participants who started learning the L2 between the ages of 10 and 16 scored significantly higher on self-reported proficiency than the group whose AoA was 17 years of age or older. This finding is congruent with Abrahamsson and Hyltenstam (2009) whose study revealed that no speaker of L2 with age of onset over 17 years old reached a native-like level (Abrahamsson & Hyltenstam, 2009). No differences were found between participants who started learning the L2 before the age of 13 when compared to those whose onset came later than that. The findings also confirmed that older participants reported significantly higher proficiency levels than younger participants. This again reflects previous research on SLA age-related variables (Dewaele, 2010).

Evidence presented in this chapter show that acculturation level is strongly and systematically linked to L2 proficiency self-ratings. The present study provides evidence that in the context of migration the L2 learner-migrant acquires the target language to the degree proportional to which they acculturate (Schumann, 1978, 1986). As high acculturation levels are associated with low levels of social and psychological distance it can be inferred that higher levels of acculturation promote increased opportunities to receive L2 input via high frequency of L2 use, which results in effective L2 intake reflected in high L2 proficiency self-ratings of both highly acculturated migrants and those who use the L2 more frequently (cf. Gass & Selinker, 2008). The present study supports previous findings that high frequency of L2 use and immersion in the L2 speaking culture are positively linked with higher L2 self-reported proficiency ratings (Dewaele, 2010; Ożanska-Ponikwia, 2013; Ożanska-Ponikwia & Dewaele, 2012; Taguchi, 2008). A similar tendency with respect to L2 proficiency ratings was found in migrants who had lived in the UK for longer, which confirms previous findings on the effect of length of domicile on the L2 attainment (Bialystok, 1997) and on cognitive restructuring and processes of 'renaming the world' in bilinguals (Pavlenko, 2011: 199).

Age at migration, motivation and education level were found to be unrelated to self-reported proficiency levels in the participants. This could be partially linked to the profile of the sample which consisted of young adults with higher level academic qualifications. Context of acquisition and gender did not have any significant effects on the self-reported proficiency in L2 either. This is in contrast with previous findings where higher education level and female gender were linked to higher self-reported proficiency scores (Dewaele, 2010). It is possible that migration and acculturation neutralise the effect of education and gender.

Qualitative analyses of open questions and interviews generally confirmed the statistical results. A majority of participants declared that length of domicile had a tremendous effect on their English skills and confidence when using the L2. Many participants declared experiencing initial linguistic disorientation due to different accents and dialects of English used in the UK. Testimonies of highly acculturated participants also revealed a post-migration realisation of the importance of acquiring cultural and communicative competence. L2 attainment is therefore linked to cultural awareness and a full, confident and competent use of the L2. It could be hypothesised that L2 learning in the circumstances of migration is understood more through the prism of cultural and integrative competence, rather than merely linguistic competence. The experience and use of the L2 in different contexts potentially enables the learner/user to reach high levels of L2 attainment through minimising the distance between them and the surrounding cultural reality and *bringing the L2 to life*. One of the participants reported this by saying:

MI118: *Living in an English speaking country without the ability to speak English [proficiently] is like window shopping: you see stuff, but you can't touch it, get it, feel it, smell it and so on.*

Feedback from open questions and interviews also revealed that participants started perceiving L2 words as more emotional which provides support for the concept of emotional acculturation as found by De Leersnyder *et al.* (2011). One of the respondents illustrated this phenomenon by saying:

MI63: *My level of understanding and 'feeling' of the language (English) changed dramatically over the years. I am unable to recall the feelings or emotional response now, bearing in mind the time that's passed, but the notion of going from 'emotional emptiness' to the total opposite seems reasonable. My 'feeling' for Polish language has definitely deteriorated over the years, there are words that seem to carry more meaning in English and the Polish equivalents do not feel adequate.*

This supports findings by Schrauf (2009) who concluded that not only exposure but the engagement in the L2 serves as one of the main predictors of the level of proficiency in the L2. The present study also adds to the earlier evidence provided by Graham and Brown (1996), Jiang *et al.* (2009) Maple (1982) and Schrauf (2009) that increased levels of acculturation and cultural immersion are strongly linked to higher levels of proficiency in the L2.

Conclusion

The findings suggest that the high level of attainment in the L2 is tightly linked with acculturation level and age of onset (Hyltenstam, 2014; Schumann, 1986). It should be noted that participants who took part in this study were highly educated and were professionally or academically active following migration. It is very likely that the participants had high levels of meta-linguistic awareness and thus were able to offer relevant feedback and reflect on their L2 learning (Dewaele, 2010; Wilson & Dewaele, 2010).

Participants underlined the importance of cultural awareness and sociocultural understanding in the process of SLA following migration. Feedback from open questions and interviews highlighted the discrepancy between language learning in the home country and language acquisition in the country where the language is spoken on a daily basis. The findings showed that acculturation oriented variables, namely, acculturation level and length of domicile, are closely linked to self-reported proficiency level in the L2. Higher levels of acculturation and longer domicile in the L2-speaking country correspond to higher self-reported proficiency levels in migrants and an increased perception of the L2 as emotional. Also SLA-oriented variables such as frequency of L2 use, age of onset and current age, proved to be linked to self-reported proficiency scores. High frequency of L2 use, higher current age and lower age of acquisition were linked to higher self-reported proficiency scores. Acculturation turned out to have the strongest effect on high level of attainment in English L2. What this study shows is that acculturation is a powerful variable in the processes of SLA and that it is tightly linked to the high levels of attainment in the L2.

Note

(1) *12 out of the 149 participants were residing outside the UK (Republic of Ireland, USA, Canada, Australia).

References

Abrahamsson, N. and Hyltenstam, K. (2009) Age of onset and nativelikeness in a second language: Listener perception versus linguistic scrutiny. *Language Learning* 59 (2), 249–306.

Abrahamsson, N. (2012) Age of onset and nativelike L2 ultimate attainment of morphosyntactic and phonetic intuition. *Studies in Second Language Acquisition* 34, 187–214.

Bialystok, E. (1997) The structure of age: In search of barriers to second language acquisition. *Second Language Research* 13, 116–137.

Birdsong, D. (2005) Interpreting age effects in second language acquisition. In J.F. Kroll and A.M.D. de Groot (eds) *Handbook of Bilingualism: Psycholinguistic Approaches* (pp. 109–127). Oxford: Oxford University Press.

Birdsong, D. (2006) Age and second language acquisition and processing: A selective overview. *Language Learning* 56, 9–49.

Bley-Vroman, R. (1989) What is the logical problem of foreign language learning? In S. Gass and J. Schachter (eds) *Linguistic Perspectives on Second Language Acquisition* (pp. 41–68). Cambridge: Cambridge University Press.

Boski, P. (2008) Five meanings of integration in acculturation research. *International Journal of Intercultural Relations* 32, 142–153.

Brown, H.D. (1994) *Principles of Language Learning and Teaching*. Englewood Cliffs, NJ: Prentice Hall Regents.

Brown, H.D. (2007) *Principles of Language Learning and Teaching* (5th edn). New York: Pearson Education.

Bylund, E., Abrahamsson, N. and Hyltenstam, K. (2012) Does L1 maintenance hamper L2 nativelikeness? A study of L2 ultimate attainment in early bilinguals. *Studies in Second Language Acquisition* 34, 215–241.

Clément, R., Noels, K. and Deneault, B. (2001) Interethnic contact, identity and psychological adjustment: The mediating and moderating roles of communication. *Journal of Social Issues* 57, 559–579.

Cook, V.J. and Singleton, D. (2014) *Key Topics in Second Language Acquisition*. Bristol: Multilingual Matters.

Damen, L. (1987) *Culture Learning: The Fifth Dimension in the Language Classroom*. Reading, MA: Addison-Wesley.

Debaene, E. and Harris, J. (2013) Divergence, convergence and passing for a native speaker: Variations in the use of English by Polish migrants in Ireland. In D. Singleton, V. Regan and E. Debaene (eds) *Linguistic and Cultural Acquisition in a Migrant Community*. Bristol: Multilingual Matters.

De Leersnyder, J., Mesquita, B. and Kim, H. (2011) Where do my emotions belong? A study on immigrants' emotional acculturation. *Personality & Social Psychology Bulletin* 37, 451–463.

Dervin, F. (2013) Rethinking the acculturation and assimilation of 'Others' in a 'monocultural' country: Forms of intercultural pygmalionism in two Finnish novels. *Journal of Intercultural Studies* 34 (4), 356–370.

Dewaele, J.-M. (2005) Investigating the psychological and emotional dimensions in instructed language learning: Obstacles and possibilities. *The Modern Language Journal* 89 (3), 367–380.

Dewaele, J.-M. (2009a) The cognitive perspective: The age factor. In K. Knapp and B. Seidlhofer (eds) *Handbook of Foreign Language Communication and Learning* (pp. 279–306). Berlin: Mouton De Gruyter.

Dewaele, J.-M. (2009b) The effect of age of acquisition on self-perceived proficiency and language choice among adult multilinguals. *Eurosla Yearbook* 9, 246–269.

Dewaele, J.-M. (2010) *Emotions in Multiple Languages*. Basingstoke: Palgrave Macmillan.
Dewaele, J.-M. (2011) Reflections on the emotional and psychological aspects of foreign language learning and use. *Anglistik. International Journal of English Studies* 22 (1), 23–42.
Dewaele, J.-M. (2013) Second and additional language acquisition. In L. Wei (ed.) *Applied Linguistics* (pp. 46–68). Malden, MA/Oxford: Wiley-Blackwell.
Ellis, R., (1994) *The Study of Second Language Acquisition*. Oxford: Oxford University Press.
Dörnyei, Z. and Ushioda, E. (eds) (2009) *Motivation, Language Identity and the L2 Self*. Bristol: Multilingual Matters.
Dörnyei, Z. and Ushioda, E. (2011) *Teaching and Researching Motivation* (2nd edn). Harlow: Longman.
Flege, J.E. (1999) Age of learning and second language speech. In D. Birdsong (ed.) *Second Language Acquisition and the Critical Period Hypothesis* (pp. 101–131). Mahwah, NJ: Erlbaum.
Flege, J.E., Frieda E.M. and Nozawa, T. (1997) Amount of native-language (L1) use affects the pronunciation of an L2. *Journal of Phonetics* 25, 169–186.
Flege, J.E., Munro, M.J. and MacKay, I.R.A. (1995) Factors affecting degree of perceived foreign accent in a second language. *Journal of the Acoustical Society of America* 97, 3125–3134.
Gardner, R.C. (2001) Integrative motivation and second language acquisition. In Z. Dörnyei and R. Schmidt (eds) *Motivation and Second Language Acquisition* (pp. 1–19). Honolulu, HI: University of Hawai'i, Second Language Teaching and Curriculum Centre.
Gass, S.M. and Selinker, L. (2008) *Second Language Acquisition: An Introductory Course* (3rd edn). London: Routledge.
Giles, H. and Smith, P.M. (1979) Accommodation theory: Optional levels of convergence. In H. Giles and R.N. St. Clair (eds) *Language and Social Psychology* (pp. 45–65). Oxford: Basil Blackwell.
Graham, C.R. and Brown, C. (1996) The effects of acculturation on second language proficiency in a community with a two-way bilingual program. *The Bilingual Research Journal* 20, 235–260.
Green, D.W. (1986) Control, activation and resource: A framework and a model for the control of speech in bilinguals. *Brain and Language* 27, 210–223.
Hammer, K. (2012) Web questionnaire on language use and language choice in bilinguals (E-PLUS). Unpublished manuscript, University of London.
Hansen, D. (1995) A study of the effect of the acculturation model on second language acquisition. In F.R. Eckman, D. Highland, P.W. Lee, J. Mileham and R. Weber (eds) *Second Language Acquisition Theory and Pedagogy* (pp. 305–316). Hillsdale, NJ: Lawrence Erlbaum.
Harris, C.L., Gleason, J.B, and Ayçiçegi, A. (2006) Why is a first language more emotional? Psychophysiological evidence from bilingual speakers. In A. Pavlenko (ed.) *Bilingual Minds: Emotional Experience, Expression, and Representation* (pp. 257–283). Clevedon: Multilingual Matters.
Howard, M. (2005) Second language acquisition in the study abroad context: A comparative investigation of the effects of study abroad and foreign language instruction on the L2 learner's grammatical development. In A. Housen and M. Pierrard (eds.) *Current Issues in Instructed Second Language Acquisition* (pp. 539–588). Malden, MA/Oxford: Blackwell.
Hyltenstam, K. (2014) Age and aptitude and nativelike ultimate attainment in two languages. Plenary paper presented at the annual conference of the American Association for Applied Linguistics, Portland.
Hyltenstam, K. and Abrahamsson, N. (2003) Age of onset and ultimate attainment in near-native speakers of Swedish. In K. Fraurud and K. Hyltenstam (eds)

Multilingualism in Global and Local Perspectives. Selected Papers from the 8th Nordic Conference on Bilingualism, November 1–3, 2001, Stockholm Rinkeby. Stockholm: Centre for Research on Bilingualism, Stockholm University, and Rinkeby Institute of Multilingual Research.

Jia, G., Aaronson, D. and Wu, Y. (2002) Long-term language attainment of bilingual immigrants: Predictive variables and language group differences. *Applied Psycholinguistics* 23, 599–621.

Jiang, M., Green, R.J., Henley, T.B. and Masten, W.G. (2009) Acculturation in relation to the acquisition of a second language. *Journal of Multilingual and Multicultural Development* 30 (6), 481–492.

Kelley, J.P. (1982) Interlanguage variation and social/psychological influences within a developmental stage. Unpublished MA thesis. University of California, Los Angeles.

Kopeckova, R. (2013) Segmental acquisition in Polish child and adult learners in Ireland. In D. Singleton, V. Regan and E. Debaene (eds) *Linguistic and Cultural Acquisition in a Migrant Community* (pp. 134–152). Bristol: Multilingual Matters.

Kramsch, C. (2009) *The Multilingual Subject*. Oxford: Oxford University Press.

Lenneberg, E.H. (1967) *Biological Foundations of Language*. New York: Wiley.

Lybeck, K. (2002) Cultural identification and second language pronunciation of Americans in Norway. *The Modern Language Journal* 86, 174–191.

Maple, R. (1982) Social distance and the acquisition of English as a second language: A study of Spanish-speaking adult learners. Unpublished doctoral thesis, University of Texas at Austin.

Masgoret, A.-M. and Ward, C. (2006) Culture learning approach to acculturation. In D.L. Sam and J.W. Berry. *The Cambridge Handbook of Acculturation Psychology* (pp. 58–77). Cambridge: Cambridge University Press.

Masgoret, A.-M. and Gardner, R.C. (1999) A causal model of Spanish immigrant adaptation in Canada. *Journal of Multilingual and Multicultural Development* 20, 216–236.

Mougeon, R., Nadasdi, T. and Rehner, K. (2010) *The Sociolinguistic Competence of Immersion Students*. Bristol: Multilingual Matters.

Munro, M. and Mann, V. (2005) Age of immersion as a predictor of foreign accent. *Applied Psycholinguistics* 26, 311–341.

Norton Pierce, B. (1995) Social identity, investment, and language learning. *TESOL Quarterly* 29 (1), 9–31.

Ożanska-Ponikwia, K. (2013) *Emotions from a Bilingual Point of View: Personality and Emotional Intelligence in Relation to Perception and Expression of Emotions in the L1 and L2*. Newcastle upon Tyne: Cambridge Scholars.

Ożanska-Ponikwia, K. and Dewaele, J.-M. (2012) Personality and L2 use. The advantage of being openminded and self-confident in an immigration context. *Eurosla Yearbook* 12, 112–134.

Paradis, J. (2007) Early bilingual and multilingual acquisition. In P. Auer and L. Wei (eds) *Handbook of Multilingualism and Multilingual Communication* (pp. 101–130). Berlin/New York: Mouton De Gruyter.

Pavlenko, A. (2002) Poststructuralist approaches to the study of social factors in L2. In V. Cook (ed.) *Portraits of the L2 User* (pp. 277–302). Clevedon: Multilingual Matters.

Pavlenko, A. (ed.) (2011) *Thinking and Speaking in Two Languages*. Bristol: Multilingual Matters.

Pavlenko, A. (2014) *The Bilingual Mind and What it Tells us About Language and Thought*. Cambridge: Cambridge University Press.

Pavlenko, A., Blackledge, A., Piller I. and Teutsch-Dwyer, M. (eds) (2003) *Multilingualism, Second Language Learning, and Gender*. Berlin: Mouton De Gruyter.

Redfield, R., Linton, R. and Herskovits, M. (1936) Memorandum on the study of acculturation. *American Anthropologist* 38, 149–152.

Regan, V. (2005) From speech community back to classroom: What variation analysis can tell us about the role of context in the acquisition of French as a foreign language. In J.-M. Dewaele (ed.) *Focus on French as a Foreign Language: Multidisciplinary Approaches* (pp. 191–209). Clevedon: Multilingual Matters.

Regan, V. (2013) The Bookseller and the Basketball Player: Tales from the French Polonia. In D. Singleton, V. Regan and E. Debaene (eds) *Linguistic and Cultural Acquisition in a Migrant Community* (pp. 28–48). Bristol: Multilingual Matters.

Schrauf, R.W. (2009) English use among older bilingual immigrants in linguistically concentrated neighbourhoods: Social proficiency and internal speech as intracultural variation. *Journal of Cross-Cultural Gerontology* 24, 157–179.

Schumann, J. (1978) The acculturation model for second language acquisition. In R. Gingras (ed.) *Second Language Acquisition and Foreign Language Teaching* (pp. 22–50). Arlington, VA: Center for Applied Linguistics.

Schumann, J. (1986) Research on the acculturation model for second language acquisition. *Journal of Multilingual and Multicultural Development* 7 (5), 379–392.

Singleton, D. (2003) Critical period or general age factor(s)? In M.P. Garcia Mayo and M.L. Garcia Lecumberri (eds) *Age and the Acquisition of English as a Foreign Language* (pp. 3–22). Clevedon: Multilingual Matters.

Singleton, D., Regan, V. and Debaene, E. (2013) *Linguistic and Cultural Acquisition in a Migrant Community*. Bristol: Multilingual Matters.

Spitzberg, B.H. (1988) Communication competence: Measures of perceived effectiveness. In C.H. Tardy (ed.) *A Handbook for the Study of Human Communication* (pp. 67–106). Norwood, NJ: Ablex.

Stauble, A. (1981) A comparative study of a Spanish-English and Japanese-English second language continuum: Verb phrase morphology. Unpublished doctoral dissertation. University of California, Los Angeles.

Taguchi, N. (2008) Cognition, language contact and the development of pragmatic comprehension in a Study-Abroad context. *Language Learning* 58 (1), 33–71.

Ushioda, E. (1993) *Acculturation theory and linguistic fossilization: A comparative case study*. Working Paper. Dublin: Trinity College, Centre for Language & Communication Studies (CLCS Occasional Papers).

Ward, C. and Kennedy, A. (1993) Psychological and socio-cultural adjustment during cross-cultural transitions: A comparison of secondary students at home and abroad. *International Journal of Psychology* 28, 129–147.

Wilson, R.J. and Dewaele, J.-M. (2010) The use of web questionnaires in second language acquisition and bilingualism. *Second Language Research* 26 (1), 103–123.

7 The Role of Sociopsychological Factors in Long-term L2 Achievement of L1 Chinese Learners of L2 Spanish[1]

Gisela Granena

Long-term achievement in second language (L2) acquisition is characterised by high inter-individual variability. This variability is explained by a number of factors, out of which age of first (meaningful) exposure, a biological factor, is broadly agreed to be the most reliable predictor of ultimate level of L2 attainment (Long, 1990). Many are the studies that support the existence of such maturational constraints on L2 attainment and that have shown that late L2 learners cannot score within native-speaker range, or early-learner range, unless they compensate for a late start by means of other factors such as language aptitude (Abrahamsson & Hyltenstam, 2009; DeKeyser, 2000; DeKeyser et al., 2010; Granena & Long, 2013). These are all studies carried out in naturalistic language settings with first- or second-generation immigrants and where level of achievement was examined on the basis of age of arrival in the L2 community. From these studies, it is becoming increasingly evident that multiple sensitive periods exist for different language domains (Long, 1990), and even for different language aspects, and that some of these periods are closing earlier than generally thought, as early as age three for certain morphosyntactic structures and L1–L2 pairings.

In addition to age of first exposure, or age of onset (AO), there is a broad array of other factors (see Larsen-Freeman & Long, 1991) that may not be able to override the impact of age, but that also contribute to explain the complex picture of variability in ultimate attainment. Hyltenstam and Abrahamsson (2003) argued that sociopsychological factors with no basis in biology, such as motivation to learn or appear native-like, identity and attitudes play an increasingly larger role in ultimate attainment as AO increases in order to compensate for the effects of maturation. According to them, biological factors would play a more important role before the closing of a sensitive period, whereas sociopsychological factors would be more important to explain variability after a sensitive period. There are several models that explain how second language acquisition is affected by sociopsychological factors. These models attribute differential success in SLA to factors in the affective domain and to their potential to inhibit or block the cognitive processes leading to acquisition.

One of them is Schumann's model (1975, 1978, 1986), which assumes that L2 attainment depends on two sets of factors, social and psychological. According to Schumann, children are either favourably tuned or neutral in this regard, but adult L2 learners may develop ego boundaries and attitudes that can constrain acquisition. Schumann's Acculturation Model identifies several variables that determine the social and psychological distance between the learner and the speakers of the target language. Social distance is determined by differences between the two groups of speakers at a political, social, cultural or economic level. Psychological distance is determined by (1) language shock, or the learners' fear of being ridiculed because of their imperfect L2 skills, (2) culture shock and stress, (3) ego permeability, or the learners' capacity to detach themselves from their L1 identity and (4) motivation, specifically the learners' interest in acquiring the L2 to meet and communicate with speakers of the target language.

Schumann based his claims regarding motivation on Gardner and colleagues' work (Gardner & Lambert, 1972). According to Gardner and Lambert, instrumental motivation influences L2 learning positively, but an integrative motivation creates the optimal opportunity for SLA, since it implies minimal psychological distance from the target language speakers. Gardner and Lambert's work developed into the Socio-Educational Model of second language learning (Gardner, 1985), where integrative motivation is one of the key components.

Motivation has been one of the sociopsychological factors most widely investigated. Much of the empirical work in this area has looked at attainment in phonology (L2 pronunciation) both in foreign language learning (instructional) settings and naturalistic settings (Bongaerts, 1999; Bongaerts *et al.*, 2000; Flege *et al.*, 1999; Jia *et al.*, 2002; Moyer, 1999; Oyama, 1976; Thompson, 1991). The prediction is that positive attitudes are related to higher levels of attainment. Bongaerts (1999), in fact, claimed that high motivation was crucial for late L2 learners to achieve native-like pronunciation and that this was partially explaining the success of the exceptional learners in his study together with exposure and intensive training (see also Bongaerts *et al.*, 1995, and Bongaerts *et al.*, 1997, where highly motivated Dutch learners of English, university students in the Netherlands, a formal setting, overlapped with native speakers (NSs) for pronunciation scores in read-aloud sentence tasks in which the L2 learners were given three reading opportunities).

Despite claims that sociopsychological dimensions play a role in ultimate attainment, the results of the studies have been mixed. Some studies found an effect for motivational factors, but only for one of the motivational variables examined (e.g. Moyer, 1999; Jia *et al.*, 2002). Other studies (e.g. Flege *et al.*, 1999) did find an effect but considerably smaller than for other factors such as age of arrival. Finally, other studies (Oyama, 1976; Thompson, 1991) found no effect.

Moyer (1999) investigated the role of instructional and motivational factors in the pronunciation of 24 late, very advanced and highly motivated, American learners of German as a foreign language. A panel of NSs evaluated the learners' degree of foreign accent on a series of read-aloud (controlled) tasks, with words, sentences and paragraphs, and a free-response (spontaneous) task. Results showed that the raters were able to distinguish NSs from L2 learners. The range of ratings obtained by each group was clearly differentiated and did not overlap. A regression analysis further revealed that professional motivation operationalised as current and long-term goals for studying German was a significant predictor, able to account for around 40% of the variance, whereas age of immersion, or first meaningful exposure, was only able to account for 1% of the unique variance. Other motivational/attitudinal variables such as cultural empathy, desire to sound like a NS, and type or amount of input did not correlate significantly with mean accent rating and were not included in the regression analyses. Jia *et al.* (2002) found no relationship between various motivational variables and ultimate L2 attainment as measured by a listening and a reading task, but one of the affective variables (self-consciousness) was negatively related to performance in both outcome measures.

Flege *et al.* (1999) investigated a large group of L2 learners with ages of arrival between 1 and 23 and found that integrative and instrumental motivation accounted for a significant increase in variance in participants' foreign accent ratings and grammaticality judgement test (GJT) scores. However, these only explained around 3% of the additional variance in degree of foreign accent and grammaticality judgement scores.

Finally, Oyama (1976) and Thompson (1991) found no relationship between motivation and degree of L2 foreign accent. Oyama (1976) investigated the relationship between AO, length of exposure, and degree of accent in a sample of 60 Italian L1–English L2 participants. She also administered a background questionnaire that measured sociopsychological factors such as motivation. The results indicated a strong effect for AO, but not for years of exposure. Motivational factors were not related to accent either, once AO was partialed out. In fact, motivation and self-consciousness were negatively correlated with accent, suggesting that accent was worse with higher motivation. Very similar findings were reported by Thompson (1991) with 36 NSs of Russian who arrived in the US between ages 4 and 42. In the study, age of arrival was the best indicator of pronunciation accuracy. The full model that accounted for the data included age of arrival, sex, ability to mimic and global proficiency. Motivational/attitudinal variables such as importance of English for work, importance of having good accent, and degree of integration in the L2 culture played no role as predictor variables.

Purpose of the Study

Moyer (1999) argued that non-biological factors are crucial factors often left unexamined by researchers as predictors of L2 attainment. These factors include a variety of affective, social and psychological variables, such as learner motivation, cultural empathy, self-confidence and desire to sound like a NS, which may not override the impact of age but which may contribute to explain the high inter-individual variability in long-term L2 attainment. In Moyer's (1999) study, self-perceived accentedness was not able to predict late learners' actual ultimate attainment in L2 phonology as measured by NS judge ratings, but professional motivation was a significant predictor of variation in attainment.

The present study contributed to this literature by investigating whether four of these non-biological factors, specifically four sociopsychological variables (self-assessment of perceived L2 learning success, identification with the L2 culture, satisfaction with one's own pronunciation and desire to pass as a NS), were differentially related to one another or to actual ultimate morphosyntactic attainment in early and late L2 learners.

The four sociopsychological variables examined measure Schumann's (1975, 1978, 1986) notions of social and psychological distance, specifically the extent to which learners can identify themselves with members of the target language group and the extent to which they feel confident or are at ease with their target-language learning task. The extent to which learners can identify themselves with members of the target language group was operationalised in the present study by means of two variables, identification with the L2 culture and desire to pass for a NS. These two factors indicate the learner's degree of desire to be associated with the target culture and are claimed to potentially promote or inhibit contact with the target language group, which in turn should lead to more or less successful acquisition (Schumann, 1978). The extent to which learners feel confident or at ease with their target-language learning task was operationalised in this study by means of two additional variables, self-assessment of perceived L2 learning success and satisfaction with one's own pronunciation. These two factors are internal psychological constructs involving an individual's self-perception of L2 competence and related self-evaluations. They have been claimed to indicate learners' linguistic self-confidence and to contribute to the psychological distance felt by the learner towards the target language group, a sign of adaptation in a different culture. Research by MacIntyre et al. (1997) further showed that self-perception of L2 competence was significantly correlated with actual communicative competence, especially with oral production (Clement, 1986).

Method

Participants

One hundred Chinese L1–Spanish L2 sequential bilinguals, long-term residents in Madrid (Spain), participated in the study. Half of them ($n=50$) were early bilinguals (42% males and 58% females) with AOs ranging from 3 to 6. The other half ($n=50$) were late L2 learners (34% males and 66% females) with AOs of 16 and older. AO was operationalised as the beginning of a serious and sustained process of language acquisition as the result of migration or the commencement of a formal Spanish language program. AO, therefore, could differ from age of physical arrival in the country. In this study, when age of onset and age of arrival did not overlap, formal instruction took place in adulthood, after age 16. Therefore, age of first exposure as a result of immersion in the L2-speaking country and age of first instruction still overlapped for the purposes of the current study, where adult L2 learners are defined as those with AOs of 16 and older. Participants were recruited by advertising in Chinese-Spanish newspapers, by distributing fliers in cultural centres, embassies, and language schools, and by word of mouth in the community. To qualify for the study, participants had to: (1) have Chinese as mother tongue, (2) have lived in Spain for at least five years[2] and (3) have an educational level of no less than high school. Participants were informally screened into the study via a telephone interview.[3] Table 7.1 summarises the information regarding age at testing, age of onset and length of residence for the participants.

Target structures

Six target structures that are known to be difficult for NSs of a non-Romance language (Bruhn de Garavito & Valenzuela, 2008; Collentine, 1995;

Table 7.1 Participants' information

Group	Age at Testing		Age of Onset		Length of Residence	
	M	Range	M	Range	M	Range
Early AO $n=50$	22.38 (4.45)	18-33	4.14 (1.23)	3-6	17.88 (4.49)	11-28
Late AO $n=50$	29.46 (6.38)	21-50	20.84 (4.14)	16-30	8.42 (3.14)	5-20

Note: Standard deviations appear between parentheses.

Montrul, 2004) were investigated: (1) Noun-adjective gender agreement, (2) Subject-verb number agreement, (3) Noun-adjective number agreement, (4) Subjunctive mood, (5) Perfective/imperfective aspect contrasts and (6) Passives with *ser/estar*. A pool of 360 target items was created and items were randomly assigned to each of the six language measures.

Instruments

All participants completed a detailed biographical questionnaire and four grammaticality judgement tests (GJTs) as part of a broader research project. The questionnaire included four Likert-scale questions, adapted from Moyer (1999). The first question addressed participants' perceived success with respect to the NS model: 'Do you agree that you pass as a NS of Spanish when you talk?' The second and third questions addressed participants' attitudes towards their own pronunciation and towards native-level pronunciation (i.e. concern for accuracy in pronunciation): 'Are you satisfied with your pronunciation in Spanish?', and 'Is it important for you to pass as a NS of Spanish?' Finally, the last question addressed participants' degree of identification with the L2 culture: 'To what extent do you identify with Spanish culture?' The first three questions were answered on a four-point scale, where 1 was the lowest rating ('completely disagree', 'completely unsatisfied' or 'it is not important for me') and 4 the highest rating ('completely agree', 'very satisfied' or 'it is very important for me'). The last question was answered on a five-point scale representing a continuum between [− identification] and [+ identification].

The four GJTs combined different timing (timed/untimed) and modality (visual/auditory) conditions: (1) A timed visual GJT, (2) a timed auditory GJT, (3) an untimed auditory GJT and (4) an untimed visual GJT. The four tests were administered following a 4×4 balanced Latin square to control for order and carry-over effects. Each GJT included 60 items, 10 per target structure. Half of the items in every test were grammatical and half ungrammatical.

Timed Auditory GJT. The timed auditory GJT was a computer-delivered test with sentences presented aurally. Participants indicated whether each sentence was grammatical or ungrammatical by pressing a response button within a fixed time limit. They were asked to press a key as soon as an error was detected in the sentence. Once participants pressed a key, the computer automatically moved on to the next sentence without a pause. Following R. Ellis (2005), the time limit for each item was established on the basis of NSs' average response time in a pilot study ($n=10$). Following R. Ellis as well, an additional 20% of the time taken for each sentence was added to allow for the slower processing speed of L2 learners. The time allowed for judging each sentence in the timed auditory GJT ranged between 3408.72 milliseconds (3.4 seconds) to 10045.92

(10 seconds) ($M=5807.98$, $SD=1000.76$). In terms of target structure, NSs' longest response times were on aspectual contrasts ($M=5365.09$, $SD=1156.64$), followed by gender agreement ($M=5102.60$, $SD=471.69$), the passive ($M=4988.20$, $SD=432.40$), person agreement ($M=4892.22$, $SD=608.58$), number agreement ($M=4691.73$, $SD=344.26$) and the subjunctive ($M=4000.05$, $SD=714.31$).

Each item was scored dichotomously as correct/incorrect, and percentage accuracy scores were calculated for grammatical and ungrammatical items overall, as well as for grammatical and ungrammatical items separately. Percentage scores out of total number of attempts were used due to the relatively high proportion of missing data as a result of the speeded nature of the test (10.61% of total items).

The internal consistency of the test, according to Cronbach's alpha, which measures the rank-order stability of individuals' scores on different items of the test, was .92.

Timed Visual GJT. The timed visual GJT was a computer-delivered test with sentences presented visually. Participants indicated whether each sentence was grammatical or ungrammatical by pressing a response button within a fixed time limit. Once participants pressed a key, the computer automatically moved on to the next sentence without a pause. The time limit for each item was also established by adding 20% to NSs' average response time. The time allowed for judging each sentence in the timed auditory GJT ranged between 3590.23 milliseconds (3.5 seconds) to 8587.20 (8.5 seconds) ($M=5804.37$, $SD=993.40$). In terms of target structure, NSs' longest response times were again on aspectual contrasts ($M=5289.30$, $SD=931.76$), followed by gender agreement ($M=4942.46$, $SD=844.04$), the passive ($M=4930.43$, $SD=720.62$), number agreement ($M=4742.05$, $SD=1122.58$), the subjunctive ($M=4595.84$, $SD=625.48$) and person agreement ($M=4521.77$, $SD=553.95$).

Each item was scored dichotomously as correct/incorrect, and percentage accuracy scores were calculated for grammatical and ungrammatical items overall, as well as for grammatical and ungrammatical items separately. Percentage scores out of total number of attempts were used due to the relatively high proportion of missing data as a result of the speeded nature of the test (15.67% of total items).

The internal consistency of the test, according to Cronbach's alpha, was .89.

Untimed Auditory GJT ($k=60$). The untimed auditory GJT was a computer-delivered test with sentences presented aurally. Participants were required to indicate whether each sentence was grammatical or ungrammatical by pressing a response button. Unlike its time-pressured counterpart, this test presented each sentence twice before participants were allowed to provide a response. Following DeKeyser (2000) and DeKeyser et al. (2010), each sentence was played twice, with a three-second interval between the repetitions and a six-second interval between sentence pairs.

Each item was scored dichotomously as correct/incorrect, and percentage accuracy scores were calculated for grammatical and ungrammatical items overall, as well as for grammatical and ungrammatical items separately.

The internal consistency of the test, according to Cronbach's alpha, was .89.

Untimed Visual GJT ($k=60$). The untimed visual GJT was a computer-delivered self-paced test with sentences presented visually. Participants were required to indicate whether each sentence was grammatical or ungrammatical by pressing a response button.

Each item was scored dichotomously as correct/incorrect and percentage accuracy scores were calculated for grammatical and ungrammatical items overall, as well as for grammatical and ungrammatical items separately.

The internal consistency of the test, according to Cronbach's alpha, was .85.

Procedure

Participants were tested individually by the researcher and all the tasks were administered on a laptop computer. Upon their arrival, participants were provided with the consent form of the study and had the opportunity to ask questions before signing it. Then, they filled out the biographical questionnaire. The four GJTs were administered following a balanced Latin square design. The two timed GJTs took approximately 10 minutes each, whereas the untimed auditory and untimed visual GJT took approximately 20 minutes each.

Results

Table 7.2 displays early and late learners' scores on the four Likert-scale items measuring sociopsychological factors.

Early L2 learners agreed that they could pass as NSs to a greater extent than late learners ($t(98)=12.903$, $p<.001$). They were also more satisfied with their pronunciation ($t(98)=11.261$, $p<.001$) and identified more with the L2 culture than late L2 learners ($t(98)=4.323$, $p<.001$). The only sociopsychological variable where the two groups did not differ significantly from each other, but where late L2 learners scored descriptively higher than early L2 learners even if this difference was not significant, was the importance of native-likeness (the extent to which they considered it important to pass as a NS) ($t(98)=-.897$, $p=.372$).

In order to investigate any differences in the relationships between the sociopsychological variables within each of the groups, simple bivariate correlations were computed. Tables 7.3 and 7.4 show the correlations in

Table 7.2 Descriptive statistics for sociopsychological variables

	Question 1[a]		Question 2[b]		Question 3[c]		Question 4[d]	
	M	Min.-Max.	M	Min.-Max.	M	Min.-Max.	M	Min.-Max
Early	3.68 (.51)	2.0–4.0	3.82 (.44)	2.0–4.0	3.10 (.76)	1.0–4.0	3.72 (.70)	3.0–5.0
Late	2.14 (.67)	1.0–4.0	2.64 (.60)	1.0–4.0	3.24 (.80)	1.0–4.0	3.14 (.64)	1.0–4.0

Note: Standard deviations appear between parentheses.
[a]Question 1. Do you agree that you can pass as a NS of Spanish when you talk?
[b]Question 2. Are you satisfied with your pronunciation in Spanish?
[c]Question 3. Is it important for you to pass as a NS of Spanish?
[d]Question 4. To what extent do you identify with Spanish culture?

the early and late L2 learner group, respectively. For a correlation to be significant, a p value smaller than 0.0125 was required after applying Bonferroni's correction for repeated analyses. In the early group, the only significant relationship was between perceived L2 learning success, understood as being able to pass as a NS, and satisfaction with one's own pronunciation ($p<.001$). In the late group, however, perceived L2 learning success was significantly related to all the other sociopsychological variables investigated. Late L2 learners who perceived themselves as having been more successful with respect to the NS model were also more satisfied with their pronunciation, considered it more important to pass as a NS, and identified more with the L2 culture.

The next step in the analysis involved examining the extent to which sociopsychological variables predicted ultimate morphosyntactic attainment as measured by GJTs. Table 7.5 shows the descriptive statistics for the four GJTs in each of the two L2 learner groups and Figure 7.1 a visual display of the group means. As can be observed, early L2 learners obtained higher overall scores in each of the measures and these differences were always statistically significant ($p<.001$) (but see Granena, 2013, for between-group comparisons of different types of structures).

Table 7.3 Bivariate correlations between sociopsychological variables in the early L2 learner group

	Question 1[a]	Question 2[b]	Question 3[c]	Question 4[d]
Question 1[a]	1	.65 $p<.001$	.03 $p=.829$	.26 $p=.072$
Question 2[b]	–	1	–.07 $p=.642$	.10 $p=.496$
Question 3[c]	–	–	1	.21 $p=.151$
Question 4[d]	–	–	–	1

[a]Question 1. Do you agree that you can pass as a NS of Spanish when you talk?
[b]Question 2. Are you satisfied with your pronunciation in Spanish?
[c]Question 3. Is it important for you to pass as a NS of Spanish?
[d]Question 4. To what extent do you identify with Spanish culture?

Table 7.4 Bivariate correlations between sociopsychological variables in the late L2 learner group

	Question 1[a]	Question 2[b]	Question 3[c]	Question 4[d]
Question 1[a]	1	.55 p<.001	.45 p=.001	.42 p=.003
Question 2[b]	–	1	–.03 p=.841	.19 p=.191
Question 3[c]	–	–	1	.22 p=.137
Question 4[d]	–	–	–	1

[a]Question 1. Do you agree that you can pass as a NS of Spanish when you talk?
[b]Question 2. Are you satisfied with your pronunciation in Spanish?
[c]Question 3. Is it important for you to pass as a NS of Spanish?
[d]Question 4. To what extent do you identify with Spanish culture?

Tables 7.6 and 7.7 present the correlations between the sociopsychological variables investigated and the four GJTs in the early and late L2 learner groups. In the two groups, satisfaction with one's own pronunciation was significantly related to GJT scores, specifically to untimed GJT scores. Greater satisfaction correlated with higher GJT accuracy scores. In addition, GJT scores were also related to the extent to which learners agreed that they could pass as NSs (perceived L2 success). The more they agreed that they could pass as NSs, the higher the GJT scores they obtained. However, this relationship was only significant in the early group and only for the untimed auditory GJT after applying the Bonferroni correction, despite the fact that the two sociopsychological variables in question (satisfaction with one's pronunciation and perceived L2 success) were significantly related in the two groups of L2 learners.

In order to examine the predictive power of sociopsychological factors, multiple linear regression was then run on ultimate morphosyntactic attainment. For the regression models, two equally weighted composite scores were created, one for ultimate morphosyntactic attainment, which combined the scores on the four GJTs, and one for sociopsychological factors, which combined the scores on the four Likert-type questions. The composite variables were created by converting raw scores into z-scores and adding them up. Kolmogorov-Smirnov ($K\text{-}S$) tests indicated that the two variables were normally distributed in the two groups, the early ($p=.537$ and $p=.452$) and late L2-learner group ($p=.896$ and $p=.299$). In addition to the sociopsychological composite, AO and length of residence were also added as independent factors in the regression models. Both were also normally distributed in the early ($p=.454$ and $p=.085$) and late L2 learner group ($p=.454$ and $p=.099$).

The regression analyses showed that none of the two models was significant and, therefore, that the combination of AO, length of residence and sociopsychological variables was not able to could account for variation in ultimate morphosyntactic attainment in early ($F(3, 46)=2.642$, $p=.063$) or late ($F(3, 46)=1.714$, $p=.177$) L2 learners. The adjusted R^2 was .11 in the

Table 7.5 Group mean percentage scores on GJTs

	Timed Visual GJT		Timed Auditory GJT		Untimed Visual GJT		Untimed Auditory GJT	
	M	Min.-Max.	M	Min.-Max.	M	Min.-Max.	M	Min.-Max.
Early	72.03 (10.18)	50.0-90.0	76.24 (10.07)	58.33-94.92	76.77 (9.13)	53.33-96.67	79.39 (9.73)	56.67-98.33
Late	57.88 (8.39)	41.51-71.74	57.63 (7.90)	38.33-78.38	61.27 (9.05)	46.67-91.67	60.47 (9.28)	38.33-85.0

Note: Standard deviations appear between parentheses.

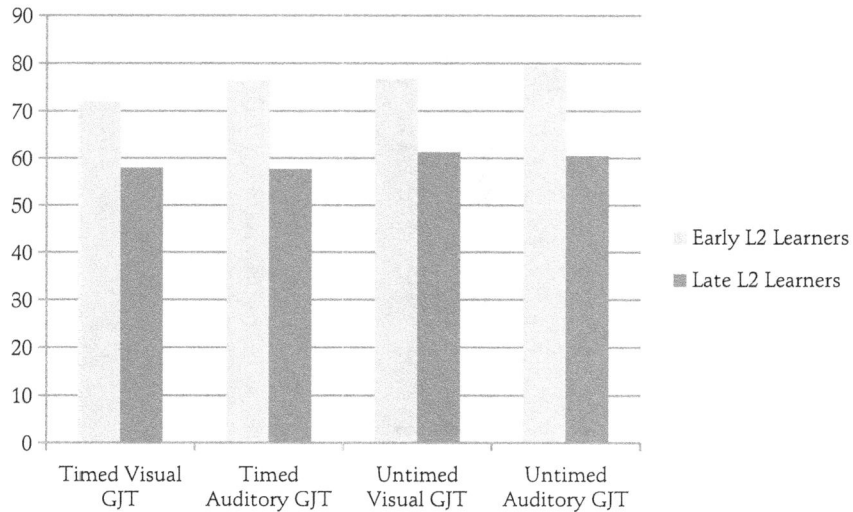

Figure 7.1 Group mean percentage GJT scores

early group and .04 in the late group, indicating that the model explained less than .05% variance in every group. Regarding the different predictors, none of them reached significance in the early group: AO ($\beta=-.228$, $p=.138$), length of residence ($\beta=.269$, $p=.082$) or sociopsychological variables ($\beta=.781$, $p=.440$). And the same results were found in the late group: AO ($\beta=-.274$, $p=.062$), length of residence ($\beta=.223$, $p=.138$) or sociopsychological variables ($\beta=.138$, $p=.347$).

Discussion

The current study investigated whether sociopsychological factors considered to be relevant for native-like attainment (self-evaluation of L2 learning success, identification with the L2 culture, satisfaction with one's own pronunciation and desire to pass as a NS) were differentially related to one another or to variation in ultimate morphosyntactic attainment in early and late L2 learners. Participants were Chinese L1–Spanish L2 sequential bilinguals. The early L2 learners had arrived in the country between ages 3 and 6, or had been born to Chinese-speaking parents who had immigrated to the country as adults. The late L2 learners had arrived after age 16. They were all well educated and well integrated, and had optimal opportunities to practice the L2. On a scale from 1 to 5, 90% of the late L2 learners rated their identification with the L2 culture as being 3 (64%) or 4 (26%) (the remaining 10% rated their identification as being 2 out of 5). Similarly, 100% of the early L2 learners rated their identification as 3 (42%), 4 (44%) or 5 (14%). Therefore, one can argue

Table 7.6 Bivariate correlations between sociopsychological variables and ultimate morphosyntactic attainment in the early L2 learner group

	Timed Visual GJT	Timed Auditory GJT	Untimed Visual GJT	Untimed Auditory GJT
Question 1[a]	.33 p=.019	.30 p=.034	.32 p=.023	.35 p=.012
Question 2[b]	.28 p=.047	.31 p=.028	.35 p=.012	.29 p=.041
Question 3[c]	.13 p=.378	-.18 p=.220	-.01 p=.965	-.04 p=.801
Question 4[d]	.15 p=.300	.24 p=.096	.21 p=.140	.25 p=.072

[a]Question 1. Do you agree that you can pass as a NS of Spanish when you talk?
[b]Question 2. Are you satisfied with your pronunciation in Spanish?
[c]Question 3. Is it important for you to pass as a NS of Spanish?
[d]Question 4. To what extent do you identify with Spanish culture?

Table 7.7 Bivariate correlations between sociopsychological variables and ultimate morphosyntactic attainment in the late L2 learner group

	Timed Visual GJT	Timed Auditory GJT	Untimed Visual GJT	Untimed Auditory GJT
Question 1[a]	-.06 p=.676	.23 p=.108	.13 p=.358	.19 p=.170
Question 2[b]	.14 p=.331	.12 p=.403	.46 p=.001	.41 p=.004
Question 3[c]	-.09 p=.510	-.08 p=.563	-.21 p=.129	-.20 p=.146
Question 4[d]	-.23 p=.096	.25 p=.088	.02 p=.881	.12 p=.427

[a]Question 1. Do you agree that you can pass as a NS of Spanish when you talk?
[b]Question 2. Are you satisfied with your pronunciation in Spanish?
[c]Question 3. Is it important for you to pass as a NS of Spanish?
[d]Question 4. To what extent do you identify with Spanish culture?

that the L2 learners in the study had positive attitudes and affect towards the target language community. From this point of view, they met the sociocultural conditions considered relevant and even necessary to acquire an L2 in a naturalistic setting (Schumann, 1978, 1986).

The results of the analyses showed that sociopsychological variables were differentially related in the two groups of L2 learners. In the early group, the only significant relationship was between the extent to which learners agreed that they could pass as NSs and degree of satisfaction with one's own pronunciation, indicating that early learners were consistent in their self-evaluations. Early L2 learners that perceived themselves as being closer to the NS model were more satisfied with their pronunciation, but did not actually consider it more important to pass as a NS. In the late group, the links between sociopsychological variables were different. Late L2 learners that self-evaluated themselves as being closer to NSs were not only more satisfied with their pronunciation, but also considered it more important to pass as NSs and identified more with the L2 culture. This suggests different affective orientations to L2 learning in early and late learners. The importance of native-likeness and acculturation in Schumann's sense only played a role in the late group. For late learners, aiming at native-likeness and feeling identified with the L2 culture seemed to actually help become, or at least, consider oneself as more native-like. For early learners, instead, native-likeness seemed to be independent from motivation to become native-like and from identification with the L2 culture. Similarly, Moyer (1999) also reported a significant correlation between the importance given to sounding native and the degree of satisfaction with one's own pronunciation in a group of late L2 learners (AOs between 11 and 27). These results indicate that the desire or motivation to become native-like and pass as a NS could be one of the distinguishing factors in the motivational profile of adult L2 learners immersed in an L2-speaking environment. In fact, almost half of the late L2 learners in the present study (42%) considered it *very* important to pass as a NS (versus 30% in the early group).

Regarding the role of sociopsychological variables in L2 attainment, correlational analyses showed that the desire to pass as a NS was not actually related to learning outcomes in morphosyntax as measured by grammaticality judgements. These are the same results that Moyer (1999) found for accent ratings. Similarly, identification with the L2 culture was not significantly related to attainment. These findings indicate that certain aspects of motivation (desire to become native-like and cultural identification) may not play a role in long-term L2 acquisition, at least as far as morphosyntactic attainment is concerned, but may be able to foster positive attitudes towards one's own L2 achievement in late learners, as the significant correlation found between these two variables and self-reported ability to pass as a NS suggests.

Self-evaluations of L2 learning success and satisfaction with one's own pronunciation, on the other hand, did relate significantly to GJT scores in correlational analyses. Early L2 learners that perceived themselves as being closer to the NS model and that had a more positive attitude towards their pronunciation also scored higher on the GJTs. Similarly, late L2 learners who were more satisfied with their pronunciation also scored higher on the GJTs. However, multiple linear regression analyses demonstrated a very weak contribution of sociopsychological factors independent of other variables (AO and length of residence). In fact the model proposed was not able to account for variation in ultimate attainment in either learner group. This finding runs contrary to Moyer (1999), where professional motivation (specifically, ambition for university-level academic jobs) accounted for 32% of the variance in attainment. These divergent findings could be due to the language domain investigated, phonology vs morphosyntax. One possibility is that motivation has greater impact on L2 phonology, since pronunciation, intonation and stress errors may mark the speaker as non-native more often than grammar errors. Consequently, motivated L2 learners aiming at sounding native-like could pay more attention to pronunciation trying to imitate NSs and this could result in more native-like accent, as Moyer found.

Finally, neither AO nor length of exposure could significantly explain outcomes in isolation, according to the regression models. This means that these factors could not offer a unique explanation of the variance in ultimate attainment. This result is similar to Moyer's (1999), where AO could not uniquely explain variance in accent ratings after controlling for motivation, and to DeKeyser (2000), DeKeyser *et al.* (2010) and Granena and Long (2013), where AO was not related to morphosyntactic attainment in early L2 learners with AOs between 3 and 6 or late L2 learners with AOs greater than 16. The fact that ultimate outcomes become statistically unpredictable from AO indicates that other learner factors should be able to explain variation. Since the sociopsychological variables investigated in this study could not offer a unique explanation of variation in morphosyntactic attainment, other factors (cognitive variables, input factors, language use or other social conditions) should be investigated.

Conclusion

This study investigated the sociopsychological profile of early and late L2 learners who were long-term residents in the L2-speaking country and the role of sociopsychological variables in ultimate morphosyntactic attainment. Findings revealed that sociopsychological variables were differentially interconnected in the two groups of L2 learners and, therefore, that early and late learners had different affective orientations to L2 learning. The desire to pass as a NS of the target language and cultural identification (i.e. an integrative orientation to language learning) were significantly related to self-reported ability to pass as a NS only in the late L2 learner group. Unlike early L2 learners, late L2 learners that perceived themselves as being more able to pass as a NS also considered it more important to pass as a NS and identified more with the L2 culture. However, the sociopsychological variables investigated were not able to predict ultimate morphosyntactic attainment. An integrative orientation to L2 learning in the type of naturalistic learning context examined may be more important to account for variation in L2 phonology, as previous studies have shown, since pronunciation, intonation and stress can mark the speaker as non-native more often than morphosyntax. Further research should be conducted following Muñoz and Singleton's (2011) call for studies that take a closer look at other social and psychological factors, especially at their relative weight in high levels of L2 attainment.

Notes

(1) This material is based upon work supported by the National Science Foundation under Grant No. 1124126.
(2) According to DeKeyser *et al.* (2010), length of residence 'turns out to be unrelated to most dependent measures, provided that it is more than 5 years, and that the dependent measures index basic grammatical proficiency (not purisms, collocations, etc.)' (p. 416).
(3) The inclusion criterion was a score of at least four on a five-point scale that rated participants' degree of native-like pronunciation: 5 – Native or near-native pronunciation. No foreign accent. 4 – Generally good pronunciation but with occasional non-native sounds. Slight foreign accent. Pronunciation does not interfere with comprehensibility. 3 – Frequent use of non-native sounds. Noticeable foreign accent. Pronunciation occasionally impedes comprehensibility. 2 – Generally poor use of native-like sounds. Strong foreign accent. Pronunciation frequently impedes comprehensibility. 1 – Very strong foreign accent. Definitely non-native. Participants rated with a three on pronunciation were also included in the study if their grammar use was native-like.

References

Abrahamsson, N. and Hyltenstam, K. (2009) Age of onset and nativelikeness in a second language: Listener perception versus linguistic scrutiny. *Language Learning* 59, 249–306.
Bongaerts, T. (1999) Ultimate attainment in L2 pronunciation: The case of very advanced late L2 learners. In D. Birdsong (ed.) *Second Language Acquisition and the Critical Period Hypothesis* (pp. 133–159). Mahwah, NJ: Lawrence Erlbaum Associates.
Bongaerts, T., Mennen, S. and van der Slik, F. (2000) Authenticity of pronunciation in naturalistic second language acquisition. The case of very advanced learners of Dutch as a second language. *Studia Linguistica* 54, 298–308.
Bongaerts, T., van Summeren, C., Planken, B. and Schils, E. (1997) Age and ultimate attainment in the pronunciation of a foreign language. *Studies in Second Language Acquisition* 19, 447–465.

Bongaerts, T., Planken, B. and Schils, E. (1995) Can late learners attain a native accent in a foreign language? A test of the critical period hypothesis. In D. Singleton and Z. Lengyel (eds) *The Age Factor in Second Language Acquisition* (pp. 30–50). Clevedon: Multilingual Matters.

Bruhn de Garavito, C. and Valenzuela, E. (2008) Eventive and stative passives in Spanish L2 acquisition: A matter of aspect. *Bilingualism: Language and Cognition* 11, 323–336.

Clement, R. (1986) Second language proficiency and acculturation: An investigation of the effects of language status and individual characteristics. *Journal of Language & Social Psychology* 5, 271–290.

Collentine, J. (1995) The development of complex syntax and mood-selection abilities by intermediate-level learners of Spanish. *Hispania* 78, 122–135.

DeKeyser, R.M. (2000) The robustness of critical period effects in second language acquisition. *Studies in Second Language Acquisition* 22, 499–533.

DeKeyser, R.M., Alfi-Shabtay, I. and Ravid, D. (2010) Cross-linguistic evidence for the nature of age-effects in second language acquisition. *Applied Psycholinguistics* 31, 413–438.

Ellis, R. (2005) Measuring implicit and explicit knowledge of a second language. A psychometric study. *Studies in Second Language Acquisition* 27, 141–172.

Flege, J., Yeni-Komshian, G. and Liu, S. (1999) Age constraints on second-language acquisition. *Journal of Memory and Language* 41, 78–104.

Gardner, R.C. (1985) *Social Psychology and Second Language Learning: The Role of Attitudes and Motivation*. London: Edward Arnold.

Gardner, R.C. and Lambert, W.E. (1972) *Attitudes and Motivation in Second-Language Learning*. Rowley: Newbury House Publishers.

Granena, G. (2013) Individual differences in sequence learning ability and SLA in early childhood and adulthood. *Language Learning* 63, 665–703.

Granena, G. and Long, M.H. (2013) Age of onset, length of residence, aptitude and ultimate L2 attainment in three linguistic domains. *Second Language Research* 29, 311–343.

Hyltenstam, K. and Abrahamsson, N. (2003) Maturational constraints in SLA. In C.J. Doughty and M.H. Long (eds) *The Handbook of Second Language Acquisition* (pp. 539–588). Oxford: Blackwell.

Jia, G., Aaronson, D. and Wu, Y. (2002) Long-term language attainment of bilingual immigrants: Predictive variables and language group differences. *Applied Psycholinguistics* 23, 599–621.

Larsen-Freeman, D. and Long, M.H. (1991) *An Introduction to Second Language Acquisition Research*. London: Longman.

Long, M.H. (1990) Maturational constraints on language development. *Studies in Second Language Acquisition* 12, 251–285.

MacIntyre, P.D., Noels, K.A. and Clement, R. (1997) Biases in self-ratings of second language proficiency: The role of language anxiety. *Language Learning* 47, 265–287.

Montrul, S. (2004) *The Acquisition of Spanish: Morphosyntactic Development in Monolingual and Bilingual L1 Acquisition and Adult L2 Acquisition*. Amsterdam: John Benjamins.

Moyer, A. (1999) Ultimate attainment in L2 phonology: The critical factors of age, motivation and instruction. *Studies in Second Language Acquisition* 21, 81–108.

Muñoz, C. and Singleton, D. (2011) A critical review of age-related research on L2 ultimate attainment. *Language Teaching* 44, 1–35.

Oyama, S. (1976) A sensitive period for the acquisition of a nonnative phonological system. *Journal of Psycholinguistic Research* 5, 261–283.

Schumann, J.H. (1975) Affective factors and the problem of age in second language acquisition. *Language Learning* 25, 209–235.

Schumann, J.H. (1978) The relationship of pidginization, creolization, and decreolization to second language acquisition. *Language Learning* 28, 367–379.
Schumann, J.H. (1986) Research on acculturation model for L2 acquisition. *Journal of Multilingual and Multicultural Development* 7, 379–397.
Thompson, I. (1991) Foreign accents revisited: The English pronunciation of Russian immigrants. *Language Learning* 41, 177–204.

Concluding Chapter: What Can SLA Learn From Cultural Migrants?

Fanny Forsberg Lundell and Inge Bartning

The seven chapters included in the present volume all deal with migrants who have specific types of motives for their migration, i.e. cultural ones. The purpose of studying such migrants was to investigate whether the motive behind migration had an impact on their L2 attainment. Some of the studies include learners with a variety of socio-psychological motives (Diskin & Regan, Granena, and Hammer & Dewaele), which allow for conclusions to be drawn regarding the effect of cultural motives. Others focus only on cultural migrants and do not include points of comparison. To this end, it was thought a good idea to begin this concluding chapter with a brief comparison with the state-of-the-art regarding adult learners' possibilities of nativelike attainment, which was presented in the Introduction. Furthermore, a particular model of SLA research will be addressed, i.e. the Acculturation model. What does the current volume imply for this model? Finally, some societal implications will be discussed as well as new research avenues.

Linking the Findings in this Volume to the Current SLA State-of-the-Art

In the Introduction, it was claimed that most of the research in SLA using data from long-residency migrants is related to the Critical Period Hypothesis (see e.g. Long, 2013a). A very good example of this type of study is Abrahamsson and Hyltenstam's seminal study from 2009, which concludes that complete, scrutinised nativelikeness is unlikely to occur after puberty. Our volume is not about the critical period hypothesis and we are not questioning the robust research findings which point to certain (often subtle) differences between L1 and L2 speakers. However, what could be questioned, according to us, is the exclusive focus on the Critical Period Hypothesis when discussing adult L2 attainment. We believe that such a focus tends to obscure the fact that many late L2 learners reach very high levels of L2 attainment and are highly functional in their L2 in their everyday lives. We believe that the CPH researchers are aware of this last fact, but, nevertheless, tend to focus on learner deficiencies in their search for confirmation of the CPH. Even researchers, such as Birdsong, who question the existence of the CPH, still relate to it in that they try to reject the existence of such a period. It is thus not a problem of scientific rigour but of scientific rhetoric, in our view. It is about what questions are being asked and what questions have been left out so far. In this volume, studying a growing group of people, adults who decide, out of their free will, to move to another country based on curiosity and interest, our intent has been to explore all the possibilities that L2 users in a favourable context actually have.

First of all, it should be underlined, again, that the studies included in this volume have not been designed together. They are not the fruit of a common research project or research agenda, but rather constitute a compilation of researchers happening to focus on similar topics. This means that the studies do not allow for similar conclusions to be drawn. Some of them include several linguistic features, whereas others only focus on one.

The studies which take the cultural migrant as a point of departure (Edmonds & Guesle-Coquelet, Erman & Lewis, Forsberg Lundell & Bartning and Gudmundson & Bardel) include, only in part, similar features. Rather than focusing on *production* of target features, Edmonds and Guesle-Coquelet have examined their participants' *perception* of their *tu/vous* use and potential difficulties. Their study seems to suggest that this feature does not appear to pose problems for the cultural migrants who consider themselves highly integrated, but it does pose a problem for those who feel less integrated, with some expressing the wish to abolish this distinction in French. Integration thus seems to play an important role, for this type of language feature, which emphasises the strong link between language and culture. Erman and Lewis conclude that their participants reach nativelikeness on multi-word structures in a role play, but not in a retelling task. As regards lexical diversity, they do not reach nativelikeness in any of the tasks. This points to the somewhat narrow character of L2 user speech – it is situationally dependent. It would, however, be interesting to know if a lack of MWSs or lack of lexical diversity influences the perceived communicative proficiency to the same extent? In Forsberg Lundell and Bartning's study, which is somewhat different since it focusses solely on four individuals, it becomes clear that nativelikeness seems within reach for one of four long-residency users. The feature for which nativelikeness is the most difficult is that of perceived nativelikeness, which most likely equals global phonology. However, most participants score within the native range as regards formulaic sequences (what Erman & Lewis label MWSs) and fluency. It should, in addition, be noted that even though all participants do not reach scores within the native range, the results are overall high and usually fall, if not within the native range, one standard deviation below the native range (which has sometimes been used as a sign of nativelikeness, see Mizrahi & Laufer, 2010). Finally, Gudmundson and Bardel's study, which concentrates on two aspects of vocabulary and analyses in detail the production of one Swedish L2 user of Italian, shows that her lexical sophistication is actually higher than that of the native controls, but her lexical variation is within the lower native results, though still within the native range. These results thus suggest that nativelikeness within this domain is attainable. We would conclude that the cultural migrants included in the present volume manifest nativelikeness in some respects, especially as regards pragmatics and vocabulary. Phonology, on the other hand, is probably more subject to maturational constraints, although one L2 user does fall within the native range for perceived nativelikeness.

Diskin and Regan's study differs somewhat from the four studies above since it does not include only cultural migrants, but also participants with more traditional migratory backgrounds. They find that cultural migrants stand out in their significantly higher use of discourse pragmatic markers (DPMs) than the other types of migrants. At a qualitative level, however, even the cultural migrants do not display a similar use of the discourse marker 'like' as the native speaker. They interpret this as some sort of distance towards Irish identity.

Two studies (Granena and Hammer & Dewaele) analyse the 'cultural theme' from another point of view. Instead of studying what cultural migrants do, they investigate the effect of acculturation on L2 attainment. They both take Schumann's Acculturation model (1986) as a point of departure, but have used different methodologies. Granena's study's operationalisation of the Acculturation model consists of four questions related to two aspects of Schumann's model: *the extent to which learners can identify themselves with members of the target language group* and *the extent to which they feel confident or are at ease with their target-language learning task*. Relating these independent variables with results on four different GJTs, in different modes, Granena found some correlations, but a regression analysis showed low predictive power of the independent variables. Granena is probably right when she herself suggests that neither the independent nor the dependent variables were suitable for the purpose of her research. In contrast, Hammer and Dewaele find strong correlations between acculturation, operationalised as one general question and self-perceived L2 attainment. They thus employ more holistic measurements which, in this case, seem more suitable.

In sum, when comparing the results from the current volume, with the SLA state-of-the-art for ultimate attainment in adults, two main things can be observed. First, it should be noted that nativelikeness seems within reach for several aspects of lexis, but can be situationally dependent. Pragmatics also seems to be an area that, for certain phenomena, is within nativelike reach for the L2 users. Phonology stands out as the most difficult factor (but is only measured globally by Forsberg Lundell

& Bartning). In general, it is important to note that the studies in the present volume generally study limited phenomena and not nativelikeness across the board such as Marinova-Todd (2003) or Abrahamsson and Hyltenstam (2009). Second, it should be observed that the Acculturation model has been used by two of the studies, with convincing results for one of them. This suggests an actualisation of this model, which has not been thoroughly investigated, especially not during the last few decades. Does this point to a revival of the Acculturation model?

Societal Implications and the Future of Acculturation

Although not all of the studies in the volume have tested the Acculturation model in an explicit way, most of them lend some indirect support to the model. The fact that participants, who are, as it seems, well-integrated and who have positive affect towards their host community reach high levels as reported in this volume, suggests that the factors included in the acculturation model do play a part. Furthermore, it has become clear that the participants in many of the studies perceive culture as a decisive factor. In Edmonds and Guesle-Coquelet's study, the more well-integrated participants did not seem to have problems with the TU/VOUS-distinction, whereas those who did not feel well integrated also displayed discomfort with the cultural aspect of the TU/VOUS-distinction. In Hammer and Dewaele's study, the qualitative part of the study revealed several testimonies emphasising the link between language and culture and the importance of target culture integration. In sum, 'culture' seems to play an important part in the language learning and use of these people, which is most certainly characteristic of high levels of L2 attainment. It is quite obvious that beginner or intermediate proficiency is not necessarily related to host country integration. Relating to the debate regarding linguistic tests and citizenship, it is clear that a level corresponding to B1 (which is the required level for citizenship in the UK, A2 in the Netherlands) will not correspond to a culturally well-integrated person in most cases. This question is indeed very complex, but it would be interesting to see what linguistic correlates would correspond to a certain CEFR-level as has been explored in the SLATE group (see Bartning *et al.*, 2010) and how these linguistic correlates relate to cultural competence.

However, there is a completely opposite tendency in society today as well, which would go against concepts such as 'acculturation' and 'linguistic citizenship' and that is, notably that of 'globalisation'. If we believe that cultural differences are diminishing and that the national state is obsolete, with borders being questioned, what is the future of a notion such as 'acculturation'? For acculturation to take place, there presumably has to be a well-defined target language community with a common language. Can we acculturate into a global culture? Will we all speak lingua franca English or, say, lingua franca Chinese? Work within the area of Global Englishes could perhaps shed a light on this (see Graddol, 2012; Melchers & Shaw, 2013). English is probably spoken by more L2 users than native speakers,[1] and what happens with the link between culture and language in such a case? Will we in fact, due to the power of globalisation, perceive a less pronounced relationship between culture and language? Will 'cultures' situate themselves at other levels than those of nation and language, such as subfields of interest for example skateboarding, environmental issues or architecture? These are exciting and important questions that need to be posed. Nevertheless, the powerful link between language and culture which is demonstrated in the present volume suggests that it would be quite a long way to go before this connection between communication and common habits and mentalities disappears.

New Research Avenues

While providing fascinating and rigorous studies regarding the human capacity to acquire a language to a nativelike level later in life, CPH research has had a natural tendency to focus on deficiencies and linguistic detail and has somehow not primarily been connected to the notion of communicative competence or adequacy. Nevertheless, having studied cultural migrants, we come to similar conclusions as CPH proponents for some measures (phonology, GJT), although a large variation has been observed. It should also be admitted that participant groups are quite modest in size as well. Nevertheless, the studies in this volume have shown that cultural migrants attain nativelike levels in areas such as lexis and pragmatics, areas that should indeed be very important for communicative proficiency. As argued in the chapter by Forsberg Lundell and Bartning (this volume), CPH research is often methodologically rigorous but tends to take into account very subtle measures, often tapping the speakers' competence rather than their performance. As Long (2013b) points out, one should make a distinction between basic research and applied research and CPH research mainly belong in the former category. However, if we are interested in the possibilities of adult speakers to learn an additional language later in life, especially if we think of their possibilities to function in society, we would be more interested in their communicative proficiency than in their grammatical intuition or VOT (voice onset time). On the basis of this we suggest that an interesting way forward would be to study the relationship between communicative efficiency in adult high-level L2 use and the linguistic correlates. Which are they and are they attainable for late starters? In our view, an exciting and useful way forward, would be combining studies on nativelikeness with studies on communicative proficiency, worlds that have not really met to date. This type of knowledge would presumably be highly valuable to our current societies as well. For this purpose, it would also be useful to study different migratory contexts. Diskin and Regan (this volume) divide their migrants based on migratory experience, which to us seems highly relevant. The division also yielded interesting differences, with cultural migrants using more DPMs. One suggestion would be to study migrants with different migratory experiences in several geographical contexts, to continue examining the possibilities of adult learners to acquire the communicative proficiency needed in order to lead a highly functional life in the L2.

As the Acculturation model suggests, not only societal factors are at play, but also psychological factors at the individual level. It would, as a consequence, be interesting to study not only the different contexts mentioned above, but also to include different psychological factors that affect adult L2 learning. As for these variational factors, empirical results point to the factor 'language aptitude' playing an important role for late learners (Abrahamsson & Hyltenstam, 2008; Granena, 2013; Long, 2013a). Forsberg Lundell and Sandgren (2013) use, in addition to a language aptitude test, a personality test. These researchers looked for correlations between a productive collocation test, a language aptitude test (LLAMA, Meara, 2005), a grammatical judgement test (GJT) and the personality test Multicultural Personality Questionnaire (MPQ). The study showed strong correlations between the LLAMA subtest of phonetic memory and collocations. It also showed significant correlations between collocations and personality features such as open-mindedness and cultural empathy. Another study, Ibrahim et al. (2008), investigates two populations of Hebrew L2 learners in Israel: Russian L1 and Arabic L1. They found that the degree of nativelike pronunciation was linked to empathy in the Russian L1 group, but not in the Arabic L1 group. The researchers suggest that learning Hebrew is plausibly more affected by social tensions for the Arabic L1 learners and that these override personality factors. Such results point to an intricate relationship between societal and psychological factors affecting adult L2 learning and use.

In sum, we look forward to new studies within the next decade, connecting migration studies and second language acquisition, relating societal and psychological measures to linguistic measures which are related to high-level communicative proficiency in an L2.

Note

(1) According to Wikipedia, English has roughly 505 million L2 speakers and 350 L1 speakers, http://en.wikipedia.org/wiki/List_of_languages_by_total_number_of_speakers

References

Abrahamsson, N. and Hyltenstam, K. (2008) The robustness of aptitude effects in near-native second language acquisition. *Studies in Second Language Acquisition* 30 (4), 481–509.

Abrahamsson, N. and Hyltenstam, K. (2009) Age of L2 acquisition and degree of nativelikeness – Listener perception vs linguistic scrutiny. *Language Learning* 58 (3), 249–306.

Bartning, I., Martin, M. and Vedder, I. (eds) (2010) *Communicative Proficiency and Linguistic Development. Intersections Between SLA and Language Testing Research*. EUROSLA Monograph series 1.

Forsberg Lundell, F. and Sandgren, M. (2013) High-level proficiency in late L2 acquisition – Relationships between collocational production, language aptitude and personality. In G. Granena and M. Long (eds) *Sensitive Periods, Language Aptitude and Ultimate L2 Attainment* (pp. 231–259). Amsterdam: John Benjamins.

Graddol, D. (2012) The impact of macro socioeconomic trends on the future of the English language. Doctoral dissertation. English Department, Stockholm University.

Granena, G. (this volume) The role of sociopsychological factors in long-term L2 achievement.

Granena, G. (2013) Reexamining the robustness of aptitude in second language acquisition. In G. Granena and M. Long (eds) *Sensitive Periods, Language Aptitude and Ultimate L2 Attainment* (pp. 179–205). Amsterdam: John Benjamins.

Gudmundson, A. and Bardel, C. (this volume) Beyond nativelike? The lexical profile of a cultural migrant.

Ibrahim, R., Eviatar, Z. and Leikin, M. (2008) Speaking Hebrew with an accent: Empathic capacity or other nonpersonal factors. *International Journal of Bilingualism* 12 (3), 195–207.

Long, M. (2013a) Maturational constraints on child and adult SLA. In G. Granena and M. Long (eds) *Sensitive Periods, Language Aptitude, and Ultimate Attainment* (pp. 3–42). Amsterdam: John Benjamins.

Long, M. (2013b) Some implications of research findings on sensitive periods in language learning for educational policy and practice. In G. Granena and M. Long (eds) *Sensitive Periods, Language Aptitude, and Ultimate Attainment* (pp. 259–272). Amsterdam: John Benjamins.

Marinova-Todd, S. (2003) Comprehensive analysis of ultimate attainment in adult second language acquisition. Unpublished doctoral dissertation. Harvard University.

Meara, P. (2005) *LLAMA Language Aptitude Tests*. Swansea, UK: Lognostics.

Melchers, G. and Shaw, P. (2013) *World Englishes*. New York: Routledge.

Mizrahi, E. and Laufer, B. (2010) Lexical competence of highly advanced L2 users: Is their collocation knowledge as good as their productive vocabulary size? Paper presented at Eurosla 20, Reggio Emilia, Italy.

Schumann, J.H. (1986) Research on the acculturation model for second language acquisition. *Journal of Multilingual and Multicultural Development* 6 (5), 379–392.

Index

Academic migrants 10, 138, 156
Accent 197, 205, 206, 216, 217, 218
Acculturation 9–10, 18, 169, 178–189, 195–202, 216, 221, 223–224, 226
Acculturation model 4, 10, 18, 178, 182–184, 200, 202, 204, 212, 220–221, 223–224, 226–227
Address system 83
Advanced learner 17, 60, 67, 117
Advanced stage 60
Affective 3, 79, 183, 184, 204, 205, 206, 216, 217
Age of onset 3, 10–11, 63, 179–180, 186–188, 191, 195–196, 198, 203, 207
Anaphors 66
Antonomy 67
Aptitude test 68–69, 71–72, 74–75, 77, 226
Aspect 3, 59
Asymmetrical address situations 85
Auditory GJ-test 66

Bilingual 10, 62, 74–75, 77, 79, 178–181, 184

Chain migrants 10, 138
Cognates 7, 9, 30, 32, 33, 34, 116, 117, 118, 122, 123, 124, 125, 126, 130, 131
Cognitive aptitude 79
Collocation 67–69, 75, 116–117, 123, 126, 154, 218, 226, 228
Collocation test 67–69, 226
Common European Framework for Languages 90, 147
Complex utterances 65
Compound nouns 67
Corpaix corpus 66
Critical period 3, 78, 179, 221
Cross-linguistic similarity 117
C-test 68
Cultural empathy 79, 205–206, 226
Cultural migrant 1–12, 17–18, 22–23, 25, 31, 33–34, 62, 75, 77–78, 83–84, 87–91, 93, 95, 99, 103–104, 120, 138, 152, 154, 156, 161, 168, 170–173, 221–223, 225

Degree of deference 85
Degree of formality 86
Discourse-pragmatic markers 9, 10, 138, 140, 142
DPMs 138, 140, 141, 142, 145, 146, 147, 152, 153, 154, 156, 158, 164, 169, 171, 174, 223, 226

Economic migrants 10, 138, 161, 165, 168, 170, 172
Education level 10, 182, 188, 193, 197
Ego permeability 204
Emic 193
Exposure 8, 9, 78, 119, 121, 130, 147, 158, 170, 180, 185, 198, 203, 204, 205, 207, 217

First-order indexicality 85
Fixed expressions 67
Fluency 60–61, 66, 69, 74, 78, 116, 145, 149, 170, 181, 222
Formulaic language 8, 59, 69, 86, 115–116, 120
Formulaic sequences 60–61, 64–65, 69, 72, 79, 116–117, 222
Fragile zone 59
Free association 67
Frequency bands 18, 30, 66, 118, 126–127
Frequency of use 138, 140, 146, 154, 156, 158, 163, 164, 181
Frequency-based measure 66

Gender 3, 10, 65, 73, 88, 138, 145, 148, 154, 165, 171, 172, 182, 186, 187, 193, 197
Gender agreement 65
Gender assignment 65
GJT 3, 11, 59, 66, 71, 205, 206, 208–212, 217, 223, 225
Globalisation 1, 119, 138, 185, 224, 225
Grammatical inference 69
Grammatical intuition 59, 61, 225
Grammaticality judgment test 66, 71

High-level proficiency 4, 59, 60, 62, 115
Highly proficient stage 60
Host country 10, 182, 186, 187, 224
Hyponomy 67

Identity 10, 76, 83, 170, 173, 184, 185,
    203, 204, 223
Idiomaticity 65
Immersion 78, 84, 178, 181, 196, 198,
    205, 207
Immersion settings 84
Imparfait 65
Individual profiles 7
Information structure 60
Innate talent 68
Input 18, 79, 116, 119, 130, 183, 186, 196,
    205, 217
Integrative motivation 152, 168, 186, 204
Irish English 10, 138, 140, 145, 148, 152,
    156, 158, 159, 169

L2 French 117, 118, 59, 60, 65, 115
L2 Self 185, 196
L2 use 79, 115, 180–181, 183, 185–187,
    192, 195–196, 198
L2 vocabulary 18, 115
Language aptitude 7–8, 60–61, 68–69,
    71–72, 74–75, 78–79, 81, 178, 203,
    226–227
Language background 73–75, 77
Language community 4, 88, 116, 122, 123,
    131, 182, 183, 216, 225
Language socialization 84
Late-onset language learning 79
Length of residence 3, 8, 10–11, 138, 173,
    185–186, 207, 212, 214, 217
Lexical formulaic sequences 64, 72
Lexical Oral Production Profile (LOPP) 7
Lexical richness 8, 22, 59–61, 66, 69, 72,
    74–75, 78, 118
Lifestyle 1, 6, 22, 75, 77, 87, 91
Linguistic evaluation 72, 74–75, 76
Listener test 60–61
LLAMA B 69
LLAMA D 69
LLAMA E 69
LLAMA F 69
LLAMA test 68, 71–72, 77, 226
Longitudinal studies 79
Lexical variation 7, 17, 19, 23–25, 27, 33, 223
Lexical sophistication 7, 17–19, 22–27,
    33, 223

Maturational constraints 3, 203, 223
Mental grammar 66
Metalinguistic awareness 66
Meta-pragmatic awareness 87
Migration studies 1, 4, 5, 137,
    183, 226
Migratory experience 9, 10, 137, 138, 150,
    172, 226
MLR (Mean Length of Run) 78
Mobility 139
Mood/mode 65
Morphosyntactic errors 72
Morphosyntactic intuition 11, 180
Morphosyntax 11, 60–61, 65, 69, 216,
    217–218
Motivation 3–6, 10, 18, 137, 151–152, 168,
    170, 172, 183, 185, 187–188, 190–191,
    197, 203–206, 216–217
Multiword structures 9, 115–116, 118,
    120, 123, 126,
MWSs 9, 115, 116, 117, 118, 121, 122, 123,
    124, 125, 126, 130, 131, 222
Multicultural Personality Questionnaire
    229

Native judges 64
Native-like attainment 4, 59, 64, 180, 214
Native-like performance 78
Native-like preference 65
Native-like speaker 8, 78
Native-likeness 2–3, 7–8, 11, 59–61, 64,
    71, 78, 178–180, 210, 216
Naturalistic 2, 68, 181, 188, 192, 203,
    204, 216, 218
Near-native 60, 90, 218
NP agreement 66

Open-mindedness 79, 226

Pass-as-a-native test 62
Passé composé 65
Perceived nativelikeness 222, 223
Personality factors 79, 226
Personality test 226
Phonetic intuition 180
Phonetic memory 226
Phrasal cognate 124, 125, 126, 130
Polyglot 75
Pragmatic markers 9, 10, 141
Productive collocation test 67, 226
Productive knowledge 69
Professional experience 69

Pronominal terms of address 84
Pronunciation 11, 17, 31, 59, 180, 184, 195, 204, 205, 206, 208, 210, 211, 212, 214, 216, 217, 218, 226

Qualifier formulaic sequences 65
Quotatives 10, 140, 147, 148, 152, 164, 172

Receptive deep knowledge test 67, 71, 74
Receptive vocabulary 117
Reported usage 8, 84, 86–89, 93, 103
Restricted exchangeability criterion 65, 123

Second-order indexicality 85, 86
Second-person address 83
Selection restrictions 67
Self-assessed integration 91, 99
Self-assessment 174, 206
Self-perceived 11, 179, 181, 182, 187, 188, 190, 191, 192, 193, 196, 206, 223
Self-reported integration 87, 91
Self-reported proficiency 10, 179, 186–187, 189–190, 195–198
Sensitive periods 79, 203
Silent morphology 66
Single word 9, 115, 117, 122, 126, 128, 130, 131
Social deixis 103–104
Socio-biographical profiles 8, 10, 64, 72, 91, 182, 187, 188
Socio-economic 188
Sociolinguistic 8, 9, 10, 17, 83, 84, 86, 87, 103, 104, 138, 145, 146, 148, 150, 151, 155, 169, 171, 174, 181, 185, 187
Sociolinguistic competence 8, 84, 86–87, 103–104, 146

Sociopsychological 203, 204, 205, 206, 210, 211, 212, 214, 216, 217, 218
Sound perception 78
Speech style 78
Spoken data 61–62, 64
Subject/verb agreement 65–66
Supra-word constructions 86
Synonymy 67

Target language community 4, 88, 116, 131, 182–183, 216, 225
Target language country 4, 20, 32, 64, 120
Tense 3, 59, 65
The critical period hypothesis 2–3, 179, 221
The InterFra corpus 60
The Modern Language Aptitude test (MLAT test) 69
The noun phrase 65
The phraseological tradition 65
The verb phrase 65
Thematic words 30, 31, 32, 188
Timed auditory GJT 208
TMA 66
Transfer 10, 29, 34, 117, 171, 173
Translation equivalent 117, 126
Transnational 5, 137, 173
Trilingual 76

Ultimate attainment 3, 59–60, 71, 176, 181–182, 203–204, 206, 217, 223
Untimed auditory GJT 208, 209, 212

Variationist approach 86
Verb constructions 66

White migration 1
Word association test 75
Word pairs 67
Written data 60, 71

For Product Safety Concerns and Information please contact our EU Authorised Representative:

Easy Access System Europe

Mustamäe tee 50

10621 Tallinn

Estonia

gpsr.requests@easproject.com

www.ingramcontent.com/pod-product-compliance
Lightning Source LLC
Chambersburg PA
CBHW070603300426
44113CB00010B/1372